Human Behaviour in Organisations

Human Behaviour in Organisations

Ivan T. Robertson

BSc, PhD, ABPsS
Lecturer in Occupational Psychology,
Department of Management Sciences,
University of Manchester Institute of Science and Technology

Cary L. Cooper

BS, MBA, PhD, MSc, FBPsS
Professor of Organisational Psychology,
Department of Management Sciences,
University of Manchester Institute of Science and Technology

Pitman

PITMAN PUBLISHING LIMITED
128 Long Acre, London WC2E 9AN

A Longman Group Company

© Pitman Publishing Ltd 1983

First published in Great Britain 1983
Reprinted 1986

British Library Cataloguing in Publication Data
Robertson, Ivan T.
　Human behaviour in organisations.—
　1. Organizational behavior
　I. Title　　2. Cooper, Cary L.
　158.7　　　HD58.7

ISBN 0-273-02608-9

Printed and bound in Great Britain
at The Bath Press, Avon

Foreword

In recent years business practice has been undergoing major and fundamental changes for a variety of economic, social and technological reasons. In parallel with these changes the developments in education for business at all levels have also been extensive and far-reaching. In particular this is true at the advanced levels for courses leading to (*a*) the first degrees of the Council for National Academic Awards and of the Universities, (*b*) the higher awards of the Business Education Council and its Scottish equivalent, and (*c*) examinations of the relevant professional bodies. Many such courses are now offered in educational institutions which include the Polytechnics, the Universities, the Colleges and Institutes of Higher Education, the Further Education Colleges and the Scottish Central Institutions. In addition to these developments in curricular design there have been important advances in educational and teaching methods.

Macdonald & Evans already have a large involvement in meeting the needs of students and staff in Business Education through their BEC series and Handbook series. The publishers have now decided to complement these with their Higher Business Education series.

The new series is intended to be one of major educational significance and will cover all aspects of Higher Business Education. It will be designed for student and staff use with all of the advanced courses at all of the educational institutions mentioned above. Each book in the series will have both a planned part in the series and be complete in itself, and each will adopt a thematic and problem-solving approach.

The editorial team have chosen authors who are experienced people from technological institutions and from professional practice and will collaborate with them to ensure that the books are authoritative and written in a style which will make them easy to use and which will assist the students to learn effectively from such use.

The editorial team will welcome criticisms on each of the books so that improvements may be made at the reprint stages to ensure a closer achievement of the objectives of the books and all the series.

Edwin Kerr
General Editor

Preface

This book is intended for students of management taking a course in occupational psychology, including students on BEC courses, undergraduates at polytechnics and universities, diploma students and others. For a fairly simple but useful way of looking at human behaviour in organisations three levels of description may be utilised: individuals, groups and the total organisation. The more *macro* issues concerning groups and organisations are largely the concern of organisational psychologists and others, such as organisational sociologists. The other, *micro*, end of the scale includes, for example, the detailed design of individual work stations or man/machine systems (ergonomics). In a work of this nature some selection of topics is necessary, and inevitably some areas of occupational psychology have not been covered. The authors have based their selection partly on their own knowledge and expertise, and their most important criterion throughout has been to provide as reasonably balanced a view of human behaviour in organisations as possible. This has meant that some important macro and micro issues such as organisation development and ergonomics receive little attention. Our aim has been to capture the middle ground and provide good coverage of some central topics rather than attempt to deal with every aspect of occupational psychology.

Although many fields of occupational psychology are providing increasingly independent theoretical and empirical advances, there are still strong links between occupational psychology and research and theory in the more fundamental aspects of scientific, academic psychology. These links are reflected in the fact that various chapters in this book provide introductory material in some of the relevant areas of basic psychology, such as personality, learning and motivation, as well as examining their relevance to organisational behaviour.

The book is divided into four main sections, and although the book may be read progressively in chapter order, many readers will no doubt prefer not to be constrained in this way. Each chapter, as far as possible, forms a self-contained and coherent whole.

Part One (Chapters 1–2) looks at some macro issues concerning organisations and groups. This provides an overview of the organisational and social context for the remainder of the book. Part Two (Chapters 3–5) deals with individual issues, such as human intellectual qualities, attitudes, personality and motivation. Part Three (Chapters 6–10) is concerned with particular issues in organisational life, including personnel selection practices (i.e. fitting the person to the job) and aspects of job redesign to improve the quality of working life (i.e. fitting the job to the person). The final part of the book, Part Four (Chapters 11–14) includes a chapter on the psychology of human learning, memory and skilled performance, and then examines some of the different perspectives for understanding and influencing human development and change in organisations.

1983   ITR
                                                             CLC

Acknowledgments

This book could not have been written without the help and assistance of many people. A strong expression of gratitude is due to the staff and students in the Department of Management Sciences at UMIST, who provided the positive climate and intellectual stimulation needed. Students and staff involved in the various psychology courses within the Department have had a particular influence on the shape and contents of the book.

We also gratefully extend our thanks to those scholars, researchers and practitioners who have carried out much of the work reported in the book, without whose dedication and ingenuity our chosen field of study would be much the poorer. Our thanks must also go to Macdonald & Evans for commissioning and producing the work and to the following publishers who have generously allowed us to make use of their copyright material:

Academic Press for the figure [Fig. 20] from J.R. Hackman and G.R. Oldham, "Motivation through the design of work: Test of a theory." *Organizational Behaviour and Human Performance.* © 1976 Academic Press, New York. Reprinted by permission.

Addison-Wesley for the figure [Fig. 5] from J.P. Kotter, *Organizational Dynamics.* © 1978 Addison-Wesley, Reading, M.A. Figure 3.1. Reprinted with permission.

The American Association for the Advancement of Science for the figure [Table V] from "Genetics and intelligence: A review" by L. Erlenmeyer-Kimling and L.G. Jarvik from *Science*, Vol. 142, December 1963.

The British Psychological Society for tables from Work Sample Tests: [Tables XI and XII] "Validity, adverse impact and applicant reaction" by I.T. Robertson and R.S. Kandola in *Journal of Occupational Psychology,* Vol. 55, 1982; table [Table II] from "Covariation of cognitive styles intelligence and achievement" by D.J. Satterly in *British Journal of Educational Psychology,* Vol. 49, 1979; figure [Fig. 18] from "A case study of repertory grids used in vocational guidance" by J.M. Smith, J. Hartley and B. Stewart in *Journal of Occupational Psychology,* Vol. 51, 1978; table [Table I] from "Who are we? An analysis of the division of occupational psychology 1981 register of members" by Z. Wedderburn in *Occupational Psychology Newsletter,* No. 10, September 1982.

Her Majesty's Stationery Office for the figure [Fig. 4] from *Management and Technology* by J. Woodward, 1958.

Holt, Rinehart & Winston for tables [Table XIII and Fig. 39] from *The Conditions of Learning* (3rd Edition) by R.M. Gagné, ©

1977 by Holt Rinehart and Winston, and from *Principles of Instructional Design* by R.M. Gagné and L.J. Briggs, © 1974 by Holt, Rinehart and Winston. Both reprinted by permission of Holt, Rinehart and Winston, CBS College Publishing.

Industrial Training Research Unit for a segment [Fig. 40] from *CRAMP: A Guide to Training Decisions. A User's Manual,* 1981.

Institute of Personnel Management for tables [Tables IX and X] from *Testing People at Work* by F. Sneath, M. Thakur and B. Medjuck, 1976.

McGraw-Hill for figure [Fig. 13] from *The Nature of Human Intelligence* by J.P. Guilford, 1967 © McGraw-Hill, New York; figure [Fig. 28] from *Personnel Testing* by R.M. Guion, 1965© McGraw-Hill, New York; and figure [Fig. 21] from *Perspectives on Behavior in Organizations* by J.R. Hackman, E.E. Lawler and L.W. Porter, 1977 © McGraw-Hill, New York. All reprinted by permission.

National Foundation for Educational Research Publishing Company Limited for items [Fig. 9] from the AH5 Group Test of High Grade Intelligence.

The Editors of *Personnel Psychology* for figure [Fig. 30] from "The employment interview: A summary and review of recent literature" by R.D. Arvey and J.E. Campion in *Personnel Psychology,* Vol. 35, 1982; tables [Fig. 31] from "The biographical item: Can it be improved?" by J.J. Asher in *Personnel Psychology,* Vol. 25, 1972, [Table VIII] "The validity of aptitude tests in personnel selection" by E.E. Ghiselli in *Personnel Psychology,* Vol. 26, 1973, and [Table VII] "Social and situational determinants of interview decisions: Implications for the employment interview" by N. Schmitt in *Personnel Psychology,* Vol. 29, 1976.

Saxon House, D.C. Heath Ltd for figure [Fig. 2] from *Organisation Structure in Its Context* by D.S. Pugh and D.J. Hickson, 1976.

Scott, Foresman for figure [Table XIV] from *Organisational Behaviour Modification* by Fred Luthans and Robert Kreitner, copyright © 1975 by Scott, Foresman and Company. Reprinted by permission.

NOTE: Every effort has been made to contact all copyright holders, but if any have been inadvertently overlooked, the publishers will be pleased to make the necessary arrangement at the earliest opportunity.

Last, but by no means least, our thanks go to Kath Wilkinson who typed and retyped the various drafts and final manuscripts, employing considerable skill and good humour.

Contents

PART THREE: ISSUES AND PRACTICES IN
ORGANISATIONAL LIFE

PART FOUR: LEARNING, DEVELOPMENT AND BEHAVIOUR
CHANGE IN ORGANISATIONS

To Kathy, Susannah, and James; Rachel, Beth, Scott, and Laura

Introduction

Social and behavioural scientists from many disciplines such as sociology, economics, psychology and political science have contributed to our understanding of organisational life. Since this book focuses on *human behaviour* in organisations, much of the material presented is drawn from the work of psychologists and, in particular, from the work of those psychologists who specialise in the industrial/organisational field.

Traditional industrial psychology developed from attempts to apply the theories, techniques and procedures of psychology to the practical problems of work behaviour. One major and lasting impact has been in the field of personnel selection. The use of psychological knowledge to aid the personnel selection process first took place on a wide scale during the First World War. In the United States a massive programme of psychological testing was instituted and the results were used to help to allocate service personnel to jobs and training courses in line with their abilities and aptitudes. During the Second World War, psychological techniques were used widely in both the United States and the United Kingdom. Subsequently, their use has spread into industry, commerce and the public service, and today personnel selection is one of the major areas of activity for applied psychologists interested in work behaviour. Other major areas of activity which fall within the scope of traditional industrial psychology include training, personnel appraisal and job analysis.

Organisational psychology, at least as a specific name for an area of research and practice, has a shorter but no less interesting history. It represents an attempt by psychologists to broaden their expertise and conceptual frameworks in an effort to cope with the full complexity of the person-related aspects of life within organisations. Although traditional industrial psychology had and still has an important contribution to make, some psychologists and others outside the discipline were critical of work in the field for a variety of reasons, including a lack of theoretical basis, an apparent unquestioning acceptance of many of the customs and practices within organisations and a narrow, over-restrictive range of interests which did not pay sufficient attention to the social and interpersonal issues involved in organisational behaviour. Argyris (1976) provides an interesting exploration of these and other issues. Increasingly from about the 1950s onwards, scholars in a variety of disciplines, particularly sociology and social psychology, began to take an interest in developing some scientific understanding of the nature of modern organisations. This, and no doubt many other factors, concerned with changes in the social and scientific environment, led psychologists to widen their spheres of interest to include topics concerned with most aspects of organisational behaviour. In the United States the change was reflected in a change of name for the relevant division of the American Psychological Association (APA). In 1973, Division 14 of the APA changed its name from Division of Industrial Psychology to Division of Industrial and Organisational Psychology.

In Great Britain the term occupational psychology has been employed for some time and its current usage seems to encompass both industrial and organisational psychology. The British Psychological Society's (BPS's) Division of Occupational Psychology (concerned with the professional activities of occupational psychologists) was formed in 1971, although its origins can be traced back at least to the 1930s and are linked with pioneering work carried out by the Industrial Health Research Board and the National Institute of Industrial Psychology. The BPS's Section of Occupational Psychology (concerned with scientific aspects of occupational psychology) was formed some time before the division. As noted above, it seems that in Britain the term occupational psychology is, to a large extent, synonymous with industrial/organisational psychology. A recent survey of the activities of members of the Division of Occupational Psychology

TABLE I. THE TOP FIVE AREAS OF COMPETENT PRACTICE FOR MEMBERS OF THE DIVISION OF OCCUPATIONAL PSYCHOLOGY

Area	Members endorsing each area as "A current area of competent practice"	
	Number	Per cent
Personnel selection	123	59
Interview techniques	108	52
Career and management development	102	49
Identification of training needs	97	47
Organisational behaviour and development	97	47

Source: Wedderburn (1982).

(Wedderburn, 1982) demonstrates this. Although the survey indicates that the top five areas of competent practice for occupational psychologists show a bias towards industrial psychology (*see* Table I), new headings suggested for inclusion by respondents include a large number of topics in the organisational psychology field. As Wedderburn (1982) points out: "Perhaps the most apt comment on these suggested new areas is that they indicate that occupational psychology is continuing to grow and develop and stretch out of the classification system" (p. 11).

PART ONE

Organisations and Groups

CHAPTER ONE

Organisations

OBJECTIVES

In modern society most people spend their working lives in an organisation of some sort and therefore have first-hand experience of organisational life. This chapter considers some of the research findings and theoretical work that help to provide a better understanding of the nature of organisations. An examination of the structural aspects of organisations revealed by organisation charts and other formal documents leads to a consideration of some of the complex interrelationships that exist between factors such as organisation structure, technology and environment. The second half of the chapter discusses the use of systems concepts as a means for describing and gaining insights into organisations. Finally, contemporary, open systems approaches to organisation theory are outlined.

CHARACTERISTICS OF ORGANISATIONS

An organisation is "a collection of interacting and interdependent individuals who work toward common goals and whose relationships are determined according to a certain structure" (Duncan, 1981, p. 5). This definition provides a useful starting-point for an examination of organisations, although as this chapter and many other chapters throughout the book demonstrate, the nature of organisations and the behaviour of the people who create them and work in them are so complex that any brief definition is bound to be imperfect. The above definition does, however, make some important points, which can be elaborated upon:

(*a*) Organisations are human creations and fundamentally they consist of people, rather than buildings, equipment, machinery, etc.

(*b*) The term "organisation" is general and not restricted to industrial or commercial firms. Educational and medical institutions, social clubs and a wide range of other organised human activities fall within the definition.

(*c*) People within organisations must, to some extent, be working to common goals and co-ordinate their activities to this end. This does not, however, mean that everyone in the organisation has the same set of goals and priorities, nor that all the goals are explicit and clear to everyone.

(*d*) Although relationships between people are determined according to a *certain* structure, informal or unofficial groups and structures can be at least as important as the formal organisation structure.

FORMAL ORGANISATION STRUCTURE

The structure of an organisation is often depicted with the aid of an organisation chart; a typical chart (*see* Fig. 1) provides an indication of the formal relationships between the management, supervisory and other staff in the organisation. Such charts indicate the overall shape of the organisation and provide an outline of the formal decision-making structure. Usually, for instance, positions higher up the chart have more power and authority than those lower down. The lines linking the positions in the chart show the formal channels of communication used to exercise this authority, and the overall shape of the chart also shows the number of levels of authority that exist within the organisation. A wide, flat chart, for example, depicts an organisation with few levels of authority where the vertical distance between the most junior and most senior position is relatively small. A narrow, tall chart shows the opposite case of an organisation with many levels of authority.

Roles not people

Organisation charts show the relationships between specific jobs or roles within the organisation. In some cases named individuals are shown to be the holders of specific positions, but the basic function of the chart is to represent the organisation structure, regardless of the particular people who fill the positions shown. This distinction between roles and people is supported in an extreme form by structural sociologists such as Perrow, who argue that in the design and analysis of organisations it makes sense to focus on "The roles people play rather than the personalities in the roles" (Perrow, 1970, p. 2). Others (e.g. Argyris, 1974) argue that individual personalities are important considerations. The widespread use of organisation charts suggests that there is at least some value in making a distinction between organisational roles and the individuals who fill them. The interrelationships between factors such as organisation structure and the people who work within the organisation is a theme that will be explored at various stages in this chapter.

Specialisation (division of labour)

In many organisations, it is impossible for one person to carry out all of the tasks involved and some degree of specialisation or division of labour usually takes place. Division of labour involves dividing up the activities of the organisation and distributing tasks amongst people, so that everyone does not find himself doing the

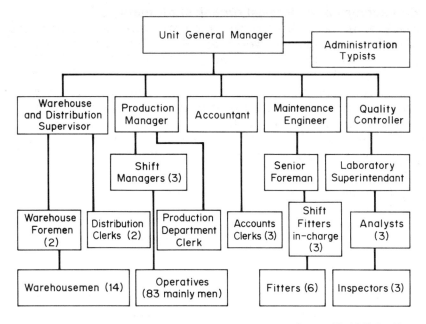

Courtesy Mr J.R.K. Berridge.

Fig. 1. *The organisation chart for Savor Products Unit—a sub-unit of Ashbourne Pure Foods Ltd.*

same collection of tasks. The basic division of labour used by most organisations is shown by the horizontal divisions in the organisation chart (*see* Fig. 1 *above*). Often the required specialisation is achieved not only by allocating different tasks to individuals but by dividing the organisation into separate departments or sub-units either on a functional basis (e.g. Sales, Marketing, Personnel), a product basis or perhaps into geographical regions.

Organisation charts reflect not only the horizontal division of labour that is a feature of modern organisations but also show that organisations are subdivided on a vertical basis. The organisation chart reveals the chain(s) of command in the organisation and it is usually possible to trace a chain of command through from the most junior to the most senior member of the organisation. In some organisations authority and decision-making may be "centralised" and be allocated to a relatively small number of people, while in others authority is "decentralised".

A further characteristic of organisation structure is span of control. At its simplest, the span of control of a manager or supervisor is indicated by the number of subordinates reporting directly to that person, and it is usually revealed on a comprehensive organisation chart.

Bureaucracy and classical organisation theory

Many of the aspects of organisation structure considered above were first examined in work carried out by early organisation theorists and management scientists such as Taylor (1911), Fayol (1930) and Weber (1947), who developed their ideas about organisations during the early part of the twentieth century. Weber, for example, produced a series of publications concerned with the structure of organisations and the exercise of power and authority within them. He proposed the "bureaucratic" model of organisations where work is organised and conducted on an entirely rational basis. Some of the essential features of a bureaucracy are:

(*a*) specialisation or division of labour;
(*b*) a hierarchy of authority;
(*c*) written rules and regulations; and
(*d*) rational application of rules and procedures.

Since Weber's time bureaucracy has become a derogatory term associated with the excessive and often completely irrational use of rules and regulations. In many ways, however, Weber's work represents the beginning of modern theories of organisations, and many of the issues addressed by Weber and other "classical" theorists are of lasting importance.

Dimensions of organisation structure

Much of the work of the early organisation theorists such as Weber was concerned with the ways in which organisations should be structured to ensure maximum efficiency, and structural aspects are still important when an attempt is made to build up a comprehensive picture of an organisation.

A long-term series of studies begun at the University of Aston in Birmingham examined various aspects of organisation structure and, by extensive studies of real organisations, have attempted to identify some of the major dimensions of structure. The structural variables examined by the Aston team were:

(*a*) *Specialisation*. The extent to which specialised tasks and roles are allocated to members of the organisation.

(*b*) *Standardisation*. The extent to which an organisation has standard procedures.

(*c*) *Formalisation*. The degree to which rules, procedures, instructions, etc., are written down.

(*d*) *Centralisation*. The degree to which certain aspects of authority and decision-making are located at the top of the organisational hierarchy.

(*e*) *Configuration*. The shape of the organisation's role structure (e.g. whether the chain of command is long or short).

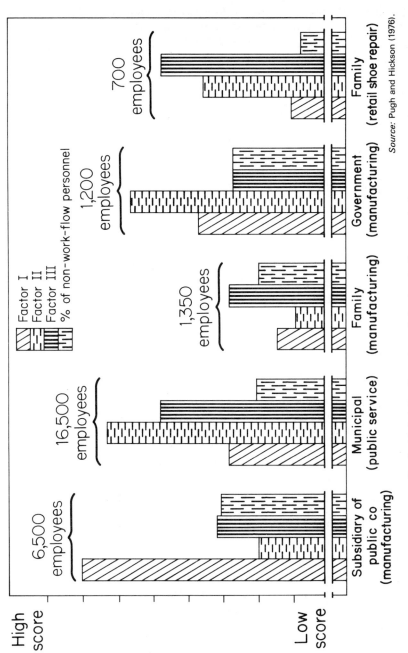

Fig. 2. *Underlying dimensions of structure in five organisations.*

Source: Pugh and Hickson (1976).

After considerable data collection and analysis the researchers were able to show that three underlying factors seemed to underpin the variations in organisation structure that they observed. These underlying factors are summarised in Payne and Pugh (1976). They are:

(*a*) *Structuring of activities.* The extent to which employee behaviour is defined by specialised jobs, routines, procedures, etc. (factor I).

(*b*) *Concentration of authority.* The degree to which the authority to take decisions is concentrated at the higher levels in the organisation's hierarchy (factor II).

(*c*) *Line control of work-flow.* The degree to which control is exercised through line personnel or through impersonal procedures (factor III).

Some examples of organisations with differing structural characteristics are given in Fig. 2. Others (e.g. James and Jones, 1976) have proposed slightly different sets of organisation structure variables (*see* Fig. 3).

The "Aston" studies	*An alternative classification*
(*see* Payne and Pugh, 1971)	(*see* James and Jones, 1976)
SPECIALISATION	SPECIALISATION
CENTRALISATION	CENTRALISATION
CONFIGURATION	Span of control
	Size
	Interdependence of components
STANDARDISATION	STANDARDISATION
FORMALISATION	PERVASIVENESS OF RULES

Fig. 3. *Major dimensions of organisation structure.*

Whichever structural factors are considered, it must be emphasised that factors such as specialisation or standardisation are concerned with the structure of the organisation only and do not provide direct evidence of how members of the organisation behave in practice. As Pugh and Hickson (1976) note:

". . . none of the variables of structure are directly related with individual behaviour in the organisation. Specialisation is concerned with the existence of separate functions and roles, not whether the individuals in them trespass outside their territories or not; standardisation is concerned with the existence of procedures, not whether they are conformed to. . . ." (p. 185).

STRUCTURE, TECHNOLOGY AND ENVIRONMENT

The fact that organisations can be described by using certain basic concepts of structural form raises the possibility that some structures will be more efficient than others. Woodward (1958) carried out research designed to examine the links between organisational success, size and structural form. The research examined 100 British organisations ranging in size from 250 to over 1,000 employees. The commercial success of each firm was assessed and relationships between commercial success and structural form were examined. The analysis, in the first instance, established no correlations between the structural factors and successful performance. Subsequently the researchers grouped the organisations into categories on the basis of the production methods (or technology) that they were using. Organisations were categorised into three groups:

(a) *Small batch and unit production,* where products are designed and manufactured on a "custom-made" basis, involving the production of single units or small batches, often to customer specifications, e.g. prototype electronic equipment.

(b) *Large batch and mass production,* where standard products are manufactured in large quantities, e.g. motor-car production lines.

(c) *Process production,* such as the continuous flow production of liquids or gases in the chemical industry.

When the organisations were regrouped on the basis of technology various links with the structural factors became apparent (*see* Fig. 4). As Fig. 4 reveals, organisations in the different categories showed marked differences in span of control. The research also established links between technology and the number of levels in the management hierarchy, and the ratio of managers and supervisory staff to other personnel.

The most important point is that the successful organisations in each category had *different structures.* For example, the spans of control of successful organisations in the unit production category were lower than those in the mass-production category. For the present purposes the main issues of interest are the demonstration that in the sample of organisations studied:

(a) there was no general link between organisational success and structural form; and

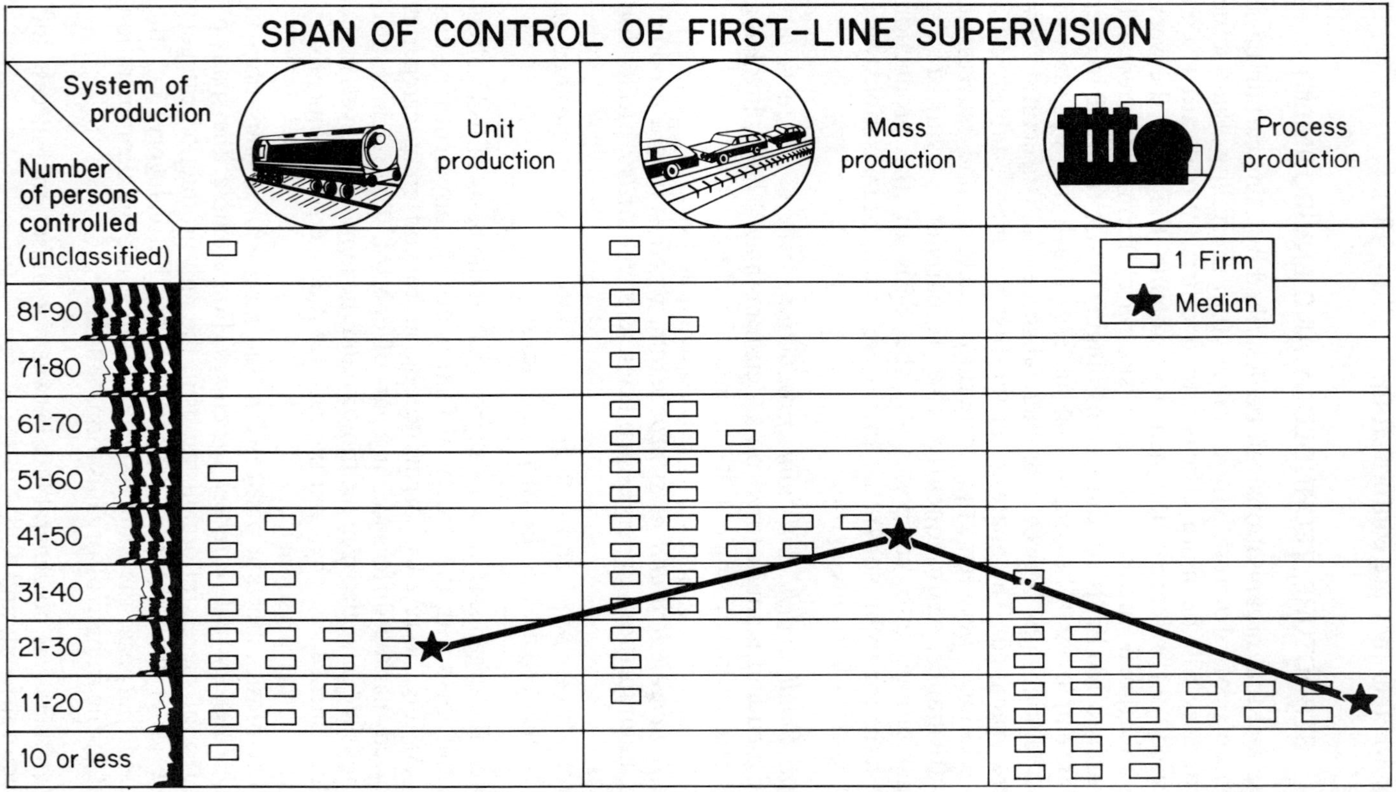

SPAN OF CONTROL OF FIRST-LINE SUPERVISION

Number of persons controlled	System of production	Unit production	Mass production	Process production

☐ 1 Firm
★ Median

Source: Woodward (1958).

Fig. 4. *Illustrative results from Woodward's study.*

(*b*) successful organisations had different structural forms, depending on the technology that they were using.

Woodward herself recognised many imperfections in the study carried out (Woodward, 1965). The specific findings and methodology of the study have also been criticised by others (e.g. Davis and Taylor, 1976). Nevertheless, the study represented a landmark in research in organisations.

A substantial amount of further research has been done to examine technology structure relationships (*see*, e.g., Pugh and Hickson, 1976). An examination of the available work reveals that although structure and technology seem to be related, it is not clear whether structure influences technology, technology influences structure or how much other factors have affected both (*see* Bedeian, 1980, for a review). Regardless of the detailed relationship between technology and structure, it is clear that there is no single, ideal structural form for all organisations.

Other researchers have shown how factors other than structure can be linked with aspects of organisational design and management. Burns and Stalker (1961), for example, have shown that organisations tend to use different management practices depending on the environmental conditions (e.g. rate of technological change in the industry concerned), and Lawrence and Lorsch (1967) have examined the links between environmental factors and effective organisation design.

The findings of both Lawrence and Lorsch and Burns and Stalker suggest that different types of organisations are likely to be successful in different environments, and few people would dispute that organisational success is dependent, to some extent, on the existence of a good match between the organisation's characteristics and the surrounding environment. Some evidence does, however, suggest that the need for a good organisation-environment match is not a critical determinant of an organisation's success. Taken as a whole, the evidence concerning organisation-environment interaction provides some rather conflicting results (Filley *et al.*, 1976). It has been suggested (e.g. Weick, 1977) that organisations do not respond to the external environment as it actually is, but to the perception of the environment built up by the members of the organisation. The perceived environment may or may not correspond with "reality", and this subjective interpretation of the environment could explain some of the conflicting research results that have been obtained.

Notwithstanding the complexities of many of the issues for the moment, it is clear that there are many complex links between factors such as organisation structure, technology, environment and the individuals and groups who work within the organisation. Any attempt to develop a comprehensive view of organisations must take this aspect into account.

ORGANISATIONS AS COMPLEX OPEN SYSTEMS

The view of an organisation provided by a static organisation chart and reflected in the structural dimensions of organisations is clearly incomplete and does not provide a comprehensive picture. In an attempt to describe organisations more adequately, many writers make use of ideas derived from *systems theory*. An open system in its simplest form involves an input, a transformation process and an output. A "closed" system, by contrast, does not involve inputs and outputs and is independent of external forces. Organisations that are part of the social and economic fabric of the environment in which they exist, should clearly be represented as open systems. Thus a system view of an organisation manufacturing motor cars (*see* Fig. 5) would involve an *input* of goods and materials and the use of mass-production technology to transform the *inputs* into motor cars, the *outputs*. Other organisations have different inputs, transformation processes and outputs.

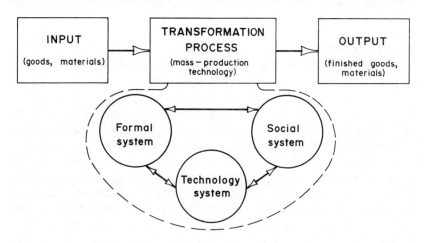

Fig. 5. *An open system view of an organisation.*

One important feature of the systems approach is that a particular system may be subdivided into smaller sub-systems. Many organisations (including car factories) could, for instance, be subdivided into a *formal system*, involving the formal or structural aspects of organisations discussed earlier, a *technology or produc-*

tion system, and a *social system*, concerned with the individuals and groups of employees within the organisation (*see* Fig. 5). Each sub-system interacts with every other sub-system, and the organisation also interacts with the external environment. In turn the sub-systems in Fig. 5 could be further subdivided, and of course the organisation itself is merely a sub-system of other super-systems—the economic system of the country, for example.

Describing organisations with the aid of systems concepts highlights two important issues:

(*a*) *Interaction and interrelatedness.* Ackoff and Emery (1972) define a system as "a set of interrelated elements, each of which is related directly or indirectly to every other element, and no subset of which is unrelated to any other subset". Using systems concepts to understand organisations helps to emphasise the point that any aspect of the organisation, e.g. structure, technology, individuals, work groups, departments, etc., cannot be considered as separate, self-contained elements or units of analysis. The elements or sub-systems in the organisation system are part of a complex, interconnected network.

(*b*) *Levels of analysis.* Any system is part of a wider super-system *and* can be subdivided into sub-systems. For example, the social system of an organisation could be considered as a whole, subdivided into systems based on groups of workers, or broken down into individual (single person) systems. Which level of analysis is most useful?

Although some writers have proposed a specific answer to this question (e.g. Katz and Kahn, 1978), it seems that the important contribution of the systems approach is that it draws attention to the problems of levels of analysis rather than that it provides a solution to the problem. In most circumstances the level of analysis that is most useful depends on the problem being addressed and, just as there is no ideal organisation to adopt, there is no ideal level of analysis for all purposes. This view is confirmed to some extent by the fact that organisational psychologists and sociologists have made use of systems concepts to study organisations at various levels of analysis. Katz and Kahn (1978) provide a thorough discussion of the use of systems theory to gain insights into some important psychological aspects of organisations. They also cover most of the more technical aspects of systems theory that have been omitted from the above discussion.

Systems theory in its strongest and most technical form makes detailed proposals about the properties of systems and the processes involved in system survival, growth and decay. Buckley (1967) and

Silverman (1970) have provided some strong criticism of the use of systems theories in the study of organisations. They are critical, for instance, of the fact that some systems theorists appear to consider organisations as "natural" systems which are capable of initiating action and, for example, attempt to ensure their own survival. In other words, some theorists treat organisations as if they were living organisms capable of an independent life of their own. As Silverman points out, when discussing the influences of the environment, "Organisations do not react to their environment, their members do" (p. 37).

Silverman is also concerned that the models developed by systems theorists may represent the important features of organisations from the theorists' (observer's) point of view but fail to capture adequately the way in which the organisational factors involved are seen by members of the organisation: "People act in terms of their own and not the observer's definition of the situation" (Ibid.).

Many organisational psychologists use systems ideas in a fairly dilute form, often merely to indicate the interaction and interrelatedness of organisational factors and to identify different variables and possible levels of analysis. They do not necessarily employ many of the more technical and often more controversial aspects of systems theory. Payne and Pugh (1971), for instance, make some use of systems ideas to present "a framework for behaviour in organisations" (p. 375). Their framework incorporates a series of interlocking systems divided into four different levels of analysis:

(a) organisation;
(b) department or segment within organisation;
(c) work team or group;
(d) individual.

They suggest that the main purpose of the framework is to provide an indication of the main features, in organisational life, the levels of analysis and interrelationships involved. This somewhat non-technical way of using systems concepts (which is also apparent in the model proposed by Kotter (1978) and described later in this chapter) does seem to provide a helpful way of conceptualising organisational variables.

Socio-technical systems
A good demonstration of the interacting nature of social and technological systems is provided in some work carried out by the

Tavistock Institute of Human Relations (Trist and Bamforth, 1951). The research examined the consequences of changes in methods of production in British coal-mines. The traditional method of mining, known as the short-wall method, involved small groups of eight to ten men working together as a team. The teams worked fairly independently of each other and each one concentrated on removing coal from a small section of the coal-face. The teams were very tightly knit systems and close relationships often formed between team members; competition between teams, however, was often fierce. The bonds of friendship and enmity were reflected both at work and in the wider community.

Improvements in mining technology led to the installation of new mechanical coal-cutting and removing systems. To operate the new equipment the small teams of miners were reorganised into much larger groups of forty to fifty, divided into specialised task groups and reporting to a single supervisor. These much larger social groups created as a consequence of the new technology were associated with many unsatisfactory changes. The new working procedures (the long-wall method) caused miners to be spread out over much larger distances, making supervision difficult. The social and psychological experiences that were associated with the earlier small teams were never adequately replaced under the new system.

Also, under the long-wall method, more extensive division of labour (specialisation) was introduced and miners became responsible for a more limited range of tasks than under the short-wall method. By and large the miners found this reduction in the scope of their jobs distasteful. With the long-wall method, low productivity predominated. The Tavistock researchers suggested that a "composite" long-wall method would be a better means of organising production. Under the composite method the new technology was used, but aspects of the earlier short-wall method were also incorporated. For example, groups were allowed to select their own members and job rotation was allowed in order to introduce more variety into the work. The composite method, which paid attention to the interacting nature of the social and technical system, produced higher output, less absenteeism and was estimated to be working at 95 per cent of its potential. The conventional long-wall method had lower output, higher absenteeism and worked to only 78 per cent of its potential.

Some more recent socio-technical systems research (Trist et al., 1977) has examined the changes in quality of working life that can result from attempts to make the best possible match between social and technical systems. Quality of working life is considered in detail in Chapter 10.

Major elements of organisational dynamics

So far four different and interrelated elements of organisational dynamics have been mentioned: formal (structural) organisational characteristics, technology, environment and social systems. Kotter (1978) has integrated these and other aspects into an overall framework for examining organisations (*see* Fig. 6). The following notes apply to Fig. 6:

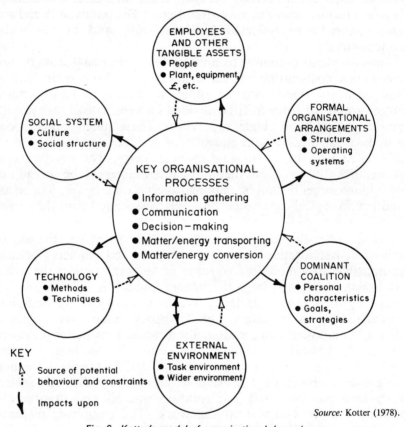

Source: Kotter (1978).

Fig. 6. *Kotter's model of organisational dynamics.*

(*a*) *Key organisational processes.* The major information-gathering, communication, decision-making, matter/energy transporting and matter/energy converting actions of the organisation's employees and machines.

(*b*) *External environment.* An organisation's *task* environment includes suppliers (of labour, information, materials and so on), markets, competitors and other factors related to the organisation's current products and services. The *wider* environment includes factors such as public attitudes, the economic and political systems, laws, etc.

(*c*) *Employees and other tangible assets.* Employees, plant and offices, equipment, tools, etc.

(*d*) *Formal organisational arrangements.* Formal systems explicitly designed to regulate the actions of employees (and machines).

(*e*) *The social system. Culture* (i.e. values and norms shared by employees) and *structure* (i.e. relationships between employees in terms of such variables as power, affiliation and trust.

(*f*) *Technology.* The major techniques that are used by employees while engaging in organisational processes and that are programmed into an organisation's machines.

(*g*) *The dominant coalition.* The objectives and strategies, the personal characteristics and the internal relationships of that minimum group of co-operating employees who oversee the organisation as a whole and control its basic policy-making.

Schein (1980) comments as follows on Kotter's work.

> In summary, Kotter's model provides a systematic check list of elements to analyse . . . types of interactions among elements to consider. . . . This type of model takes the open systems point of view to its logical conclusion in identifying the wide variety of interactions that must be analysed if adaptability is to be maximised (pp. 227-8).

In this respect, Kotter's model is in keeping with most contemporary attempts to deal with organisations in that it does not attempt to provide a total picture of every possible element involved, nor does it seek to understand or explain all of the possible interconnections and interrelationships, a task that is well beyond our current state of knowledge and perhaps always will be.

QUESTIONS

1. What are some of the main dimensions of organisation structure?

2. How do organisation structure, environment and technology interact?

3. What does the open-systems approach to organisations involve?

4. What are the strengths and weaknesses of the systems approach to organisations?

CHAPTER TWO

Group Behaviour

OBJECTIVES

Since group behaviour is so important a part of our everyday life, particularly in the work-place, this chapter will focus on various aspects of such behaviour. We shall look at the reasons why people join groups, how they interact with people in groups (both verbally and non-verbally) and at the different roles that people play in the course of interacting. Finally, the chapter examines how groups monitor all this—that is, how they control the behaviour of their members.

GROUPS

Organisations are composed not only of individual people but of groupings of people. It is vital for an understanding of organisation behaviour, therefore, to appreciate fully group behaviour. With this aim we shall explore the answers to the following four questions:

(*a*) Why do people join groups or come to be in various groupings?
(*b*) How do people interact with one another and in groups?
(*c*) What roles do people play in groups?
(*d*) How are groups managed?

Group membership

There is a wide variety of reasons why people join groups or find themselves as members of a group (Argyle, 1973). Some of these reasons are conscious and deliberate, while others are a result of circumstance or situation. One of the primary motivations why people group together is *to achieve some task that they could not accomplish alone*, e.g. to build an aeroplane, to manufacture steel, etc. Primitive man was forced to join with his fellow men to search for food and to protect himself against the elements, etc. This process has grown only by degree over the centuries and is still the basis for most groupings.

Second, some people are motivated to affiliate to a group *by their need for friendship, support and companionship*. This is most obvious in social clubs of one sort or another, but is also very much present in work organisations, with the formation of "informal" social groupings among workers and managers alike. The original Hawthorne studies (Roethlisberger and Dickson, 1939) are full of such examples.

A third reason some people may join groups is to put themselves in a position of *power*, either because they have strong needs to control others or because they want the *status* or respect that goes with a leadership role. Frequently, people who join groups for these sorts of reasons are unaware of them or would prefer not to be aware of them. Nevertheless, an awareness of this "motivation need" may be important for an understanding of particular situations that may occur in an organisation, e.g. long-term industrial disputes where neither side is prepared to give way (Cooper, 1982).

Fourth, a person may join a group *for the warmth and psychological security it provides*, or what Argyle (1973) refers to as the "need to be dependent". The famous Harlow (1962) monkey study illustrates this motivation. In his research Harlow reared baby monkeys with different surrogate mothers—one was a monkey made of steel wire, while the other was of a soft terry cloth. Even though both surrogates provided the babies with milk, all the babies preferred the "warm and cuddly" mother, constantly seeking her out for comfort. Some people enter relationships and groups to be dependent, submissive or to be taken care of.

An extension of the foregoing is the way some people affiliate with others not so much to maintain a psychological dependency role, but as a method of self-protection—protection that only a group could provide. This is particularly the case with trade-union membership, for example. It is an attempt to protect oneself by communal effort against the use of control or power from others perceived to be a threat or who have "means control" over one.

Finally, group membership can provide an individual with a sense of self-identity. The 1982 rail strike in Britain revealed a very strong sense of identity among the train-drivers of ASLEF, which helped to keep the strike alive for such a long period of time. As Argyle (1967) suggests, "through group membership a person can develop or confirm some feelings of who he is, can gain some status, and thereby enhance his sense of self-esteem".

HOW DO PEOPLE INTERACT IN GROUPS?

Now that we have some idea of why people group together, it is necessary to understand the various ways in which people interact in groups. It is important to appreciate the subtleties of social interaction, if we are accurately to diagnose group and organisational behaviour. As Handy (1976) has suggested, one of the primary roles of managers in organisations is as a GP, since managers are the "first recipients of problems" that require solutions or decisions. In carrying out this role, managers must be able to identify the symptoms in the group, department or division of the organisation and the possible cause or source of the problems. This requires a thorough understanding of human behaviour, particularly at the interpersonal and group levels (Cooper and Alderfer, 1978).

Verbal interaction

People in groups interact in a variety of ways, both verbally and non-verbally. When they interact verbally, the content of what they say is frequently not as important as "how they say it". These interactions have been referred to as the non-linguistic aspects of speech, involving as they do such characteristics as accents, speech errors, intonation and voice quality, interruptions, silence, etc. The correct understanding of all of these is critical to an effective interaction. If we misjudge the social or regional implications of a particular accent, it can be damaging, thwarting a smooth-flowing encounter with another person. One can, for example, say to someone in a calm and unemotional manner that "I'm really not upset or angry", or one can use the same words in a way that indicates the opposite. The actual content of the communications in many cases is less important than the *style* or other *non-linguistic aspects of the speech,* as many industrial relations experts have come to appreciate after numerous instances of prolonged and unresolved industrial conflicts.

Non-verbal forms of interaction

There is a range of ways in which people communicate to one another in groups. First, one can use *body contact* as a kind of social act. One can express aggression through pushing or affection through touching lightly or by less obvious symbolic gestures such as "patting on the back" for reward or comfort. In organisational terms, the Hawthorn studies (Roethlisberger and Dickson, 1939) found that some workers used "arm punching" as a means of controlling the output of workers so as not to exceed the piece-work norms established in the work group.

Second, *eye movement, gaze and contact* can serve as an extremely important adjunct to social communication. Eye contact can serve a number of very useful purposes. First, it can serve as a mechanism of "information seeking". As Argyle (1967) suggests, "the main reason why people look at the end of their utterances is they need feedback on the other's responses"—are they still listening to what I am saying, was my last message received, or do I have permission to carry on speaking? Of course, we may also avoid eye contact when we do not want the distractions of new information to be fed into our brain at a time when we are trying to think of or verbalise a difficult concept. Second, direction of gaze can be a social signal. It can be used:

(*a*) as a method of initiating an interaction;
(*b*) to show someone that you are attracted or interested in him;
(*c*) as acknowledgment or rejection of a relationship;
(*d*) as a sign of one's sincerity; or
(*e*) in the case of looking up after speaking, as a sign that one has completed a particular speech and that the other person can now speak.

The social interpretations of any particular gaze depend on the length of the gaze, the intensity of the gaze (which one picks up from other non-verbal signals such as facial expression) and the timing of the gaze (when precisely it occurs and for how long during the course of verbal interaction). Since normal eye contact occurs something like 50 per cent of the time during an average conversation, its significance as a communication tool is obvious, and the accurate diagnosis of human behaviour within organisations depends on picking up such subtle interpersonal cues. Indeed, in the myriad of interview situations one finds oneself in at work, the non-verbal forms of interaction are critical.

A third form of non-verbal interaction is *physical proximity* and *position*. The amount of space we put between ourselves and others, although done unconsciously, communicates a great deal about the type of relationship one has or the type one would like to have *vis-à-vis* the other person. Hall (1963) has suggested that there are four zones of personal space that people use in interaction with others:

(*a*) the "intimate" (which involves direct body contact);
(*b*) the "casual personal" (within 5 feet);
(*c*) the "social consultative" (between 5 and 10 feet away); and
(*d*) the "public" zone.

"It is obvious that if you like or want to have a close relationship with someone you will position yourself closer to them than if you don't" (Mehrabian, 1968). In group situations people tend to position themselves opposite to people with whom they are in an authority role, and next to people with whom they have an informal relationship (Sommer, 1961). The position of people either in a one-to-one relationship or in a group situation is highly revealing of status relationships, role differentiation and differences in inter-personal liking between those involved.

In organisational terms, the spatial environment of work plays a very important part in job satisfaction and general well-being. For example, a case study by Richards abd Dobyns (1957) illustrates the impact of the spatial and physical environment and limited opportunities for social interaction on a work group's satisfaction and, consequently, on its productivity.

Workers in a voucher-check filing unit in an insurance company worked together well, kept up with the work load and expressed feelings of satisfaction. Their work area was inside a wire cage surrounded by filing cabinets and boxes through which the group's supervisor could not see them. For efficiency purposes, the cage was moved to a new area in which the filing cabinets were arranged so that supervisors could see into the cage and restrict worker interaction. The workers could no longer engage in social activities which had been important to them (talking, eating together, playing games, etc.). Their output declined drastically, the amount of time spent in non-work activities increased substantially and the workers expressed considerable dissatisfaction with the new set-up.

It can be seen that the new socio-technical or spatial environment had an unforeseen consequence of blocking the needs of the workers to interact and develop closer personal relationships. The supervisor's ability to intrude on the social space of the workers was a significant factor in the decline of satisfaction and productivity.

Argyle and Dean (1965) claim that there is an approach-avoidance theory of proximity, whereby individuals are "both attracted and repelled by another, and take up positions corresponding to an equilibrium position". According to them, "if two people like one another, the approach forces would be stronger and greater proximity results".

Lastly, another form of non-verbal interaction is *facial expression* and *gestures*. The movements of your hands, body, feet and other parts of your body can tell another person a great deal about you. It can tell him if you are anxious or relaxed, if you consider yourself to be his equal, subordinate or superordinate, etc. As far as facial expressions are concerned, there are a variety of roles they can play in human interaction. Argyle (1973) suggests the following: "(a) it shows the emotional state of an interactor, though he may try to conceal this, (b) it provides continuous feedback on whether he understands, is surprised, agrees, etc., with what is being said . . ., (c) it indicates attitudes to others . . ., (d) it can act as a meta communication, modifying or commenting on what is being said or done at the time".

Indeed, Schlosberg (1952) suggested that facial expressions could be ranged in a circular pattern from *love* at one point to *anger* at the opposite side (*see* Fig. 7). He suggested that one can easily discriminate between emotions on people's faces that are further apart in this circle, but that one would find it increasingly more

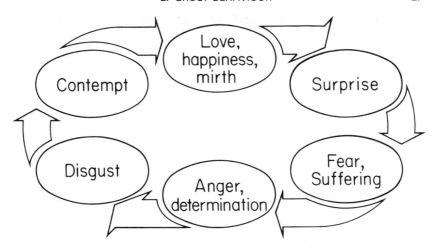

Fig. 7. *Schlosberg's (1952) circle of emotions.*

difficult to distinguish between those which were closer together, e.g. between love and surprise or anger and fear. As Argyle (1973) suggests, "the face appears to be the main region for communicating emotions; it is the area that is looked at during interaction, it signals emotion fairly clearly and there are innate patterns of expression". What he meant by this latter point was that facial expressions which depict an emotion are to some extent "culture bound", e.g. the Japanese may smile a great deal while interacting even if they do not particularly like the person with whom they are dealing, or the American who uses the Christian name of somebody in a first encounter, even if he has no close personal relationship or does not intend to have one.

Gestures are also an important component in the course of social interaction. Indeed, gestures are really a language in themselves, as witnessed by the deaf or by various cultures such as the American Indians or by the Japanese in their kabuki theatre. Argyle (1973) suggests that hand gestures serve a number of quite distinct functions in the process of social interaction:

(*a*) they sometimes replace speech, such as for the deaf or for ground staff at an airport who are trying to communicate to the pilot where to park his aircraft, etc.;

(*b*) they are frequently used to emphasise a point or to illustrate non-verbally a point made verbally; and

(*c*) they may provide the speaker with an opportunity of releasing tension—that is, they can indicate the emotional state of the speaker. One might judge, for example, the nervousness of a particular lecturer by his hand movements prior to and during a lecture.

Krout's (1954)'early studies are quite interesting in respect to (c). He examined the hand movements of 100 subjects after asking them some personal questions. He found that when he aroused fear in his subjects, they tended to place their hands to their nose; but that when on the other hand he aroused aggression, they made fist gestures. He found, in other words, that in a particular culture there were standard hand movements and gestures associated with particular emotional states and that these were understood by most people of that culture.

Body gestures also seem to convey some sort of emotional state. One can see from the illustrations below that there are a number of postures that can communicate a number of different emotional states. The early work of Sarbin and Hardyk (1953) on stick figures confirms this. They presented a series of stick figures in different body poses or postures and asked subjects to describe what the stick character might be feeling at that moment. Their results are shown in Fig. 8.

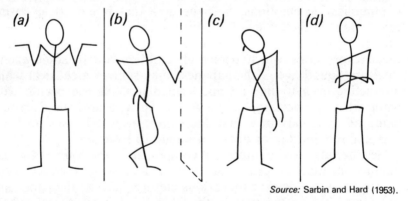

Source: Sarbin and Hard (1953).

Fig. 8. *Stick characters: (a) doubtful, questioning, resigned; (b) casual, self-satisfied; (c) shy, modest; (d) dominating, suspicious.*

WHAT ROLES DO PEOPLE PLAY IN GROUPS?

As well as understanding the processes of social interaction, it is important to be aware of the variety of roles that are played in groups. As Handy (1976) has indicated, "the definition of any individual's role in any situation will be a combination of the *role expectations* that the members of the role set have of the focal role". In other words, the particular roles we play depend on the people around us, *what* they think we should do and *how* they think we should do it. We tend to play out a series of roles in life, from the very early years throughout adulthood. Bossard and Boll (1956), for example, did a study in which they found a variety of roles among 100 families with six or more children. In these families there were children who played the "responsible" role (looking after the young children), others who played "not well" (as a method of gaining attention), or "studious", or "spoiled", etc. Each of these roles fulfilled some function in the family and, once they were reinforced over a number of years, they developed into expected patterns of behaviour, which in a circular process were constantly reinforced again and again.

Much of the early research into role differentiation has suggested that there are two basic roles in all human groups—that of the task leader and of the social emotional specialist (Slater, 1955). Effectively, one person in a group takes on the various behaviours which are necessary for achieving the goals of the group, while the other takes on the role of resolving interpersonal differences, releasing tension, showing solidarity, etc. This has been termed the "hypothesis of two complementary leaders" theory. The approach has been elaborated on by many. For example, Wallen (1963) has suggested that there are three roles in groups, played by a number of different people in a group. They are friend/helper, strong fighter and logical thinker. This approach tends to divide the Slater role of task leader into two: strong fighter and logical thinker. Wallen argues that all groups need a combination of these three roles to be effective; an over-emphasis on any one can have detrimental effects.

Most academics involved in group behaviour would accept that the essence of Wallen's and Slater's differentiation is probably present in all groups. They would, however, also suggest that there are many other roles present in human groups. For example, Handy (1976) highlights at least three other very important adjunct roles to the standard two or three: the comedian, the commentator and the deviant. The *comedian* is the person who acts as a "willing butt for other members of the group and in particular the Chairman". The *commentator*, on the other hand, is a threat to the group, because he "takes it upon himself to maintain an occasional commentary on the proceedings". The *deviant* tends to draw attention to himself by disagreeing with group decisions or the group leader. This serves a very useful purpose in the group, since it provides the group with a focus for their own coherence.

There are many more roles in groups, and Eric Berne in his humorous book *Games People Play* highlights the variety of interpersonal roles human beings use at work, in the home and in organisations.

The difficulties that many people experience in groups occur when there is role ambiguity or conflict. Role ambiguity exists when an individual has inadequate information about his role. For example, in the context of work where there is a lack of clarity about the work objectives associated with the role, about colleagues' work expectation of the work role, and about the scope and responsibilities of the job. French and Caplan (1970) found, at one of NASA's bases, in a sample 205 volunteer engineers, scientists and administrators, that role ambiguity was significantly related to low job satisfaction and to feelings of job-related threat to one's mental and physical health. This was also related to increased blood pressure, pulse rate and physiological strain.

Role conflict, on the other hand, exists when an individual in a particular work role is torn by conflicting job demands or by doing things he really does not want to do, or does not think are part of the job or role specification. The most frequent manifestation of such conflict is when a person is caught between two groups of people who demand different kinds of behaviour, or who see the job as entailing different functions. In organisational terms, the most potentially conflicting roles are those of the shop steward or foreman. Indeed, Margolis and Kroes (1974) found that foremen are seven times more likely to develop ulcers than shop-floor workers.

HOW DO GROUPS MANAGE THEMSELVES?

We have discovered why people join groups, how they behave in them, and we have outlined the various roles they may play while working together. Now we shall explore how groups manage themselves, or more appropriately how they manage to keep together! The process of group maintenance is carried out by group norms—that is, rules of behaviour which govern appropriate and inappropriate ways of acting. As Krech et al. (1962) suggest: "Norms are rules of behaviour, proper ways of acting, which have been accepted as legitimate by members of the group. These rules or standards of behaviour to which members are expected to conform are, for the most part, derived from the goals which a group has set for itself." Although all groups have a normative structure of "rights and wrongs" of behaviour, to which all members adhere or for which they are punished, many of the members may be consciously unaware of them. On a day-to-day basis, people in groups simply adhere to these unwritten but fully accepted codes of behaviour or suffer the consequence of punishment or group rejection or eviction.

The classic Hawthorne studies illustrate this concept, as described by Schein (1965):

> In the late 1920s a group of girls who assemble telephone equipment were the subjects of a series of studies undertaken to determine the effect on their output of working conditions, length of working day, number and length of rest pause, etc. . . . . The girls, especially chosen for the study, were placed in a special room under a supervisor and were carefully observed (p. 31).
>
> The group as a whole had some "norms", certain ideas of what was a proper and fair way for things to be. Several of these norms concerned the production rate of the group and could best be described by the concept of a "fair day's work for a fair day's pay". In other words, the group had established the norm of how much production was "fair", namely, 6,000 units, a figure which satisfied management but well below what the men could have produced had fatigue been the only limiting factor . . . . Being deviant in either direction elicited kidding rebukes, social pressure to get back into line and social ostracism if the person did not respond to the pressure (p. 33).

Indeed, as it happens, the workers were colluding to establish a rate of production much lower than they could actually achieve, so that greater piece-rate incentives or bonuses could be earned.

When an individual finds that his behaviour deviates from the group's norms, he has four options: to leave the group, to conform to the norms, to try to change the norms or to remain in a deviant role. The option that a particular individual takes will depend on his own personality, the support of others in the group, the strength of feelings he has about the particular issue on which he is asked to conform, etc. However, the power of groups to exercise control over their members is great. Sherif (1935) found this in his early studies on the auto-kinetic effect. Here each student was asked to judge in what direction and how far a dot of light in a darkened room moved. The light actually does not move, but only appears to do so. Under these conditions, each student develops a range in which he makes his estimates. It was found by Sherif that if an individual made judgments about the movement of this light when others were present, that the student's judgments were in the direction and distance of the judgments around him, even if his original estimates, made when alone, were in the opposite direction! That is, the individual student was strongly influenced by the group's judgments.

In summary, we have seen that there is a variety of aspects of group behaviour which influence its development and effectiveness. We have been exploring the factors that are "givens" in the situation and not the many unpredictable intervening variables, such as leadership style of a formal leader, the psychometric make-up of the individual group members, the motivation of members, etc. To predict group behaviour is an almost impossible task, but at least we can be more aware of some of the dynamics and processes that make them up. As Handy (1976) has suggested: "Groups there must be. Individuals must be co-ordinated and their skills and abilities meshed and merged. But let us not be mesmerised. Let us realise that a proper understanding of groups will demonstrate how difficult they are to manage. Let us pay more attention to their creation and be more realistic about their outcomes."

QUESTIONS

1. Why do people join groups?
2. Why do people interact in groups?
3. What roles do people play in groups?
4. How do groups manage themselves?

PART TWO

Individuals

CHAPTER THREE

Human Intellectual Qualities: Intelligence and Cognitive Style

OBJECTIVES

As Chapter 7 reveals, psychological tests of intelligence and ability have found widespread use within organisational settings. This chapter considers some of the fundamental research from which these tests were derived and examines a wide range of other related issues. The measurement and structure of intelligence are considered first and the view that intelligence consists of a general factor (involved in all mental abilities) and various more specific factors is developed. Next, some of the current controversies concerning the genetic or environmental basis of intelligence and racial-ethnic differences in intelligence test scores are examined. Some of the criticisms concerning the use of tests are also considered. Intelligence is primarily concerned with intellectual capacity; the final section of this chapter examines individual differences in intellectual strategy and style, which may help to enrich and broaden our view of human intellectual qualities.

THE MEASUREMENT AND STRUCTURE OF INTELLIGENCE

In the early years of the twentieth century two French psychologists, Alfred Binet and Théodore Simon, developed what is generally accepted as the first satisfactory test of human intelligence. At the turn of the nineteenth century France, in common with other industrialised nations, had introduced compulsory education. Most of the children entering the schools seemed well able to benefit from the regular schools. Some were perhaps in need of special help, but could be dealt with by the regular system. A third group, however, were retarded to the point of being unable to benefit from the regular system. It was not always easy to identify the children in need of special treatment, and the test developed by Binet and Simon was intended to help in identifying these children by assessing their intellectual capabilities.

The approach adopted by Binet and Simon is still the basis for contemporary intelligence tests. In essence, Binet and Simon considered that intelligence could be measured by assessing a person's ability to answer a carefully selected collection of questions. Although the questions in modern tests (*see* Fig. 9) sometimes differ from those used by Binet and Simon, the principle of *sampling behaviour* on a carefully selected set of tasks is still at the basis of most tests. Clearly, by *sampling* behaviour one runs the risk of drawing false conclusions about a person—perhaps because of the particular questions asked, circumstances in which the test is

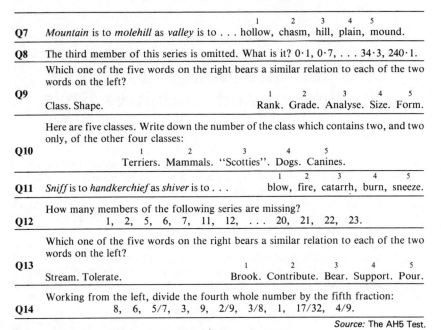

Fig. 9. *Some items from an intelligence test.*

taken, or for various other reasons. Binet and Simon certainly recognised that test scores alone were not enough and they proposed that, before any decision about a child was taken, other types of assessment should be made.

Since the pioneering work of Binet and Simon psychologists have carried out a considerable amount of work in their attempts to measure intelligence and to understand its structure. Much of this work makes use of statistical methods, developed to aid research into human intelligence. These statistical methods (the principal ones are correlation and factor analysis) are now used in many disciplines. Some elementary grasp of these methods is essential to an understanding of the psychology of human mental abilities, and at appropriate points in this chapter both correlation and factor analysis are outlined.

Correlation

An early British researcher, Francis Galton, was interested in the extent to which human mental abilities are inherited from parents. To investigate the influence of heredity Galton examined the similarity that occurred between people who were related. The rationale of his thinking was that if a particular factor (such as intelligence) is influenced by heredity, one would expect unrelated people to show much less similarity than, say, brothers or sisters (siblings). The similarities in question are often a matter of degree (i.e. there is some relationship but they are not identical). Consider, for example, the relationship between the heights of mothers and their daughters. To examine the relationship graphically, one could construct a scatter diagram (scattergram) and plot one variable against the other (*see* Fig. 10). Closely related variables will produce

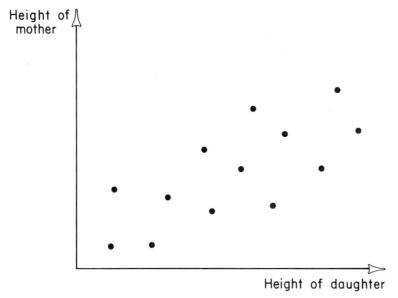

Fig. 10. *A scattergram of the relationship between two variables.*

a thin cigar-shaped distribution of points (*see* Fig. 11 (*a*) or (*b*)), and variables that are unrelated will produce a circular distribution (*see* Fig. 11 (*c*)).

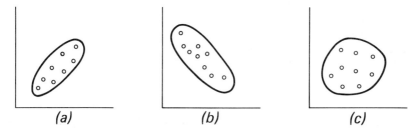

Fig. 11. *A scattergram of related and unrelated variables: (a) positively related variables; (b) negatively related variables; (c) unrelated variables.*

This relationship may be expressed more concisely in a mathematical rather than graphical form—as a correlation coefficient. Correlation coefficients can vary between $+1.00$ and -1.00. When the coefficient is zero, there is no relationship between the variables (*see* Fig. 11 (*c*)). Fig. 11(*a*) shows a *positive correlation coefficient*. When the coefficient is positive (between 0 and $+1.0$), the variables increase together. When the coefficient is negative (*see* Fig. 11 (*b*)), one variable decreases as the other increases.

It must be remembered that a correlation coefficient expresses the degree of relationship between two variables. It does not follow that if two variables are correlated that there is any direct link between them. There would, for example, be a correlation throughout the year between the incidence of games of cricket and the number of butterflies in the air. Both happen to be more prevalent in summer, but one does not cause the other.

Structure of intelligence

Human beings are capable of showing considerable ability in a wide range of pursuits. For some (e.g. a bookmaker's clerk), considerable numerical skill is required; for others (e.g. a journalist), the ability to use words correctly and fluently is important; while yet others (e.g. an architect) need the ability to visualise objects in three dimensions. It would be possible to suggest many further occupational areas and associated abilities. The important point, however, is that it may be superficial to consider intelligence as a single or unitary attribute that can be represented by one overall measure.

Table II shows a typical correlation matrix derived by

TABLE II. CORRELATIONS BETWEEN SOME INTELLECTUAL TESTS

	Maths	*English*	*Geography*	*IQ*
Maths test				
English test	$+.51$			
Geography test	$+.52$	$+.34$		
IQ test	$+.55$	$+.50$	$+.48$	

Source: Adapted from Satterly (1979).

intercorrelating the results of a group of people in a collection of tests. Notice that although some of the correlations are smaller than others, none of them is negative. In other words people who do well in one test, do well (or at least not very badly) in the others. The results in Table II are typical of those obtained when people are tested on a wide range of intellectual tasks.

Results such as this led Spearman (1927) to propose the so-called two-factor theory of the structure of intelligence. This suggested that an underlying factor of general intelligence—"g"—was helpful in performance in all areas of human ability. The existence of such a factor would explain why there is a persistent positive correlation between such a wide range of tests of human intellectual ability. Spearman explained the fact that performance in different types of test varied by proposing that, as well as "g", there were a series of test specific factors—"s".

Other researchers, notably Thurstone (1938), opposed Spearman's view. The view of Thurstone was that intelligence is made up of a loosely related set of "primary abilities" and that the relationships between the various aspects of human performance could be explained more effectively by these underlying primary abilities than by a general factor or "g". Thurstone proposed twelve or so "primary mental abilities", including:

(a) *Verbal comprehension* (v)—important in reading, comprehension and verbal reasoning.

(b) *Space or visualisation* (s)—concerned with the perception and visualisation of objects in space.

(c) *Number* (N)—the speed and accuracy of straightforward arithmetic calculation.

Factor analysis
Investigations of the structure of human abilities usually involved the use of a statistical technique known as factor analysis. Factor analysis is a mathematical technique that can be used to analyse a correlation matrix. It will show how each of the tests used to produce the original correlation matrix can be divided up and allocated to a smaller collection of underlying factors. The following example might aid understanding. Table III shows a correlation matrix. To simplify things the actual correlation coefficients have not been given, but merely an indication of where the correlations have high values.

The correlations between the tests in group A (1-3) are high, as are the correlations between the tests in group B. The correlations of tests from group A with tests from group B are only moderate. What this pattern of correlations suggests is:

(a) that the tests in group A all have something in common (probably a "verbal" factor); and

(b) the tests in group B also have something in common (probably a "spatial" factor).

TABLE III. SIZES OF CORRELATIONS IN A CORRELATION MATRIX

		A			B		
		1	2	3	4	5	6
1	Verbal reasoning	X					
2	Vocabulary		X				
3	Spelling	High		X			
4	Spatial reasoning				X		
5	Drawing accuracy					X	
6	Geometry				High		X

Notice also that all of the tests are correlated positively with each other (the correlations in the hatched areas although lower are still positive). These positive correlations between all of the tests suggest:

(c) the existence of some factor common to all tests (presumably "g").

Table IV shows how a factor analysis for this matrix might appear. The factor analysis provides a numerical statement of the factors underlying the correlation matrix, and the loading of each test on each factor indicates the extent to which the test involves this factor. The first test (verbal reasoning), for example, loads heavily on factor I ("g"), less heavily on factor II (verbal) and not at all on factor III (spatial).

A hierarchy of abilities

The factor analysis in Table IV produces both a general intelligence factor (which would offer support for Spearman) and some specific factors (supporting Thurstone). Some of the differences between the theories of Spearman and his followers and Thurstone and his were due to the use of different techniques of factor analysis, the use of different samples for investigation and so on. In fact a

TABLE IV. THE RESULTS OF A FACTOR ANALYSIS

	FACTORS		
	I (g)	II (verbal)	III (spatial)
Verbal reasoning	0.6	0.5	
Vocabulary	0.7	0.4	
Spelling	0.8	0.3	
Spatial reasoning	0.4		0.6
Drawing accuracy	0.5		0.5
Geometry	0.5		0.7

reconciliation of the two theories is not as difficult as it might at first seem.

The "compromise" theory was proposed by Burt (1940) and elaborated by Vernon (1961, 1969). The hierarchical organisation of mental abilities that they proposed (see Fig. 12) incorporates both general and specific factors. At the top of the hierarchy is "g" the broad general ability factor that is involved in all intellectual performance. But intellectual performance is not explained by "g" alone. Differences of intermediate generality are also important, between verbal-numerical-educational (v:ed), for example, and practical-mechanical-spatial-physical (k:m) factors. In turn the major group factors may be subdivided into increasingly less general minor and specific factors. In general, psychologists in Britain have adopted the hierarchical view of mental abilities. American psychologists have been inclined to adopt a view more in line with Thurstone's original ideas and have continued to search for related specific abilities. Guilford (1967), for instance, has developed a "structure of the intellect" model that classifies abilities by operation, product and content (see Fig. 13). Guilford

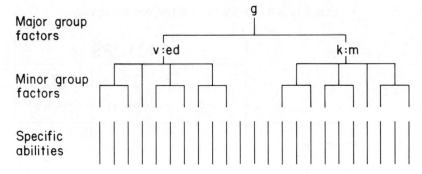

Fig. 12. *The hierarchical structure of human abilities.*

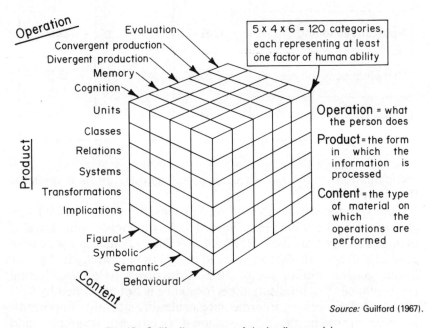

Source: Guilford (1967).

Fig. 13. *Guilford's structure of the intellect model.*

argues and has attempted to demonstrate that it should be possible to produce tests that are independent (i.e. not intercorrelated) for each cell in the cube shown in Fig. 13, i.e. 120 separate abilities in all. Guilford's work has aroused considerable interest, but the theory has not been widely accepted.

INTELLIGENCE AND INTELLIGENCE TESTS

So far we have managed to discuss the underlying structure of intelligence without directly confronting the problem of what intelligence actually is! The defining of intelligence presents problems for psychologists, and to this day there is no universally accepted definition. Many psychologists will settle for the definition first proposed by Boring (1923): "Intelligence is what intelligence tests measure" (p. 35). In fact this definition is not as meaningless as it seems at first sight. Tests of general intelligence are designed to examine the ability of people to carry out certain mental operations. The various tests of general intelligence—"g"—are all interrelated and people obtain similar scores in different tests. Thus "g" is a quality that can be measured reliably and with some precision; but as Eysenck and Kamin (1981) have pointed out, ". . . we cannot at this stage say that "g" is the same as the term is understood by the man in the street" (p. 25). Eysenck, however, clearly considers that what intelligence tests measure is pretty close to what most people think of as intelligence. Others such as Kamin (Eysenck and Kamin, 1981) hold a different view and argue that IQ tests do not provide a good measure of what most people regard as intelligence.

Both of these authors are eminent psychologists but hold quite different views about our current ability to measure intelligence. They do not disagree that the available tests measure something with reasonable accuracy—they disagree fundamentally about what such tests do measure.

Regardless of whether the available tests measure what we think of as intelligence or some other qualities, as Chapter 7 demonstrates, tests of intelligence and specific abilities have been used with some success in personnel selection. Many tests of specific abilities (mechanical, verbal, numerical, etc.) and of "g" can be used to provide quite good predictions of people's competence in certain jobs. Chapter 7 also indicates, however, that the use of psychological tests in personnel selection and other fields is coming under increasing criticism. Tests have been criticised on various grounds. One criticism is based on the argument that intelligence tests do not measure pure underlying intelligence but a mixture of it and of taught or acquired knowledge.

Vernon (1956) distinguishes between intelligence and attainments in the following way: " . . . the former refers to the more general qualities of thinking—comprehension, level of concept development, reasoning and grasping relations—qualities which seem to be acquired largely in the course of normal development without specific tuition; whereas the latter refers more to knowledge and skills which are directly trained" (p. 157).

Unfortunately, it is one thing to make such a distinction in writing but quite another to put it into practice by developing tests that are "pure" tests of one or other factor. Proponents of intelligence tests believe that this can be done; others consider that it has not been done properly and is probably impossible. Tests are also coming under the close scrutiny of employment lawyers. Recently the American Supreme Court ruled that a test had been used unfairly to select someone for a job because the organisation involved could not show that the test was clearly and directly job-related. Indeed, in the United States, the use of tests for personnel selection is being abandoned fairly rapidly because of rulings such as this. It seems likely that employment law in Britain will also challenge the possible inappropriate use of tests.

In the personnel selection context, tests are also criticised because they are biased in favour of certain ethnic or cultural groups. Consider Vernon's description of intelligence given above—as qualities which seem to be acquired largely in the course of normal development. What is the "normal environment" in which this "normal development" takes place? White middle-class family groups, some critics would say! The argument of cultural bias asserts that the intellectual development that takes place naturally is dependent on the specific environmental and cultural background in which a person develops; so that perfectly bright and intelligent people from certain socio-economic or ethnic backgrounds will fail to develop the normal qualities assessed in the tests. The consequence will be that, despite their underlying intelligence, the tests will label them as unintelligent.

A rational and unbiased examination of the advantages and disadvantages of psychological tests in the light of criticisms such as the ones raised above can only be of value to both the science of psychology and to society. The future of such tests within our society remains to be seen.

THE DETERMINANTS OF INTELLIGENCE

The major interests of the early researcher, Francis Galton, concerned the extent to which mental abilities are inherited. For example, in some early research he showed that there was a very strong tendency for "success", or at least eminence in society, to run in families. (Galton himself was related to Charles Darwin.) To Galton this tendency was consistent with the proposal that intelligence was passed on by heredity from parents to children. Of course, one could also point out that being a member of a successful or eminent family provides much greater opportunities for educational, social or economic advancement. In conflict with Galton, one could argue that it is these *environmental* advantages that are passed on rather than any superior genetic material.

Much research has been conducted in attempts to explore the influence of heredity and environment on IQ. One method of approach involves examining the test scores obtained by people with identical or similar heredity (e.g. twins or brothers or sisters) and scores obtained by unrelated people. Identical (monozygotic) twins originate from a single fertilised egg which divides into two, and therefore they are identical genetically. Fraternal twins are no more similar genetically than ordinary brothers and sisters (siblings). If genetic factors are involved in the determination of IQ, the scores of identical twins would be expected to show higher correlations than pairs of ordinary siblings who, in turn, should be more similar than unrelated people. Many studies have indeed found this to be the case. Table V provides data summarising the results from a number of studies. As Table V shows, there is evidence to suggest that genetic factors are involved. The data, however, also suggest that environmental factors play a role. For example, the correlation between fraternal twins appears to be greater than that between ordinary siblings. We have seen that fraternal twins are no more similar genetically than ordinary siblings. Correlations also arise between unrelated children who have been reared together. Environmental influences seem to be a possible cause of these sorts of effects.

At face value, the most convincing pieces of evidence supporting the influence of genetic factors are the correlations for identical and fraternal twins. The argument suggests that all twins, whether identical or fraternal, share a similar environment. The higher correlations between identical twins must therefore be due to greater genetic similarities. Some researchers, however, have pointed to possible flaws in this argument (Anastasi, 1971; Kamin, 1974) by suggesting that, because they look alike, identical twins may be treated as more alike by other people. Fraternal twins look less similar and are treated less similarly. Thus identical twins have more in common than fraternal twins from the point of view of both genetics *and* environment. If this argument is accepted (not all researchers do accept it, e.g. Scarr and Carter-Saltzman, 1979), the results in Table V are much less conclusive.

A wide collection of other studies involving, for example, the relationship between adopted children, adopted parents and biological parents (e.g. Skodak and Skeels, 1949), or surveys of the changes in IQ associated with changes in environmental conditions (e.g. Wheeler, 1942), have provided further evidence in the debate. Most psychologists accept that both environmental and inherited

TABLE V. CORRELATION COEFFICIENTS FOR "INTELLIGENCE" TEST SCORES FROM 52 STUDIES

(Correlation coefficients obtained in each study are indicated by dark circles. Medians are shown by vertical lines intersecting the horizontal lines which represent the ranges.)
Source: Erlenmeyer-Kimling and Jarvik (1963).

factors are involved. Many also accept that, for each individual person, heredity may set certain upper and lower limits to intellectual capacity and that environmental factors determine how far towards the upper or lower limit a particular person will go. The extent of genetic and environmental influences is still unresolved.

Race and IQ

The debate concerning heredity or environment is by no means new but has recently assumed new importance, partly because of fresh research evidence and techniques of analysis and partly because of the potential social consequences of one view or another. One of the important current controversies concerns the fact that differences in IQ have been found between different racial-ethnic groups. Loehlin *et al.* (1975), for example, have shown that the average score of the American black people is about fifteen points below that of American whites. The difference in scores is not disputed. The controversy rages aaround what causes the difference—genetic factors or environmental ones. In other words, are some racial ethnic groups genetically predisposed to produce lower IQ scores or are the differences the result of socio-economic and other environmental disadvantages?

Several studies point to the possibility that environmental disadvantages rather than genetic factors are responsible for the observed differences in IQ scores. One study examined the IQs of illegitimate offspring of American armed forces personnel in Germany. The average IQs for a group of children with black fathers was about the same as that for a group fathered by white servicemen (Loehlin *et al.*, 1975). Studies of interracial adoption also provide evidence of environmental influences. As with the earlier debate on heredity versus environment, when evidence which apparently supports one position or the other has been uncovered, criticisms, alternative interpretations and countercriticisms have followed. The balance of evidence does seem to favour the view that genetic differences are less important than environmental factors. However, not all researchers would support this view. Some such as Leon Kamin not only reject the genetic arguments, but argue that in any case the debate is not about true "intelligence" but merely IQ test scores. He argues, as noted earlier, that current IQ tests do not measure true intelligence at all, and that to understand what causes differences in test scores is not the same as understanding differences in intelligence. Such a viewpoint has not prevented Kamin from joining the debate over the influence of genetic or environmental factors. A useful discussion of many of the key issues involved is provided in a recent book that debates the problem (Eysenck and Kamin, 1981).

COGNITIVE STYLE

Divergent thinking and creativity

Guilford (1967) has pointed out that most tests of intelligence call for convergent thinking, i.e. the components of each question point to one single, correct solution. He argued that attention should also be paid to divergent thinking; the sort needed for problems where there is not a single correct solution—but many correct ones. It can be argued that many problems of everyday life are of this open-ended nature rather than the closed, convergent problems typical of intelligence tests. Divergent thinking is measured by tests that require the respondents to answer questions that do not have a single, correct answer. The Uses of Objects Tests, for instance, ask for as many uses as possible to be given for common objects such as a brick or a paper-clip. Responses can be scored for fluency (number of responses), originality (number of unusual responses) and flexibility (number of times that the respondent moves from one type of response to another).

Hudson (1966) has shown that people who display divergent thinking qualities in such tests tend to specialise in the Arts, while convergers prefer the Sciences. One important issue involves establishing whether divergent thinking tests do measure something that is different from the factors measured by intelligence tests.

The relationship between divergent thinking tests and intelligence tests has been studied with conflicting results. Wallach and Kogan (1965) found little relationship between the two, whereas Getzels and Jackson (1962) did find positive correlations, although even in their study the correlations are not large. The available evidence does seem to suggest that divergence is a distinct though elusive characteristic of thinking. Divergent thinking seems to be involved in what most people refer to as creativity, with which it is sometimes seen as if it were identical. It seems more likely, however, that divergent thinking alone is not sufficient for creativity (Entwistle, 1981). As Entwistle notes, ". . . the conclusion must be that knowledge, reasoning and divergent thinking are used in combination in creative production" (p. 157). In other words, both divergent thinking (idea generation, etc.) and the more analytical "closing-down" of ideas needed for obtaining high scores in traditional intelligence tests or ability tests are involved in creativity.

Intelligence and ability tests are designed to measure the *capacity* of people to solve certain kinds of problems. Other tests, such as those of convergent-divergent thinking, are less concerned with capacity and relate more to the *styles* or *strategies* of thinking that people adopt. Recent research results have shown that there are considerable differences in the cognitive (thinking) styles that people adopt.

Pask (1976) has examined the different strategies that people adopt when learning new material or solving complex problems. Some people (Pask calls them Holists) approach the material in a very broad, somewhat divergent manner and will for instance examine many aspects of a problem more or less simultaneously. Others (Serialists) adopt a narrow, systematic step-by-step approach. Pask and colleagues have observed holist and serialist strategies over a wide range of environments and with many different subjects.

Field dependence

Witkin (1976; Witkin *et. al.*, 1977) has identified a cognitive style dimension that has become well known and widely used. Witkin's research began with an interest in perceptual factors but developed into an attempt to conceptualise and measure an aspect of cognitive style known as field dependence-independence. The difference between the field dependent and independent styles lies in the extent to which the person analyses incoming information. Field independent people take an analytical, structured approach to material, whereas field dependent people take a less analytical approach and tend to perceive things in a more global fashion. The styles can be identified by use of the Embedded Figures Test, where the respondent is required to identify a specific figure embedded in a more complex figure. Field independent people have less difficulty in finding the embedded figure, whereas field dependent people have great difficulty, even with simple items. This distinction between field dependence and independence has been detected in many test situations. Witkin *et al.* (1977) provide an excellent review of much of the work.

Another well-known cognitive style dimension is the reflective-impulsive distinction made by Kagan (e.g. Kagan *et al.,* 1964). A series of studies, mostly with children, have demonstrated a consistent tendency on the part of individuals towards either fast or slow decision times for problems with high response uncertainty. In a range of different situations (e.g. the Matching Familiar Figures Test—*see* Fig. 14), some people impulsively report the first hypothesis that occurs to them, a response that often produces the incorrect answer. Reflective people delay before responding—and their response is usually correct. The reflective style is characterised by an attempt to consider the differential validity of all answers, fewer errors and greater persistence with difficult tasks. Impulsivity is reflected in a lack of concern about mistakes and rapid decision-making.

Fig. 14. *Kagan's matching familiar figures test—the task is to find the figure that matches "A".*

Similarities and differences—Styles A and B

At an intuitive level the similarities between some of the dimensions discussed above is clear: focusing strategies, serialist learning, field independence—all seem to suggest a narrow analytic and orderly approach to information processing. Entwistle (1981) considers some of the empirical and theoretical links between various aspects of human information processing and tentatively suggests two major cognitive styles providing relationships between a number of previously distinct dimensions (*see* Fig. 15). Style A is an holistic, field dependent, divergent mode of processing, while B is a serial, field independent, analytical mode. Entwistle admits that this unification is based on sparse evidence, but the patterns of cognitive processing that he suggests do have some appeal.

Style A	*Style B*
Holist	Serialist
Divergent	Convergent
Impulsive	Reflective
Field dependent	Field independent
etc.	etc.

Fig. 15. *Styles A and B.*

Mintzberg (1976), Robey and Taggart (1981) have discussed the possible importance of cognitive styles for management performance. They point out that management (and other) education and practice in Western cultures stresses the importance of the analytic, systematic approach to thinking and problem-solving (i.e. Entwistle's Style B). They argue that more emphasis should be given to the other more divergent approach, both in management practice and education.

Robey and Taggart (1981) make the following points:

> There may be nothing "natural" about the analytic decision style acquired through traditional management education. Rather, this style may well be a function of our entire educational process, beginning in kindergarten.
>
> . . . we are suggesting that opportunities to explore the full range of decision styles and strategies should be made available in business school curricula. We believe that managers can be more effective if they are aware of several styles and strategies (within a sound theoretical framework) and if they learn to use them appropriately (p. 194).

The ideas of these authors concerning information processing style are interesting and have considerable intuitive appeal, but it must be stressed that firm evidence to support their views is not yet available. Nevertheless, Robey and Taggart may have a point when they argue for a movement away from many people's traditional view of management as an entirely logical, analytical activity and stress that some attempt to encompass a much wider range of information processing styles and strategies is "a major challenge for management education in the 1980s" (ibid.).

QUESTIONS

1. How can the statistical techniques of correlation and factor analysis help in the examination of the structure of intelligence?

2. Outline the hierarchical view of the structure of intelligence.

3. What do IQ tests measure?

4. What evidence is there that genetic and/or environmental factors influence IQ? What are the implications of this?

5. How does cognitive style differ from intelligence?

CHAPTER FOUR

Attitudes and Attitude Change

OBJECTIVES

This chapter examines the area of attitudes and attitude change. In the first place it provides a comprehensive definition of an attitude. Second, it explores the various research findings in the area of attitude change, highlighting the following: characteristics of the change agent; form and content of the persuasive communication; the context in which the persuasive communication is presented; the influence of the group; and the situation in which attitude change takes place. In addition, it briefly discusses how we measure attitudes.

WHAT IS AN ATTITUDE?

The concept *attitude* refers, as Secord and Backman (1969) define it, to "certain regularities of an individual's feelings, thoughts and predispositions to act toward some aspect of his environment". Feelings represent the *affective*, thoughts the *cognitive*, and predispositions act as the *behavioural* component.

Attitudes can be held about the physical world around us (e.g. the Sydney Opera House), about hypothetical constructs (e.g. worker participation, flexible rostering, etc.) and about other people (e.g. your boss, mother-in-law, the Prime Minister, etc.). The three components of an attitude can be illustrated by looking at a person's attitude towards, for example, racial integration. The affective component of the attitude is his emotional *feelings*, for instance, in support of segregated housing/schooling for the different races. This component may be inferred from his angry behaviour when he argues with an antagonist of such a policy, or empirically from his measured high blood pressure or galvanic skin response when confronted with newspaper commentaries on the subject. The cognitive component of the attitude consists of his *ideas* about racial integration. This component is inferred from what he says he will do or in fact what he does. Does he allow his children to attend racially mixed schools? Will he live in an integrated residential area?

There is a difference between an *attitude* and an *opinion*. An opinion or belief differs from an attitude in that neither contains an affective or feeling component which is fundamental to an attitude or value system (which is a constellation of interrelated attitudes). Fishbein and Ajzen (1975) provide an informative overview of much of the recent work concerning attitudes, beliefs and behaviour.

The cognitive aspect of the attitudinal process, therefore, is superordinate in an opinion or belief; it is much more to do with the factual or knowledge elements we have towards a particular object in our environment.

ATTITUDE CHANGE

There are a number of variables that seem to be associated with the direction and degree of attitude change:

(*a*) characteristics of the change agent;
(*b*) form and content of the persuasive communication;
(*c*) the context in which the persuasive communication is presented;
(*d*) characteristics of the person you are attempting to change;
(*e*) the nature of the group to which he/she belongs; and
(*f*) characteristics of his/her membership in the group.

Krech, Crutchfield and Ballachey (1962) have outlined a number of factors that are linked to attitude change and these must be taken into account by managers of the future. Examples of studies illustrating some of these factors are taken from Karlins and Abelson (1970).

Characteristics of the change agent
Studies have indicated that, among other characteristics, the (*a*) credibility, (*b*) attractiveness, and (*c*) group identification of the change agent (as perceived by the influencee) are important in determining effectiveness (Krech, *et al.*, 1962).

Credibility
A number of investigations have been carried out by Hovland and Weiss (1952) into the effect of an individual's evaluation of the communication upon his effectiveness. They found that a highly credible communicator was more effective in changing attitudes than a communicator with low credibility. The chief characteristics of a credible communicator are "expertness" and "trustworthiness". In addition, it has been found that a low credibility source arguing against his own best interest is equally as effective (Koeske and Crano, 1968). For instance, although the British American Tobacco Company would be low in credibility if it argued that there was no relationship between smoking and lung cancer, it would be very persuasive in changing people's attitudes if it publicly argued that "smoking definitely leads to lung cancer'. Another

technique that has been found to lead to communicator effectiveness is the phenomenon of "flogging the dead horse" – that is, agreeing with your audience on one or two issues and then attempting to change them on another (Weiss, 1957). Research indicates that when a change agent initially expresses some views that are also held by the person he is trying to influence, a bond is established between him and that person, such that it makes it difficult for the latter to disagree on subsequent influence attempts on other issues.

Karlins and Abelson (1970) illustrate the impact of communication credibility in their Dr Hans Schmidt class-room demonstration. In this experiment a lecturer was introduced as Dr Hans Schmidt, an internationally renowned research chemist. Dr Schmidt was dressed in a white lab coat and had a decidedly Germanic accent. He wanted the students to indicate when they could smell a new chemical vapour he was about to release by putting up their hands. He then proceeded to pull the stopper of a small glass beaker, apparently releasing the vapour as he did so. The hands of the students began to rise, first in the front of the hall and then throughout the lecture theatre. It was only later that the students were told that the beaker had not contained any vapour but merely distilled water, and that the so-called Dr Schmidt was a lecturer in the German Department.

This example illustrates the power of suggestibility and in particular the influence of an apparent expert or credible source of information. What would have happened, one wonders, if a fellow student in jeans had tried the same experiment?

Attractiveness

Tannenbaum (1956) and others (e.g. Rogers, 1978) have found that the amount of attitude change is directly related to the degree of attractiveness of the change agent. In Tannenbaum's work the attractiveness of the communicator was measured through the use of the semantic-differential technique. The ratings of the subjects on the following six evaluation scales were obtained: fair-unfair, dirty-clean, tasty-distasteful, good-bad, pleasant-unpleasant, worthless-valuable. Tannenbaum's results also indicate that the change agent is not effective if he advocates a position opposed to the original attitude of his audience, and that he is more effective when he advocates a position which is in the same direction as the initial attitude of the people he is trying to influence (Schuessler, 1982).

An example of a study that illustrates the impact of communicator liking/attractiveness was done by Wright (1966). In this study, male undergraduates completed an attitude questionnaire on the value of university athletics. They were then told that they would be discussing this topic with others by means of written notes to one another. What they did not know was that the group interaction was under the control of the experimenter – that is, that one member of the group was acting as a confederate with the investigator. The experiment was designed so that the confederate would get the students either to like or dislike him, and then to try to change the subjects' attitudes toward athletics. To create experimentally a favourable or unfavourable relationship between change agent and influencee, friendly and unfriendly "practice notes" were sent by the confederate to each subject in turn, prior to the actual discussion. To create a positive relationship the following notes were sent:

> I'd sure like to get acquainted with you at least a little before we start this game, but I guess that's impossible with this screwy communication set-up. You'd probably like to know a little about me too, even if we can't chat right now.

> Well, we got through one round okay. I'm kind of anxious to get started. I'm glad I can communicate directly to you; you seem like a good guy to talk to (even if it does have to be one-sided).

The unfriendly communication went as follows:

> I don't like the idea of conversing with virtual strangers, so I really have nothing to say to you. This note is just for the sake of practice, and doesn't mean I really want to communicate to you.

> I want to communicate to the guy in charge, and I guess the easiest way is to tell you to write a note on him. Write this message – and please be sure to get it right. "Person B thinks we've had enough practice to do an adequate job." Be careful of the spelling and punctuation, too.

It was found that these notes did indeed create either a positive or negative attitude towards the investigator's confederate, depending on which note was received. Then the confederate wrote notes trying to change the students' attitudes towards university athletics, after which all the students filled in another questionnaire on athletics. The main finding was that where the student *liked* the confederate he showed significantly more change in the direction of his persuasive communication toward athletics than when he disliked him. Wright (1966) concluded: ". . . make sure the person you are trying to persuade likes you in the first place, or your efforts are likely to be in vain".

Group affiliation
For a change agent to be effective he must be seen to be a significant member of the group – to be, as Krech *et al.* (1962) suggest, "one of

us". Studies carried out by Katz and Lazarsfield (1955) indicate that the person who occupies a position of influence in the word-of-mouth communication system – the opinion leader – is seen as "one of us" by the persons whom he influences. Menzel and Katz (1956) provide convincing demonstration of the role that change agents, or opinion leaders, can have. In their study they focused on the diffusion of information amongst physicians. They examined the prescribing records of a group of physicians to establish a comparison between them on the time they took to adopt a new drug after its appearance on the market. Prescribing behaviour was found to be related to the extent to which the doctor concerned was integrated into the social structure of the medical community. Those who were frequently named by colleagues as friends or discussion partners were more likely to be innovative and prescribe new drugs at an early stage. The extent of integration seemed to be more important than other factors such as age or medical school attended. Physicians who had fewer contacts within the medical community and less social support for innovative prescribing adopted the new drugs at a slower rate. The physicians who were the quickest to adopt the new drugs not only occupied influential positions within the medical community but tended to be those who were more likely to read professional journals, attend out-of-town conferences more frequently and maintain contact with a larger variety of medical institutions and societies than the others.

It can be seen, therefore, that a two-step flow of communication takes place. First, information through journals, conferences, etc., to a few people who are or who become the main status symbols of their profession, and from them to the next, larger level of information purveyors, and from that level on downwards. The behaviour of people at the bottom of any "influence pyramid" is determined to some extent by others in the professional group who are higher up and are seen to have greater "membership characteristics".

The organisation of the persuasive message

Degree of persuasion
Which is more effective – extremely stated or moderately stated information? Many of the early findings by Hovland and his associates indicate significantly greater opinion or attitude change the larger the change advocated (Hovland and Pritzker, 1957), and many of these aspects are still operative today. This relation was found to be much the same for individuals holding extreme opinions and for those holding less extreme ones. As Hovland pointed out, the generality of these findings may be limited. If the

issue is one in which the individual is deeply involved, results opposite to the above may occur. The change agent who attacks an attitude towards an issue in which a person is deeply involved is attacking an attitude which is a part of the individual's self-concept. "The advocate of extreme change will therefore be resisted and the target of the information, in defending his self-esteem, may be driven still further away from the position advocated by the communicator" (Krech, Crutchfield and Ballachey, 1962).

One-sided versus two-sided arguments
This issue was first examined by the Yale researchers (Hovland, Lumsdaine and Sheffield, 1949) in their studies of training and indoctrination films used by the American armed forces during the Second World War. One-sided and two-sided communications were used to evaluate empirically the effectiveness of messages in convincing the soldiers that a long hard war was likely with Japan. They found:

(*a*) that the two-sided presentation was more effective for men who initially held the opposed opinion that the war with Japan would be a short one (less than two years). For men who initially favoured the position of the communication (that war would last longer than two years) the one-sided presentation was more effective; and

(*b*) that better educated men were influenced less by the one-sided than by the two-sided presentation. Thus, a person who values his own independence of judgment and his own intellectual competence may view the acceptance of a one-sided communication as incompatible with maintaining self-esteem.

Another example of a study on the effectiveness of one-sided versus two-sided argument was made by McGinnies (1966):

Japanese university students were first asked to fill out attitude scales assessing their position towards two relevant international issues: (1) American handling of the Cuban missile crisis; and (2) visits by American submarines to Japanese ports. A week later each subject was exposed to one of four pro-American speeches, all presented in a similar way by a Japanese dramatic arts student. The four messages were:

(1) One sided argument – Cuban missile crisis: This presentation was based on the commentary of Ambassador Adlai Stevenson defending United States action on Cuba to the United Nations.
(2) Two sided argument – Cuban missile crisis: In this communication cognizance was taken of certain points raised by Premier Nikita Khrushchev on the matter of missile bases in Cuba.
(3) One sided argument – American submarine visits: This statement was composed from Japanese editorial comments favouring such visits.

(4) Two sided argument – American submarine visits: This speech included arguments against such visits by a "left-wing" Japanese newspaper, (quoted in Karlins and Abelson, 1970, p. 24).

The students were asked to fill out the same attitude questionnaire after hearing the arguments again. As Karlins and Abelson (1970) suggest: "McGinnies found that the two sided communication was superior to the one sided appeal for individuals initially opposed to the position advocated. For the subjects who initially agreed with the opinions of the speaker, the one sided communication tended to be more effective."

A number of other studies (Carlson and Abelson, 1956) are consistent with the above, but why might it be more effective to present two or more sides to an argument? Karlins and Abelson (1970) suggest several reasons. The most effective presentation involves those aspects that arouse needs first and those that satisfy them second. An entire volume by Hovland (*The Order of Presentation in Persuasion*, 1957) has been published for further reference.

What of primacy-recency today? Can any conclusions be drawn, any generalisations stated, concerning the order in which persuasive appeals should be presented? Rosnow and Robinson (1967) provide a very good summary:

Instead of a general "law" of primacy, or recency, we have today an assortment of miscellaneous variables, some of which tend to produce primacy, others of which to produce recency. Nonsalient, controversial topics, interesting subject matter and highly familiar issues tend toward primacy. Salient topics, uninteresting subject matter and moderately unfamiliar issues tend to yield recency.

Use of threat in attitude change

Is the use of threat effective in changing attitudes? Janis and Feshbach (1953) studied the effects of three different intensities of fear-arousing messages in an illustrated lecture on dental hygiene given to three matched groups of students. The immediate effect on these three different intensities of fear arousal showed that change in attitude and behaviour was *inversely* related to the intensity of fear arousal. The mild fear appeal produced: a 37 per cent net change in the direction sought; 22 per cent change for the moderate fear appeal; and 28 per cent change for the strong fear appeal. The fear appeal, however, was not very credible in that it included the possibility of cancer among the many consequences of poor oral hygiene habits.

A better study was carried out by Dabbs and Leventhal (1966), in which a more credible fear arousal situation seemed to me effective. In that investigation the effects of three different messages regarding tetanus were explored, both in terms of attitudes and behaviour. The students were presented with written material discussing tetanus, the contents of which were varied in the following ways (Karlins and Abelson, 1970):

(1) Fear level of the message: In the low-fear communication, tetanus was described as difficult to control and relatively easy to cure. A case history, complete with black and white photographs, told of recovery from the disease following "mild medication and throat suction procedures". In the high-fear communication, tetanus was pictured as easy to contract and difficult to cure. Another case study, this one with colour photographs, described death from tetanus "despite heavy medication and surgery to relieve throat congestion". In a third, no-fear message (control condition), the discussion of tetanus and accompanying case history were omitted from the pamphlets.

(2) Reported effectiveness of inoculation in preventing tetanus: In the low-effective message, pamphlets contained information stating that inoculations were generally effective but did not eliminate the possibility of contracting the disease. High-effectiveness material, on the other hand, presented inoculation as an "almost perfect" guarantee against tetanus.

(3) Reported painfulness of the inoculation: In the high pain message students were told that the particular shot they would receive was very painful due to the necessity of "deep intramuscular injection of tetanus toxoid and alum precipitate". In the no pain communication discussion of discomfort was excluded from the pamphlet (pp. 7/8).

Subsequent to reading this material the students were asked about their attitudes towards taking a tetanus vaccine. In addition, data were collected from the university health service to see who took the inoculation. The findings were rather interesting in that the students were not influenced in their attitudes or their shot-taking behaviour by information about the effectiveness of the vaccine or by the reported painfulness of the shot. The only factor that predicted shot-taking behaviour was the fear arousal of the message: the students who received the high fear arousal appeal were more likely both to see the benefit of the vaccine and take the inoculation. Thus it could be argued that strong fear messages which seem credible are more likely to be effective.

In addition, whether strong and mild fear appeals are more effective in producing attitude change, depends on the situation. According to Karlins and Abelson (1970), based on all the research done in the attitude change field, strong fear appeal is superior to mild ones in changing attitudes when they: "(1) pose a threat to the individual's loved ones (2) are presented by a highly credible source

(3) deal with topics relatively unfamiliar to the individual and (4) aim at the subjects with a high degree of self-esteem and/or low perceived vulnerability to danger''.

The influence of the group on attitude change
Group characteristics and group membership can influence attitude change.

(*a*) *Group characteristics.* Groups can influence individual attitude change quite dramatically, but this will depend upon, as Krech *et al.* (1962) suggest, three characteristics of the group: (*i*) the nature of the group norm, (*ii*) sanctions against the group, and (*iii*) the effectiveness of the sanctioning system.

(*i*) *Group norms.* Every group develops a normative structure to control and enforce those attitudes and behaviour that are central to the group achieving its objectives. Any deviation from such central norms is not tolerated. Most members of a group must confirm to norms (approved attitudes and behaviour) or they will suffer isolation and expulsion.

(*ii*) *Sanctions upon leaving the group.* In voluntary groups, the *cohesiveness* or overall attractiveness of the group to its members provides the source of the group's influence over its members.

(*iii*) *Effectiveness of sanctioning.* Unless agents of the group can maintain control over the members and thus detect and punish aberrent behaviour, the impact of norms may be greatly reduced.

(*b*) *Characteristics of group membership.* As Krech *et al.* (1962) suggest: ''. . . the degree to which new members of a group accept the attitudes prescribed as appropriate by the norms of the group is partly determined by membership characteristics: (1) the status of the member, (2) valuation of membership and (3) legitimacy of norm''.

Status of member
Homans (1950) has indicated in his investigations during the 1950s and 1960s the importance of the status and position of a group member and attitude change: ''To rank high in his group, a man must live up to all of its norms and the norms in question must be the actual or sanctional norms of the group, and not just those to which the group gives lip service.'' Or as Krech *et al.* (1962) suggest:

A new member of a group, unsure of his status, may conform – indeed, overconform – to win popularity. The marginal status of the social climber is probably responsible for his oft-observed social orthodoxy. The middle-class man who has ''struck it rich'' and who aspires to upper-class status will be painfully proper. The aristocrat, secure in his elite status, will be casually comfortable in violating norms to suit his convenience (p. 250).

Importance of group
Most of the studies in this area indicate that the more valued a person's membership in a group, the greater his resistance to change (Cooper, 1979).

Acceptability of norms
"The impact of a group norm upon a new member will be influenced by his beliefs about the legitimacy of the norm" (Krech *et al.*, 1962). An example of the impact of the legitimacy of norms appeared in a national study of the 1956 US presidential election. In this, Converse and Campbell (1960) assessed the impact of "political norms" of various subcultural groups (i.e. Catholics, Jews, Negroes and labour unions) in their voting behaviour. The subjects from each of these groups were asked whether they approved of organisations representing them supporting the relevant candidates in legislative programmes. As Krech *et al.* (1962) summarise:

> A substantial relation was found between belief in legitimacy of the political group norm and voting for the party (viz. Democratic) predominantly favored by the group. Of those with "strong" belief in legitimacy of the norm, 65% voted Democratic; of those with "weak" belief, only 41% voted Democratic. It was also found that members with a high degree of identification with the group tended to feel more strongly that its political activity was legitimate than did members who were less closely identified. However, for comparable amounts of identification, there still remained the above relation between belief in norm legitimacy and voting in accord with the group (p. 251).

As Converse and Campbell suggested, "the beliefs of members about the legitimacy of political norms will be influenced by perceived congruence between personal and group political positions".

The situation in which attitude change takes place
There are three such situations:

(*a*) group *versus* individual;
(*b*) commitment in public or private;
(*c*) the effect of the group.

For a long time there have been conflicting views as to whether one should attempt to change attitudes in groups or on a one-to-one basis with the isolated individual. Research has shown that it depends on the nature and composition of the group. If the group is divided on the attitude concerned, it is probably best to attempt to change the person on his/her own. But if not, as Krech *et al.* (1962) suggest, "a situation in which a communication is addressed to a group largely composed of persons favorable to the communicator's position will greatly increase the effectiveness of his communication upon the dissident minority". Kelley and Woodruff (1956) found among a group of university students that when they thought that *important* "other students" on campus approved of a particular speech (by applauding), their own attitudes towards the speech changed. This was not the case with control students who were told that the applause came from a group of people from the town whom they did not know. They found in effect that 63 per cent of the students who changed their attitudes did so when they thought the audience who applauded were high status students, whereas only 30 per cent of change was reported in the control group.

The requiring of people to commit themselves publicly to a change in attitude has long been used by change agents. One might term this requirement "the Billy Graham effect". If a person makes his stand public, he will be less likely to change his position as a result of persuasion in the opposite direction. This is demonstrated by various religious revivalist groups that encourage public commitments in the hope of preventing public reconversion or a lapse in faith. As Krech *et al.* (1962) suggest: "Public commitment has been found to be an effective procedure; private commitment has been found to be ineffective."

And, finally, considerable research has been carried out into the impact of groups on attitudes and action. Lewin's (1953) study, the first of its kind, assessed the impact of group decision-making on the attitudes of women towards certain foodstuffs. In this early investigation, Lewin divided a group of housewives into a lecture group and discussion group, the object of which was to change their attitudes towards offal – beef hearts, sweetbreads and kidneys, which normally they did not eat. The first group was lectured about the various nutritionally beneficial qualities of these meats and how they could make to be attractive. The second group was asked to discuss the subject as a group with a nutritional expert. Each group was then asked how many of its number planned to try these meats. In addition, a follow-up study was carried out on the buying behaviour of the housewives. It was found that 3 per cent of those in the lecture group had served the meats sometime after the change process, while 32 per cent of those involved in the discussion did so.

Since Lewin's study numerous other investigations have taken place to show that participating in the process of attitude change can be more effective in the long run if certain conditions prevail (e.g. they have some consensus, they support the change agent's position, etc.).

HOW DO WE MEASURE ATTITUDES?

There are numerous ways to measure attitudes. Since attitudes are hypothetical constructs, we have to infer them from what people say they think, feel or will do. By far the most common approach is by an attitude questionnaire, in which we can ask people what they think about a particular subject or person, how they feel towards it or them, or what their behaviour intentions are. The two most popular methods of attitude measure are the Thurstone and Likert techniques.

In the Thurstone approach, we generate a number of potential questionnaire items, ranging from highly favourable about the attitudes in question to highly unfavourable – for example, in terms of one's attitude towards war from "war is glorious" to "there is no conceivable justification for war". After collecting, say, about 100 such statements, we ask a sample group of those ultimately to be assessed to rate each statement on a scale from one to eleven on the degree of favourableness of the attitude statement. We then include in the final attitude questionnaire those statements where (*a*) there is a high degree of agreement between evaluators on the scale value, and (*b*) the average scale value of the item ranges up the eleven-point scale at equal intervals from one to eleven, perhaps selecting around twenty to twenty-two items in the final questionnaire, each of which is separated from the previous item by a scale value of, say, roughly half a point.

The second approach is the Likert technique, which is sometimes known as the summated scale. In this approach, one selects a large number of items that relate to the attitude object concerned (though not in terms of degree of favourableness). These items are then subjected to factor analysis, and those that are strongly inter correlated with one another are chosen for inclusion. Whereas in the Thurstone method the respondents reply with either a yes or no or not applicable, in the Likert method they utilise a five- or seven- or ten-point scale for each item in terms of strongly agree to strongly disagree. Providing respondents with a range of responses to a particular question is always preferable to a simple discreet category system (e.g. yes or no).

The difficulty with both these techniques is that they are still subject to the "social desirability effect" – that is, to respondents' giving you the socially desirable answer, as for instance "Of course I don't think war is glorious" when in fact they think just the

Description of a character you may know

Is a nineteen–year–old male.
Has a girl–friend.
Went to public school / comprehensive school.[*]
Smokes cigarettes.
Is keen on sport.
Enjoys films.

* A single version only given on each form

Whereabouts on these scales would you place this character ?
Please put a tick in the appropriate box according to where you think he would most probably
be best described on the scale.

Would vote Conservative		Would vote Labour
Is inclined to be "bossy"		Is inclined to be meek
Is a good mixer socially		Is rather shy socially
Is very studious		Is not very studious
Would assume leadership in groups		Would not assume leadership in groups
Contains his emotions		Expresses his emotions freely
Is self–confident		Is not self–confident
Is a bit effeminate		Is not at all effeminate
Is very patriotic		Is not in the least patriotic
Gets on well with his parents		Does not get on well with his parents

How much do you think he will be earning: (a) when he is thirty ?   £.................../p.a.

(b) when he is sixty ?   £.................../p.a.

What occupations is he likely to go into ?   _____

_____

_____

What sports does he take part in ?   _____

Fig. 16. *Students' questionnaire.*

opposite. There are techniques available to minimise this effect. For
example, in the questionnaire above (*see* Fig. 16) Professor Cooper
wanted to find out what university students thought of public versus
comprehensive school students. Instead of asking them directly, he
devised two questionnaires which were exactly alike, except that in

each version a single line was different — "went to comprehensive school" and "went to public school". The two versions of the questionnaire were randomly distributed among university students and the differences between the two forms were assessed, without the issue of public or comprehensive school stereotype ever being raised.

QUESTIONS

1. What is an attitude?
2. What are some of the factors that influence attitude change?
3. How do we measure attitudes?
4. How important is the change agent in attitude change?

CHAPTER FIVE

Personality, Motivation and Organisational Behaviour

OBJECTIVES

This chapter considers the related topics of personality and motivation, both of central importance for understanding human behaviour in organisations. After mentioning the contribution of Sigmund Freud, the first part of the chapter describes a person-based (Trait theory) approach to personality and a situation-based (Operant theory) approach. Next, the idea that behaviour is determined, not by person variables or situation variables alone, but by the *interaction* between the two, is introduced. An interactionist theory (Social Learning theory) is then outlined and Kelly's theory of Personal Constructs is also described. Finally, examples of how each theoretical position has been applied within organisational contexts are noted.

The second part of the chapter deals specifically with the topic of motivation at work and begins by exploring a Need theory (Maslow) and research that attempts to explore the links between human needs and the characteristics in jobs which might satisfy these needs (Herzberg, Hackman and Oldham). Next, approaches to motivation based on understanding the thinking processes involved (Expectancy theory) are outlined. The implications of this theory for managers and organisation design are described, and finally some of the similarities and differences between expectancy, operant and social learning theories are considered.

PERSONALITY THEORIES

When one observes human behaviour in organisations it becomes clear that, as with human behaviour in general, people are similar in some ways, while in other ways everyone is different. Research and theory on human personality involve attempts to establish a basis for understanding these similarities and differences.

Freud

A significant figure in early work on human personality is Sigmund Freud. Freud emphasised the role of unconscious processes in the control of behaviour and, basing his findings to a large extent on psychoanalysis of himself and his patients, he developed a comprehensive and complex theory of personality. One of the central ideas in his theoretical framework is that the eventual goal of all human behaviour is pleasure. Behaviour results from the interaction of the id, ego and super-ego. The id operates according to the pleasure principle and is the part of us that attempts to seek immediate and total satisfaction or pleasure regardless of other considerations. By contrast, the ego operates according to the reality principle and, in accordance with the demands of reality, attempts to control the id. The super-ego is concerned not with reality but morality and struggles to control behaviour in accordance with our moral values of conscience and the rules of society. The conflicts that arise between the id, ego and super-ego cause considerable psychological turmoil. Freud argued that the resulting turmoil was often resolved at the level of unconscious thought rather than in the rational, conscious mind. According to Freudian theory, human personality is determined, to a large extent, by the previous experiences of the individual, the methods used to resolve conflict and in the early experiences involved in feeding, toilet training and so on. Behaviour is controlled and determined by largely unconscious processes which are beyond direct observation.

There is widespread agreement that Freud and other workers in the psychoanalytic tradition have an important place in the development of psychology. Freud's lasting contributions were perhaps not in the detail of his theory of personality but are represented by his role in the emergence of the scientific study of human personality and his emphasis on the role of unconscious forces and previous experience on behaviour and thought. Although ideas deriving from Freudian/psychoanalytic theory are still being employed in organisational settings (e.g. Dickson, 1976; De Board, 1978), the theory does not now have a dominant role in contemporary attempts to understand personality and its relationship to organisational behaviour.

Trait views of personality
Psychoanalytic theories of human personality such as Freud's are often criticised by other psychologists for their lack of scientific rigour, lack of satisfactory definition of key concepts and the fact that the theories either do not generate testable predictions about human behaviour or, when predictions are made, that they do not work out in practice. One of the strongest critics of these theories is Eysenck (e.g. Eysenck and Wilson, 1973), who has developed an alternative approach to personality based on the rigorous application of scientific methods and statistical analysis. Eysenck, working in Britain, and the British born psychologist Cattell, working in the United States, pursue an approach that attempts to uncover the underlying personality traits which they believe can be used to explain human behaviour in a variety of different situations.

Trait theories perhaps come closest to describing the structure of personality in a way that matches our everyday use of the term.

Trait theories use words such as shy, outgoing, tense and extroverted to describe the basic factors of human personality. These basic elements—traits—represent *predispositions to behave in certain ways, in a variety of different situations.* In the United Kingdom the main exponent of this approach to personality theory and measurement is Eysenck (1970).

Trait theorists such as Eysenck (1970) and Cattell (1965) use the technique of factor analysis (*see* Chapter 3) in attempts to identify the underlying structure of human personality. Eysenck argues that personality is best understood in terms of a heirarchical organisation (*see* Fig. 17). The underlying building blocks for

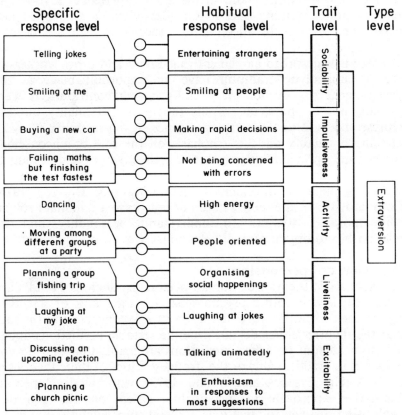

Source: Le Francois (1980). Adapted from *The Biological Basis of Personality* by H. J. Eysenck, Charles C. Thomas, 1967.

Fig. 17. *A representation of Eysenck's hierarchical structure for personality.*

personality can be represented by a small number of basic dimensions (types) that have been identified from the factor analysis of large numbers of personality questionnaires asking people how they behave and feel in various situations. Two major dimensions emerging consistently from factor analytic studies conducted by Eysenck and others are Extroversion and Neuroticism. Extraverts are lively, sociable, excitable people, and neurotics are characterised by high levels of anxiety and tension. Two important points should be borne in mind in relation to these dimensions. The first is that they are continuous dimensions and most people are not extreme in either extroversion or neuroticism. The second point is that the dimensions are *independent*; in other words, someone's position on one dimension bears no relationship to his position on the other.

As well as providing empirical evidence concerning basic human personality factors, Eysenck's work provides a theory concerning the origins and development of personality. This involves the impact of both inherited, neurological differences and environmental influences due to the processes of conditioning and socialisation. The main measuring instrument associated with Eysenck's theory is the Eysenck Personality Inventory (Eysenck and Eysenck, 1964), a self-report questionnaire that measures the factors extroversion and neuroticism.

Working in the United States, Cattell, using similar statistical techniques to those of Eysenck, also pursues a trait approach to personality. One notable difference between the two theorists is the number of stable factors that they feel need to be used to describe and measure personality structure. Although neither Cattell not Eysenck base theories entirely on data from self-report questionnaires, some of the differences between them become apparent when the questionnaires used by each of them are compared. They Eysenck Personality Inventory uses two dimensions (extroversion-introversion and neuroticism), and Eysenck recognises the existence of a third important factor—psychoticism. Cattell's main personality questionnaire (the 16PF) includes sixteen personality factors. To some extent the differences are due to the different statistical procedures that the researchers employ. It is also worth noting that both researchers agree on certain key personality factors such as extroversion and anxiety (Neuroticism).

Despite their differences, both theorists share a common belief that stable, underlying personality traits can be used to explain people's behaviour, and they both focus on the role of internal *person* variables in determining behaviour.

Behavioural approaches to personality
The explanatory concepts used in both Freudian theory and trait

approaches to personality, such as the id and ego or extroversion and introversion, concern internal, unobservable mental constructs. This view of human psychology emphasising personal rather than situational factors is rejected by behaviourists and behaviour theorists in favour of an emphasis on observable events. Some attempts have been made to reconcile behaviour theory and Freudian psychology (Dollard and Miller, 1950), and although in some ways the two approaches represent opposite ends of a spectrum, they also have similarities. One similarity is their joint affirmation that the eventual goal of human behaviour is to obtain pleasure and avoid pain. However, their mechanisms for understanding and explaining behaviour are quite different.

The most influential, modern exponent of the behavioural position is Skinner (1974), and his approach to psychology and the application of the approach in organisational settings are examined in detail in Chapter 13. The essence of the behavioural approach is that behaviour is shaped and determined, not by internal personality factors, motivation, etc., but by the process of operant conditioning, and that each person's current behaviour can be explained entirely with reference to his individual reinforcement history and specific behaviour that has been punished or rewarded. This represents an external or situational view of personality.

The interactionist view of human personality

As we have seen in their attempts to explain personality, psychologists have tended to emphasise the role of either internal (person) factors or external (situational) factors. This does not necessarily mean that such theorists do not accept the importance of both situation and person factors, merely that their focus of attention has been on one or the other.

Recent theoretical and research work has developed an important, more sophisticated concept than the idea that both people and situations are important. This is the idea that people and situations *interact* with each other to determine behaviour. This reorientation of the views of many personality theorists began with Mischel (1968). Pervin (1980) summarises succinctly the development from then on:

> Since the publication of Mischel's book and its development of this issue, considerable attention has been given to the internal-external (or person-situation) controversy. First there was the debate about whether persons or situations control behavior, then about whether persons or situations are more important, and, finally, acceptance of the view that both are important *and interact with one another* (Endler and Magnusson, 1976; Magnusson and Endler,. 1977) (p. 17).

An influential current theory that adopts an interactionist perspective is the social learning theory of Bandura (1977) and Mischel (1977). Social learning theory has its roots in a variety of earlier theories, although the strongest and clearest line of development links it with the earlier behavioural approaches of Skinner and other learning theorists such as Hull (1943). An outline of the ideas and uses of social learning theory is provided in Chapter 13, and Chapter 14 gives an example of how social learning theory can be used as a basis for understanding and improving the processes of management education.

The basis of trait theory is that there are cross-situational generalities in behaviour. In other words, personality traits explain why people behave in similar ways in different circumstances. This emphasis on the *person* as the source of individual differences contrasts most sharply with the emphasis in behaviour theory on the *situation* as the source of individual differences in behaviour. Bandura and Mischel reject the trait theory approach as inadequate because it does not explain properly the situational specificity in behaviour (i.e. people in different situations behave in different ways). They also reject Skinner's behaviourist approach because of its emphasis on reward/punishment and the situation as the only determinants of behaviour. They argue that both situational factors (e.g. rewards, punishment, the behaviour of others) and person factors (e.g. personal goals, plans and expectations) influence behaviour. Furthermore, Bandura and Mischel emphasise the *interaction* between the person and the situation. In other words, to some extent, situations determine how people think and behave, but at the same time people have some influence and help to create the situations that surround them. Mischel (1977) makes the following claim for social learning theory:

"[It] highlights the shortcoming of all simplistic theories that view behavior as the result of any narrow set of determinants, whether these are habits, traits, drives, reinforcers, constructs, instincts or genes and whether they are exclusively inside or outside the person. (quoted in Pervin, 1980, p. 361).

Social learning theory suggests that people learn how to behave, to a large extent, by observing the behaviour of others and modelling their own behaviour on that of others when they feel that the consequences will be rewarding. Behaviour is maintained, not by its immediate consequences (as traditional learning theory suggests), but by expectancies about what the behaviour will eventually lead to. Nor is behaviour determined by personality traits; it is dependent on an evaluation of the consequences of a particular response in a particular situation and whether or not it helps to achieve personal goals or plans.

Personal construct theory

One theory that deserves special mention within the context of personality research, theory and application in Great Britain is Kelly's (1955) personal construct theory. Although Kelly is American, many British researchers have made use of construct theory and the technique for analysing personality, repertory grids, which is derived from the theory (Smith and Stewart, 1977; Smith, 1980; Stewart and Stewart, 1981). According to personal construct theory our personality is determined by the nature of our *personal construct system*. Our personal constructs help us to interpret the world around us, and we use a personal construct when, for example, we classify another person as unhappy or contented. A personal construct is a bipolar descriptive term used to help us understand and classify our experience of objects, events or people in the world around us. Pleasant-horrid, safe-threatening, nervous-calm, reliable-unreliable, are all possible examples. One of the central ideas in personal construct theory is that of "constructive alternativism" (i.e. each of us uses different constructs to help us to classify and understand the world around us). In so doing we develop our own individual personal construct system and our own individual construction of reality. The extent to which we "share" constructs with others or understand their construct system represents the extent to which we understand their personalities.

In contrast to others, notably Skinner, Kelly believes that people have the capacity to represent the environment (i.e. they develop internal models relevant to the world around them—construct systems). Like social learning theory, personal construct theory emphasises the relationship between person and environment, since construct systems develop and change as a result of experience; however, the emphasis in construct theory is on the role of internal, *person* variables (i.e. constructs). The basic motivational urge of human beings, according to construct theory, is to develop and elaborate these internal models so that they provide an increasingly better basis for interpreting and predicting events in the world around us.

A person's construct system can be explored and investigated with the aid of the repertory grid techniques. Repertory grid methods provide a means of *eliciting* personal constructs by asking people to compare and contrast *elements*. These elements might be other people, job tasks, products, etc. The resulting descriptions represent their constructs. An important difference between repertory grids and other techniques for exploring human personality (e.g. questionnaires) is that the constructs that emerge from a grid should represent the individual person's own particular set of constructs. Although this individualistic means of exploring personality has considerable benefits in terms of relevance and meaning for the person concerned, it can also present problems, since it may be difficult to make comparisons between the results obtained from different people. Many sophisticated methods are available for analysis, often based on the statistical procedure of *principal components analysis* (similar to factor analysis) (*see* Slater, 1977).

PERSONALITY THEORIES IN ORGANISATIONAL CONTEXTS

The extent to which we accept or reject different views about human nature can have a profound effect on how we behave. Most people, of course, are not familiar with formal theories of personality, but many will recognise in the theories outlined above underlying ideas about human nature that resemble their own views and influence their behaviour.

The fact that there is a variety of available personality theories, each with its own set of concepts and methods, does not mean that there is total disagreement among psychologists about the nature and development of human personality. The different theoretical positions reflect, in part, the fact that personality can be examined using different concepts, levels of analysis and methods with the focus of attention on different phenomena. It should also be recognised that the various lines of theoretical development are not entirely independent of each other. Eysenck, for example, uses some of the concepts of conditioning and learning, developed by behaviour theorists to explain the development of personality traits. Like professional psychologists, managers and other members of organisations are likely to reject or accept different theories to different degrees.

Pervin (1980) provides an informative and extensive illustration of the insights that can be obtained when different theoretical frameworks and methods are used together to examine the personality of one person—in this case Jim Hersch, a student at Harvard University:

> . . . the observations obtained are different in striking and important ways, but they are not inconsistent with one another. To conclude that one knows Jim or understands his personality from just one set of observations would undoubtedly put one in the same position as the blind man who examined a small portion of the elephant and was led to a wrong conclusion on the basis of

his limited observations. In part, the data suggest that at times the theories talk about the same phenomena in different terms. However, the data also strongly suggest that each set of observations and each theory represents an incomplete picture of the whole individual. In a certain sense, each represents a glimpse of the total complexity of human personality (pp. 486/7).

This view, that each theoretical viewpoint represents a useful but incomplete understanding of human personality, is reflected in the way that the various theories have been drawn on by researchers and practitioners working in organisational settings. Different aims and goals have led investigators to make use of available theories and methods in a variety of ways. Table VI provides a brief overview comparing the different theories mentioned above and gives an indication of some typical areas of application.

Each of the theoretical positions and the measurement techniques associated with them lend themselves to different areas of application, and to a large extent the different areas in which the theories have found application reflect the differences in the theories themselves. *Trait theory*, for example, with its emphasis on relatively stable, unchanging personality characteristics, provides a viewpoint from which it makes sense to select people for jobs or other organisational roles on the basis of these stable characteristics. The personality instruments associated with trait theory (e.g. 16PF and EPI) are sometimes used to assess people for selection, career development or team-building purposes. Belbin (1981), for instance, has examined some of the links between the personality traits of members and the functioning of successful or unsuccessful work teams. Assessment centres (*see* Chapter 7), designed to select new entrants to a company or to identify promotion candidates, also make use of personality questionnaires.

Operant and social learning theories, by contrast, emphasise that people learn and change as a consequence of their experiences. This view provides a basis for attempting to change and develop human behaviour, and operant and social learning approaches are of considerable value in programmes of behaviour modification and training and development within organisations (*see* Chapters 12 and 13).

Personal construct theory assigns an important role to the individualistic and differing nature of each person's construct system and proposes that behaviour is determined by this system rather than personality traits common to all of us. Thus, in situations where it is important to see things from the perspective of the person or people concerned, construct theory can provide a suitable theoretical basis (e.g. Beck, 1980). In fact construct theory and, in particular, the associated repertory grid methods, have

TABLE VI. A COMPARISON OF PERSONALITY THEORIES

	Trait theory	Operant theory	Social learning theory	Personal construct theory
Main measuring procedure	Self-report questionnaires	Observation	Observation	Repertory grids
Causes of behaviour emphasised by the theory	Mainly "person" factors, i.e. personality traits	"Situation" factors, i.e. external rewards and punishment	"Person" and "situation" factors in continual *interaction* with each other	Mainly "person" factors, i.e. attempts to develop a more elaborate and improved personal construct system, but influenced by feedback from the environment (situation)
Sample areas of application	Personnel selection Career development Team building	Organisational behaviour modification Training/ development	Organisational behaviour modification Training/ development	Training evaluation Career development /guidance Job/task analysis

found an enormous variety of applications. This is perhaps hardly surprising, since many people would argue that to understand things from the perspective of the person concerned is the goal of all personality theories.

Stewart and Stewart (1982) provide examples of the use of repertory grids in market research, training evaluation, quality control, motivation, counselling and managerial effectiveness. Smith (1980) describes applications in job analysis, task analysis and vocational guidance. Fig. 18(a) shows part of a grid completed

	Historian	Business man	Teacher-F.E.	Clerk	Postman	Climbing Instr	Nurse	Accountant	Barrister	Naval officer	Policeman	Fireman	Jet Set Executive	Barman	Journalist	Self	Ideal self
Concerned with business and commerce	1	7	1	5	1	1	1	7	5	1	5	1	7	1	6	1	5
Using brain	7	7	7	5	4	5	6	7	7	7	7	5	7	3	7	6	6
Responsibility	4	7	7	3	2	7	6	6	7	7	7	6	7	1	6	1	6
Excitement	2	4	5	2	1	6	4	4	3	6	6	5	7	1	6	1	7
Concerned with figures	3	7	1	6	1	1	1	7	1	1	1	1	7	1	2	1	1
Have to think fast	1	7	1	2	1	4	4	6	7	7	6	5	7	1	7	4	5
Purely physical	1	1	1	1	5	7	4	1	1	3	5	7	1	3	3	1	6
Outside	1	1	1	1	1	7	1	1	1	7	6	7	2	1	7	1	7
Stay in one place	1	5	1	1	6	7	1	1	2	7	4	3	7	1	6	7	6
Teaching something	7	1	7	1	1	7	1	1	1	2	1	1	1	1	1	1	5
Solving problems	6	7	2	1	1	1	3	6	5	5	6	2	7	1	4	5	4
High pay	3	6	3	2	2	2	3	6	7	5	3	7	7	1	4	1	6
Have to meet deadlines	1	7	2	2	2	2	3	6	7	7	7	4	7	2	7	6	3

Key: Rating scale from 7—very true—to 1—very untrue.

Source: Smith et al. (1978).

Fig. 18(a) *Part of Anthony P's completed grid.*

by a young man who had been pressured by his family to study for a history degree at university (*see* Smith *et al.*, 1978). Fig. 18(b) shows a cognitive map produced by analysing the grid with one of the many computer packages available. The analysis identifies the major components in the young man's personal view of the world. As Smith *et al.* (1978) put it: "Anthony P's cognitive map makes his dilemma crystal clear. He tends to divide the occupations in his conceptual scheme into four groups, outdoor 'big-shots', indoor 'big-shots', outdoor 'small-shots' and indoor 'small-shots'. Ideally he would like to be an outdoor 'big-shot', but because of historical factors and family pressure he feels he is now becoming an 'indoor small-shot' '' (p. 101).

MOTIVATION

Whereas the study of personality involves attempting to understand

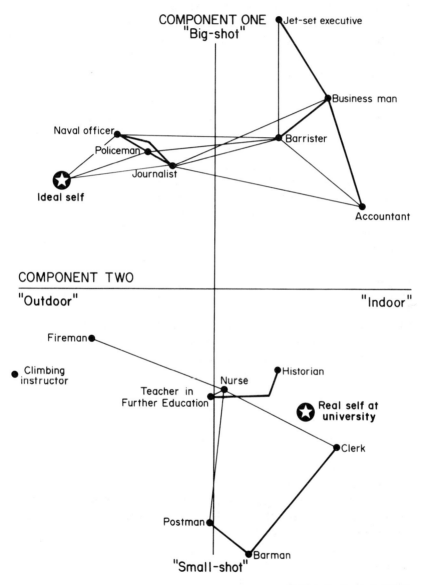

Source: Smith et al. (1978).

Fig. 18 (b). Map derived from Anthony P's completed grid.

the basis of individual differences and similarities between people, the study of motivation attempts to grasp the reasons *why* people engage in certain activities—either people in general or specific individuals. In this sense, human personality and motivation are inextricably linked, and a strong connection between views of personality and motivation theorists can often be found. Many general personality theories, for example, incorporate ideas about what motivates people and, as we shall see later in this chapter, contemporary theories concerned specifically with work motivation share considerable common ground with theories of personality.

Problems and issues concerning motivation are frequently of central importance in organisational life. Why does someone who apparently has the ability to do a job well consistently fail to perform effectively? How can a group of employees be encouraged to produce more? Can the payment of incentive bonuses be used to produce more effort? Although many issues of this sort frequently have an individual motivational basis, it must be remembered that other factors such as an inadequate training or job experience, personality characteristics, unsuitable organisation structure or inadequate supervision may also be involved. Thus, whilst motivation is unquestionably an important topic, many other factors are involved in successful performance, and one must resist any such notion that all performance problems can be understood and resolved by addressing motivational issues. Just as attempts to understand human personality emphasise both internal and external factors, explorations of motivation also recognise a distinction between internal and external factors. One means of explaining the motivation to behave in certain ways is to propose the existence of certain internal, motivational states of drive or need.

Some theories of motivation focus on the *content* of motivation and attempt to uncover needs such as hunger, security, affiliation, self-esteem, which underlie and control behaviour. Other *process* theories focus on the processes by which goals or needs exert their influence. Examples of both types of theory are given in this chapter.

Human needs and motivation

One of the most influential content theories of motivation is the need heirarchy formulated by Maslow (1954). Maslow identified five distinct need categories:

(a) physiological needs;
(b) safety and security needs;
(c) belongingness and love needs;

(d) self-esteem needs;

(e) the need to self-actualise.

Furthermore, he proposed that these needs are organised into a hierarchy (*see* Fig. 19): needs higher up the hierarchy emerge to play a prominent role in the control of behaviour only when needs lower down the hierarchy are satisfied. Thus, someone who is hungry (a physiological need) will take risks and ignore safety needs to obtain food. In the work context, safety needs such as job security or safe working conditions need to be satisfied before attention is turned to the development of friendships and good relationships with others. The highest level in the hierarchy, self-actualisation, concerns the needs for self-fulfilment and the achievement of one's full potential. What Maslow attempts to emphasise with his need hierarchy is the positive side of human nature, by stressing that despite the requirement for the satisfaction of lower level needs, humans will whenever possible, strive to achieve their potential and attain the satisfaction that is to be derived from using one's abilities and attributes to the full.

Some possible implications of the need hierarchy for organisations are fairly clear, which may be one of the reasons why

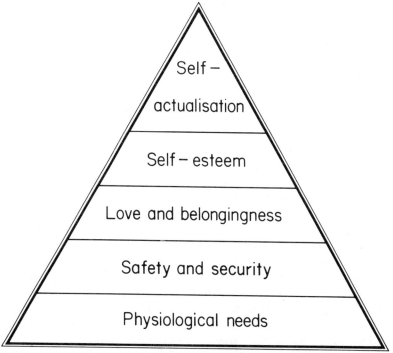

Fig. 19. *Maslow's need hierarchy. (Needs lower down the pyramid must be at least partly met before higher needs become important.)*

Maslow's theory has been so popular in management circles. First, the incentives or goals that will motivate employees will depend on their current level of need satisfaction. Second, it is probably in its best interests for the organisation to attempt to arrange working conditions and tasks so that lower level needs are met and employees are motivated by their own needs for self-actualisation.

Despite its obvious appeal and clear relevance to work in organisations, Maslow's theory has not been well supported by empirical studies of its validity. Some studies have examined the proposition that needs are organised heirarchically in the way that Maslow suggests (e.g. Lawler and Suttle, 1972; Hall and Nougaim, 1968; Rauschenberger et al., 1980; and Dachler and Hulin, 1969). The theory suggests that, as any need is satisfied, it should become less important and a higher need should predominate. The balance of evidence provides little support for this proposal.

The idea that there are five underlying needs has also been investigated with the aid of factor analysis techniques (e.g. Payne, 1970). Again, the evidence does not provide convincing support for the theory. Wahba and Bridwell (1979) review the research relating to Maslow's hierarchy and conclude that the literature "shows little clear or consistent support" (p. 52). However, they point out that some of the research designed to test the theory has drawbacks of its own and therefore may not have provided a completely fair test. Alderfer has produced a revision of Maslow's theory involving only three categories of need and less emphasis on the strict heirarchical ordering, and his reformulation has been supported by some evidence (see Alderfer, 1972).

Motivation and work

Attempts to explain motivation in terms of human needs can be of value in organisational contexts only if the job factors that are involved in the satisfaction of such needs can be identified. The two-factor theory of Herzberg represents an attempt to examine the role of various job factors and how they relate to needs. His theory is based, to a large extent, on investigations of the factors in jobs that give rise to satisfaction or dissatisfaction. In an early study (Herzberg et al., 1959) of a fairly small sample of engineers and accountants in the Pittsburgh area of the United States, employees were asked to describe incidents in their jobs which made them feel particularly good (satisfied) or bad (dissatisfied) about them. This study and subsequent similar studies (see Herzberg, 1968) indicated those factors that were related to good feelings about the job (factors such as achievement, recognition, the work itself, responsibility) and those that were related to bad feelings (factors such as company policy and administration, working conditions, supervision). These data led Herzberg to the "two-factor" theory, which proposes that two different types of factors contribute to satisfaction and dissatisfaction at work. Factors associated with good feelings about the job (motivators) are mostly derived from the job itself. The second set of factors (hygiene factors) are mostly external to the job and involve aspects of the physical or psychological environment. Some of the most important implications of Herzberg's theory concern the ideas about how satisfaction and motivation can be improved by restructuring or "enriching" jobs so that they provide people with rewarding experiences.

The core of Herzberg's proposal is that it will not be possible to *motivate* people by improving hygiene factors alone. Improvements in hygiene factors such as working conditions will perhaps decrease dissatisfaction but will not improve motivation. True motivation, according to Herzberg, derives from factors associated with the job itself and relies on offering opportunities for achievement, recognition, responsibility, etc. Like Maslow's theory Herzberg's proposals have been extremely popular in management circles, but also like Maslow's theory there is no consistent body of research evidence to support them (Dunnette *et al.*, 1967; Schneider and Locke, 1971). Indeed, some writers have been critical of many of the basic concepts of job enrichment. Fein (1979) argues that: "The simple truth is that there are no data which show that restructuring and enriching jobs will raise the will to work. . . . The intrinsic nature of the work is only one factor among many that affect worker satisfaction" (pp. 449/50).

More recently, Hackman and Oldham have proposed a job characteristics model that identifies five core job characteristics involved in job satisfaction and motivation (*see* Fig. 20). According to the model, satisfaction and motivation are controlled by the critical psychological states: meaningfulness of the work, responsibility for the outcomes of work and knowledge of the results of work. In turn, the critical psychological states are linked to the core job dimensions. *Skill variety* is concerned with the extent to which the activities of the job call for a selection of abilities and skills. *Task identity* and *significance* concern the extent to which the activities of the job form an identifiable whole and the extent to which the job has an impact on the lives or work of other people. *Autonomy* relates to the freedom and independence that the jobholder has, and *feedback* to the extent to which knowledge of results concerning individual effectiveness is provided. Hackman and Oldham have also produced the Job Diagnostic Survey (Hackman and Oldham, 1975), which provides measures of the job dimensions and other variables involved in the model.

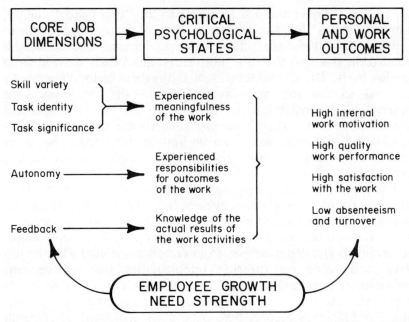

Source: Hackman and Oldham (1976).

Fig. 20. *The job characteristics model.*

Some studies have been done to attempt to examine the validity of the model (e.g. Dunham, 1976; Wall *et al.*, 1978) and mixed results have been produced. It is clear, from these studies, that further work is needed and that the job characteristics model may need some reformulation. The model does, however, provide a coherent theoretical basis for the links between job factors and their consequences for motivation and organisational behaviour.

Process theories

Motivation theories such as Maslow's need hierarchy focus on the *contents* of motivation. An alternative approach to motivation involves examining the cognitive processes that are involved. The most important process approaches to motivation make use of ideas about the *expectations* that people have about the consequences of their behaviour (e.g. Lawler, 1973). Put simply, the theory suggests that the amount of effort people are prepared to invest in a task depends on three factors:

(*a*) expectancy—whether the effort involved will produce better performance;

(*b*) instrumentality—whether the performance will pay off in terms of outcomes, e.g. promotion;

(*c*) valence—whether the possible outcomes are attractive for the individual concerned.

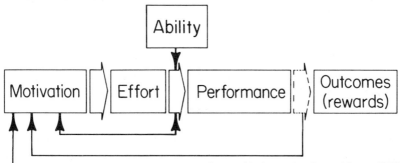

Source: Hackman, Lawler and Porter (1977).

Fig. 21. *The basic motivation—behaviour sequence according to expectancy theory. A person's motivation is a function of: (a) effort-to-performance expectancies; (b) performance-to-outcome expectancies; and (c) perceived valence of outcomes.*

As Fig. 21 suggests, a person's motivation is relected in the amount of effort that he puts into his job. Theories involving the concepts of expectancy, instrumentality and valence (usually called expectancy theory, or expectancy/valence theory) form the basis of much current research on motivation and work behaviour (*see* Steers and Porter, 1979). According to expectancy theory the following factors are involved in determining motivation, effort and, eventually, job satisfaction:

(*a*) The perceived relationship between Effort and Performance (E→P). This concerns the belief the person holds that extra effort will lead to better performance.

(*b*) The perceived relationship between Performance and Outcomes (P→O). This concerns the belief that improved job performance will lead to outcomes such as promotion, extra pay, more responsibility, etc.

(*c*) The attractiveness or Valence of the possible outcomes (V). This concerns the value of the possible outcomes for the person concerned.

Other points are worth noticing.

(*d*) Even if Motivation is high, this *may* not be reflected in performance, perhaps because of a lack of ability or an inappropriate strategy for doing the job.

(*e*) The beliefs that the person holds about links between Effort, Performance and Outcomes are modified as a result of experience—hence the feedback loop. For example, an initial belief that good performance will lead to positive outcomes such as promotion may not be borne out by experience and this may result in a reassessment of the Performance-Outcome (P→O) relationships.

Two points are worth mentioning in connection with such theories. First, they emphasise the fact that the attractiveness of specific outcomes or rewards is a very individualistic matter. What is important and attractive for one person may be irrelevant for another. Thus, although expectancy theories seek to provide a general model of the factors involved in determining effort and performance for all employees, the individual differences between people is an integral part of the theory. The second and related point is that although expectancy theories concentrate on the common *processes* involved, the *contents* of each individual's motivational system (e.g. whether extra pay or time off has higher valence) are also important. Research to evaluate expectancy theory is complex and extensive (*see* Campbell and Pritchard, 1979) but does offer some support for the idea that each of the factors involved, i.e. Expectancy, Instrumentality and Valence, are important in determining work motivation, although how each of the factors combine together to influence motivation is far from clear.

Nadler and Lawler (1979) have examined the implications that expectancy theory has for both the behaviour of individual managers and the design or organisation systems/structures.

Implications for individual managers
The following are among the chief implications for managers put forward by Nadler and Lawler (1979):

(*a*) Find out what particular outcomes or rewards are valued (have high valence) for each employee. The theory proposes that different people will value different rewards.

(*b*) Be specific about the precise behaviours that constitute good levels of performance.

(*c*) Make sure that the desired levels of performance are reachable. According to the theory, E→P expectancy influences motivation. If an employee feels that it is not possible for him to reach the performance level, even with high effort, his motivation will be low.

(*d*) Ensure that there is a direct, clear and explicit link between performance at the desired level and outcomes/rewards. In other words, employees must be able to observe and experience the

(P→O) connection. If this is not clear and seen to work, the motivating expectancies will not be created in employees' minds.

(e) Check that there are no conflicting expectancies. Once the motivating expectancies have been set up and employees have a clear grasp of the E→P and P→O relationship, it is important to check that other people or systems within the organisation are not encouraging alternative expectancies. For example, another manager might be providing rewards for lower or higher levels of performance.

(f) Ensure changes in outcome are large enough. As Nadler and Lawler put it, "Trivial rewards will result in trivial amounts of effort and thus trivial improvements in performance" (p. 223).

(g) Check that the system is treating everyone fairly. The theory is based on the idea that people are different and therefore different rewards will need to be used for different people. Nevertheless, "Good performers should see that they get more of the desired rewards than do poor performers, and others in the system should see that also" (ibid). In other words, despite the use of different rewards the system should seem to be fair and equitable to those involved.

Implications for organisations

Below are some of the main implications for organisations proposed by Nadler and Lawler (1979):

(a) Design pay and reward systems so that,

(i) *desirable* performance is rewarded (e.g. do not reward mere "membership" by linking pay with years of service; and

(ii) the relationship between performance and reward is clear. Whatever the rewards in terms of pay, promotion, etc., that result from good performance, these should be made clear and explicit rather than kept ambiguous or secret.

(b) Design tasks, jobs and roles so that people have an opportunity to satisfy their own needs through their work, but do not assume that everyone wants the same things. Some people may want "enriched" jobs with greater autonomy, feedback, etc., but some will not.

(c) "Individualise" the organisation. Expectancy theory proposes that people have different needs, valences, etc. Because of these individual differences it is important to allow people some opportunity to influence not only the type of work they do but many other aspects of organisational life, such as reward-systems, or fringe benefits offered.

Expectancy and reinforcement

When consideration is given to systematic ways in which effort and performance can be enhanced, it emerges that there are two major alternative positions within contemporary organisational behaviour research, expectancy/valence theory and reinforcement/operant theory. Both of these viewpoints are considered in the present volume. Expectancy theory has been dealt with in this chapter, and Chapter 13 is devoted to operant theory. These two viewpoints differ in various ways, but there are also similarities in that both theories emphasise the role of rewards in determining behaviour. Important differences concern the view that the two positions hold about reward scheduling. Operant theory proposes that partial reinforcement is most effective, whereas expectancy theory seems to suggest that there should be a direct and continuous link between behaviour and reward (continuous reinforcement). Some investigation of the detailed predictions derived from each position and how they work out in "live" situations would be helpful here.

One fairly clear trend which emerges from the literature on motivation is that there is a movement away from general theories, which apply equally to everyone, towards much more individual theories of motivation, which allow for the role of individual differences. In this sense motivation theories seem to be sharing more and more common ground with theories of personality. Like personality theories some motivation theories emphasise internal *person* variables such as needs or expectancies, while others concentrate on external *situation* factors such as job characteristics or rewards. Also, like personality theories, one of the most influential current theories of motivation emphasises the role of both person and situation variables. Expectancy theory, according to Nadler and Lawler (1979), assumes that, "Behaviour is determined by a combination of forces in the individual and forces in the environment. Neither the individual nor the environment alone determines behaviour" (p. 217). In the personality field, social learning theory adopts a similar position. In fact there are many striking similarities between social learning theory and expectancy theory in their joint emphasis on expectancies, individual goals and values and the influence of both person and situation factors. In fact, if we remember that social learning theory also embodies many of the ideas of operant theory, these similarities seem to represent not only a coming together of personality and motivation theory, but provide the basis for a synthesis between two previously irreconcilable positions concerning motivation: the behaviourial, reinforcement based, operant view and the views of expectancy theory which are more concerned with internal psychological processes and their consequences. Both approaches have independently been successful in improving motivation and work performance, and this emerging concensus promises even more soundly based and applicable ideas.

QUESTIONS

1. What are "trait theories" of personality? What relevance do they have to organisational behaviour?

2. Why is social learning theory described as an "interactionist" theory?

3. What is the difference between content and process theories of motivation?

4. What are the implications of expectancy-valence theory for managers and organisations?

5. Do operant and expectancy theories make the same proposals about how rewards in organisations should be administered?

PART THREE

Issues and Practices in Organisational Life

CHAPTER SIX

Fundamentals of Job Analysis, Personnel Selection and Appraisal

OBJECTIVES

The next two chapters are closely linked and together provide an overview of much of the psychological research and theory that has direct relevance to personnel practices within organisations. The present chapter is concerned with three topics that are of central importance to the work of industrial/organisational psychologists and personnel specialists: job analysis, personnel selection and appraisal. A clear understanding of a job via job analysis is a prerequisite for many personnel-related activities in organisations such as career development, job evaluation and, of course, personnel selection. The chapter outlines the main techniques for job analysis that are available and then provides a systematic introduction to the basic principles involved in the development and validation of personnel selection procedures. Finally, the topic of performance appraisal is dealt with. Particular attention is given to the types of rating scales that can be used for appraisal purposes, typical errors in the rating process and how errors might be minimised by the use of appropriate scales and training procedures.

PERSONNEL PRACTICES

Common factors

Although organisations may vary in many respects most industrial and commercial organisations share some fundamental, common practices with regard to the personnel that work within them. First, although people are allocated duties or tasks to carry out, there is often ambiguity about the specific nature and range of people's overall jobs, the qualities required to carry them out successfully and the position of jobs within the organisation. A second common factor is that most organisations have some method(s) for selecting new entrants. Third, at some stage in most organisations attempts are made to assess the extent to which people carry out their jobs effectively. These common threads of organisational life have an impact on most of us in one way or another. The key areas of technical knowledge that underlie these practices concern the techniques and procedures of job analysis, personnel selection and performance appraisal.

JOB ANALYSIS

In recent years a great deal of research effort has been put into the development of methods and techniques for job analysis. Job analysis procedures are designed to produce systematic information about jobs, including the nature of the work performed, equipment used, the working conditions and the position of the job within the organisation. It is worth noting that satisfactory job analyses are prerequisites for many decisions and activities that have a crucial influence on the lives of personnel within the organisation, including the design and validation of personnel selection procedures, training and career development schemes, job design or redesign, job evaluation, and safety. There is a wide range of techniques and procedures available for job analysis, and Blum and Naylor (1968), Prien and Ronan (1971) and McCormick (1976) provide overviews and critical examinations of some of the major techniques. Essentially, job analysis data may be divided into these four categories:

(a) written material;
(b) job holders' reports;
(c) colleagues' reports; and
(d) direct observation.

Written material

In many organisations written job descriptions are available (except for newly created jobs) and can provide the analyst with useful information. It is worth checking by observation and other methods that available descriptions are up to date and provide comprehensive information about the job. If so, a great deal of time and effort may be saved. Unfortunately, in many organisations existing job descriptions are rarely up to date, comprehensive or detailed enough. Published analyses of jobs may provide useful leads but are of limited value, since jobs analysed elsewhere are likely to be similar but not identical to the one under consideration. An accountant's, secretary's or production manager's job will vary considerably from one organisation to another, perhaps in ways that are crucial. Other written material such as production data, organisation charts, training manuals, job aids and so on may also provide useful, additional information.

Job-holders' reports

Interviews in which job-holders are asked, through careful questioning, to give a description of their main tasks and how they carry them out provide extremely useful information, and such interviews are usually an essential element in any job analysis. On the other hand it is difficult to be sure that all of the important aspects of the job have been covered by the interview and that the information provided by the job-holder is not too subjective, biased (owing to faulty memory perhaps) or even deliberately untrue.

Workers' reports may also be obtained by asking them to complete a *diary or activity record*. Since this is done on a regular basis as the job is being carried out, it avoids problems associated with faulty memory, etc. It is, however, a difficult and time-consuming procedure. Stewart (1967) provides an example of the use of this method to analyse the jobs of British managers.

Structured *task or job inventories* may also be used to collect job analysis data. These consist of lists of tasks and other relevant job features such as working conditions. In completing an inventory job-holders are asked to check (i.e. yes or no) or rate (e.g. on a seven-point scale) whether an item does or does not apply to their job. Examples of such inventories are given by Prien (1965) on clerical workers and Hemphill (1959) on executives.

Flanagan (1954) developed a procedure known as the *critical incident technique*. In brief, using this technique involves asking the interviewee to recall specific incidents of job behaviour that are characteristic of either very good or very poor performance on the job. This can provide the analyst with a clear grasp of the job behaviour(s) that are important and enable him to differentiate between good and poor job-holders—extremely useful information in the context of personnel selection!

McCormick *et al.* (1972) have produced the Position Analysis Questionnaire (PAQ), which is an example of a *structured questionnaire* approach to job analysis. The elements in the questionnaire are worker-orientated in that they focus on generalised aspects of human behaviour and are less tied to the technology of specific jobs. The PAQ consists of 189 job elements organised into six major divisions:

(*a*) information input;
(*b*) mediation processes (i.e. the mental processes of reasoning, decision-making, etc.);
(*c*) work output;
(*d*) interpersonal activities (i.e. relationships with others);
(*e*) work situation and job context; and
(*f*) miscellaneous aspects.

One problem with the PAQ is that it requires a fairly high level of reading ability on the part of respondents (Ash and Edgell, 1975). Nevertheless, the PAQ is an extremely well-researched and valuable means of analysing jobs. The development work for the PAQ was carried out in the United States by McCormick and others, and the

PAQ may come into use in Britain. Research is currently being conducted at the University of Aston to examine the PAQ as a means of job analysis and in particular the applicability of the instrument and changes that might be needed when using it within British organisations (*see* Patrick *et al.*, 1980).

A self-contained technique for analysis, which is job rather than worker orientated, has been described by Fine and Wiley (1974). Known as Functional Job Analysis (FJA), this approach makes use of a standardised language to describe what job-holders do and provides a means of examining the complexity and the orientation of the job. Orientation here is described as the extent to which the job is directed towards "data", "people" or "things" and, as a result of analysis, can be expressed in percentage terms. The basic unit of analysis in FJA is the task, i.e. an action or action sequence organised over time and designed to contribute to a specific end result or objective. Using a very similar definition of the task, Annett and others (Annett *et. al.,* 1971; Shepherd, 1976) have developed a means of analysis known as Hierarchial Task Analysis (HTA). Since HTA is particularly useful in the development of training, this procedure is discussed in more detail in Chapter 12.

A recent innovation in the job analysis literature involves the use of Kelly's (1955) *repertory grid technique* (e.g. Smith, 1980). This approach appears to have great potential for providing systematic worker orientated data. It has an advantage over other means of obtaining worker orientated data such as PAQ, in that it does not limit the responses of the job-holder by providing a prestructured set of categories.

The procedures outlined above can all be used with one job-holder at a time. In some circumstances it may be useful to collect data from groups of job-holders rather than individuals, and the techniques can all be adapted for such use.

Colleagues' reports
In addition to gleaning information directly from job-holders, it can be useful to obtain data from subordinates, peers and superiors. For example, when collecting critical incident data the views of a job-holder, a subordinate and a superior on the nature of such critical incidents might provide for interesting comparisons.

Direct observation
In any job analysis exercise some direct observation of the job being carried out is invariably helpful. It is, of course, possible that the presence of the analyst may alter the job-holder's behaviour, and as with the approaches described earlier the data obtained cannot be perfect. Yet data derived from observation, perhaps even from

participant-observation, where the analyst actually does all or some of the job, can provide insights that no other method can.

Job analyses are usually best developed by using as many different approaches and means of data collection as possible and pooling the results.

Using job analysis information

The job analysis is used in a number of ways. A *job description* can be prepared from the job analysis data. It can be useful in the selection procedure to give candidates some understanding of the job and can also be used within the organisation to provide information for training, job evaluation and other purposes (*see* Fig. 22). Bottomly (1983) provides practical guidance on the development and use of job evaluation procedures. The job analysis also provides information that might be used when recruitment advertisements, etc., are prepared to attract candidates for the job. (Detailed advice on this topic is beyond the scope of the present book but further information may be found in Fordham, 1975.)

A *personnel specification* represents the demands of the job translated into human terms. It involves listing the essential criteria that candidates must satisfy and also those criteria that would exclude candidates from consideration.

PERSONNEL SELECTION

The conceptual foundation of personnel selection has two main elements. First, the fact that there are *individual differences* between people (*see* Chapters 3, 4 and 5). This makes it sensible to attempt to match people with jobs—if everyone were the same, selection would be pointless. The second element is the proposition that it is possible to predict future (job-related) behaviour on the basis of current or past behaviour. The idea that future behaviour is predictable does not mean that it is possible to predict future job success with absolute accuracy or that human behaviour is, or can ever be, entirely predictable. It implies that systematic selection procedures can produce a more efficient work-force than a random matching of people with jobs.

Before going further it is worth making a distinction between the two major ways in which people and jobs might be matched. These are: *selection* and *placement*.

Selection concerns the process of choosing, from a sample of job applicants, the person(s) who seem(s) best suited to the available job(s). In other words, a selection procedure determines who does, or does not, enter the organisation *and* matches people with jobs.

JOB DESCRIPTION: WOOD MACHINIST

1. JOB TITLE   WOOD MACHINIST (trencher)

2. LOCATION   MILL SHOP

3. NUMBER IN JOB   8

4. PURPOSE OF JOB
To take pre-cut and pre-planed wood and to cut trenches of specified dimensions at specified positions.

5. RESPONSIBILITIES
Responsible to the Mill Shop foreman.

6. RELATIONSHIPS

Works largely on own, but has some contact with the operatives performing previous and subsequent operations. Sometimes required to train new operatives.

7. PHYSICAL CONDITIONS

The Mill Shop is dry, well lit and ventilated but there is no heating at any time of year. Noise levels can be high. Work is performed in standing position. Some lifting and carrying is involved.

8. OUTLINE OF THE JOB

8.1 Transport batch of wood from previous process by pulling along trolley.

8.2 Check with plan the position of the trenches: change cutters on trencher if necessary.

8.3 Take small batches of wood to bench: place in position under trenching machine using pre-set guides. Pull cutters of trencher forward, keeping hands clear of cutters.

8.4 Restack trenched wood neatly and safely.

8.5 When batch is completed, pull cart to next operative.

8.6 Complete simple forms.

9. SAFETY ASPECTS

The work involves a number of serious potential hazards.

9.1 Falling stacks of wood.

9.2 Injury from the cutters of the trenching machine.

10. SALARY AND CONDITIONS OF SERVICE

Salary: Flat rate of £55.00 per week plus monthly group bonus.

Holidays: Three weeks per year plus Bank Holidays.

Hours: Monday - Friday   9.00 a.m. - 5.00 p.m.
                Saturdays   8.30 a.m. - 12.30 p.m.

Breaks: Afternoon and morning breaks of 15 minutes.
                Lunch-break of 1 hour.

Overtime: Usually available.

Courtesy Dr J.M. Smith.

Fig. 22. *An illustrative job description.*

By contrast, placement involves dealing with people who are already in the organisation and need to be matched with jobs. This might take place after changes in the internal structure of the organisation, or for example when a group of general management trainees are recruited. Placement involves examining the characteristics of people within the organisation, looking at the available jobs and making the best match possible.

This chapter is concerned specifically with the process of selection, although most of the principles and practices described could be applied equally well to placement problems.

The selection system

The key stage in the personnel selection process occurs when the selection decision is taken and a candidate is either offered a position within the company or turned away. At this point various pieces of evidence concerning the current or past performance of candidates (e.g. behaviour at an interview, psychological test scores or references), usually referred to as *predictors*, are used to decide whether or not a candidate is suitable for the job in question. Although the selection decision is the key stage in the selection process, there are many other important elements in the selection process leading up to and following the selection decision itself.

Fig. 23 provides an outline of the main elements involved in designing a personnel selection procedure. The process begins with a *job analysis,* followed by the choice of *selection instruments.* Information on the *work performance* of job-holders is then used to examine the *validity* of the selection instruments (i.e. whether high and low scores on the selection instruments are associated with good and poor work performance).

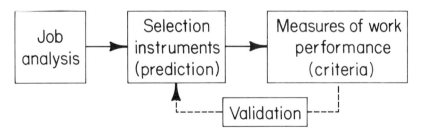

Fig. 23. *The main elements in the personnel selection system.*

A thorough job analysis provides a basis for suggesting that candidates who satisfy particular selection criteria are likely to be suitable for the job in question. The analysis may suggest, for example, that certain personality and dispositional characteristics are desirable together with specific previous experience, technical qualifications and levels of intelligence and specific abilities (*see* Chapter 3). The next stage in the process is to identify selection instruments (e.g. intelligence tests, group discussion exercises, interviews, application forms) that can be used to examine whether candidates meet the required criteria or not. The advantages and disadvantages of various selection instruments as *predictors* will be examined in the next chapter, but first another issue must be addressed.

VALIDITY AND RELIABILITY

Job analysis may suggest that certain selection criteria are appropriate but does not (and cannot) provide any definite evidence that candidates who meet the criteria actually turn out to be better employees than candidates who do not. Such evidence is obtained by examining the validity and reliability of the proposed predictors.

Criterion-related validity

Criterion-related validity refers to the strength of the relationship between the *predictor* (e.g. psychological test scores or interview ratings) and the *criterion* (i.e. subsequent work behaviour, indicated by measures such as output figures or supervisors' ratings). Criterion-related validity is high if candidates who obtain high *predictor* scores obtain high *criterion* scores AND candidates who obtain low scores on a predictor also obtain low criterion scores. Fig. 24 shows a scatterplot of some hypothetical data obtained by using two predictors:

(*a*) a job knowledge test score; and
(*b*) an intelligence test score.

and one criterion (work performance) measure:

(*c*) average number of units produced per day.

Inspection of the scatterplot in Fig. 24 shows that the criterion-related validity of the intelligence test appears to be quite good. Participants' scores in this test correspond closely with the number of units produced. Although the predictor and criterion scores are obviously closely related, it is worth noting that the correspondence is not perfect. For perfect correspondence all of the points would lie exactly on the diagonal line drawn in on Fig. 24 (*b*). For the job knowledge test there is no correspondence at all and, as Fig. 24 (*a*) clearly shows, the points are distributed more or less in a circle and

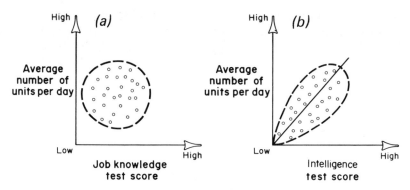

Fig. 24. *Some hypothetical predictor and criterion scores: (a) job knowledge test; (b) intelligence test.*

high scores on one variable can be associated with *either* high or low scores on the other variable.

The strength of the relationship between predictor scores and criterion scores is usually expressed as a correlation coefficient (referred to as a validity coefficient). Perfect correlation between two variables will produce a correlation of 1. No correlation at all will produce a coefficient of 0.

Correlation and prediction
When the correlation between variables is high it is possible to predict the score of one when supplied with someone's score on the other. Consider for example Fig. 25, where the predictor-criterion relationship is perfect, i.e. a validity (correlation) coefficient of + 1.0. In the case of a candidate, it would be possible to obtain his

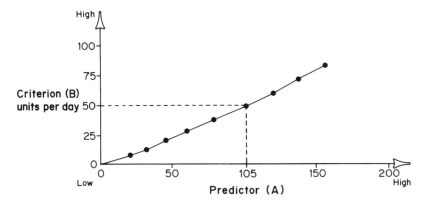

Fig. 25. *Prediction of criterion score from predictor score.*

score on predictor A and thus predict his score on the criterion. If the organisation wished to select staff who would produce an average of at least fifty units per day, what should be done?

As Fig. 25 shows, if *only* people who obtained a score of above 105 on predictor A were offered jobs by the organisation, all future employees would be likely to produce fifty units (or more) per day. Unfortunately, in practice selection can rarely be conducted in such an idealised and clear-cut fashion and there are a number of practical problems that must be considered.

Less than perfect predictor-criterion relationships

Research (e.g. Ghiselli, 1966, 1973) has shown that it is most unusual in practical situations to obtain validity coefficients much in excess of $+0.5$—much less the coefficient of $+1.0$ that will allow perfect prediction. Nevertheless, as will be shown in a later section of the present chapter on "Utility", validity coefficients of considerably less than $+1.0$ can provide a basis for improved personnel selection.

Theoretically the ideal way to collect criterion-related validity data is to use a *predictive (or follow-up) design*. This design involves collecting predictor information (e.g. interview ratings, test scores) for candidates and then following up the candidates (e.g. during their first year of employment) to gather criterion data on their work performance. One important feature emerging from data collected in this way is that the work performance of people with both high *and* low predictor scores needs to be examined. The true relationship between predictor and criterion scores can be established only by allowing candidates with the full range of predictor scores to be given an opportunity to conduct the job. Candidates with poor scores on the predictor may be capable of satisfactory job performance. What this means in practice is that the predictor scores should not be used to take selection decisions until *after* a validity study has been conducted. In other words, until the relationship between predictor and criterion is firmly established, candidates should be offered employment *regardless of their performance on the predictors*. Often this is a difficult step for an organisation to take. If job analysis and other information (in the absence of validity data) suggest that the use of certain predictors should improve their selection decisions, many organisations would not be happy to allow candidates with low scores on these predictors to enter employment. Sometimes it is possible to convince an organisation not to use the results of potential predictors and to continue to use their existing methods while a validation study is carried out. Often, however, organisations cannot accept the constraints of a complete predictive validity (follow-up) design and some compromise is needed.

Another practical problem with the predictive validity design is that of ensuring that the predictor results obtained by new employees are not revealed to other members of the organisation before a validity study has been conducted. Obviously a supervisor who is given a new employee with either a high or low predictor score could be affected by these results. The supervisor's behaviour towards the new employee might be influenced and/or estimates of the new employee's work performance could be biased.

An alternative design for conducting criterion-related validity studies is the *concurrent design*. In the concurrent design, predictor data are obtained from existing employees on whom criterion data are already available. One advantage of the concurrent design is that the organisation is not required to collect predictor data from candidates (for employment) without making use of the data for selection decisions. Predictor data are collected from existing employees only. A second advantage of the concurrent design is that there is no time delay between the collection of predictor and criterion data. Existing employees' predictor scores are correlated with their criterion performance. The criterion data are likely to be already available, or at least they can be collected quickly. There is certainly no need to wait for the lengthy follow-up period involved with the predictive design. Fig. 26 compares the two designs in a hypothetical situation and indicates the considerable differences in time scales and data collection effort that can occur.

Because of these advantages the concurrent design is attractive to many organisations. However, there are disadvantages. The workers presently employed by an organisation provide a population that may be very different from the population of job applicants. Current job-holders have already survived existing company selection procedures and represent a preselected group of people who have been with the organisation for some time. No data are available on people who were not hired by the company, nor on those who were hired but have subsequently left it. Thus the concurrent sample is incomplete and not representative of the potential work-force. If, as a result of a concurrent validity study, a link between, say, scores in an arithmetic test and job performance is established, it is difficult to be sure if the people tested come to the job with such skills or whether arithmetic skills are acquired as a result of training and job experience. Such problems make it hard to be certain about the actual predictive value of results derived from a concurrent validity study. One important point to make about any validity study, regardless of whether predictive or concurrent

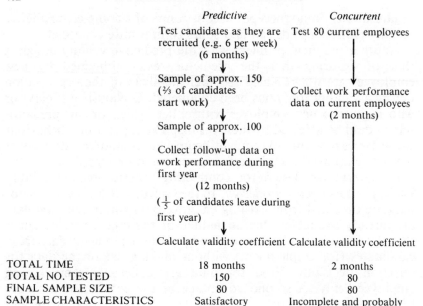

Fig. 26. *A comparison of predictive and concurrent designs.*

procedures are used, concerns the fact that the initial validity study should always be followed by a "cross-validation" study on a second sample of people—to cross-check the results obtained. For studies that involve relatively few predictors this requirement is perhaps not essential and represents a "counsel of perfection". However, when a study has investigated many possible predictors and those with the strongest predictor-criterion relationship are to be used for selection purposes, cross-validation is more important. The more potential predictors are used, the more likely it becomes that random or chance variations will produce apparent relationships between some of these predictors and the criterion measure(s). Relationships due to chance would be unlikely to occur again in the cross-validation sample—only "real" relationships would produce the same results in both samples.

Other types of validity
Criterion-related validity is the most important type of validity as far as selection is concerned, but there are other important types of validity as well.

Face validity
A selection test or procedure displays face validity if it "looks right" as common sense. Requiring an applicant for a carpenter's

job to make a "T-joint" from two pieces of wood would show face validity. On the other hand, asking the applicant to carry out a test of general intelligence would probably have much less face validity for the candidate, since the link between that test and job performance would probably be less clear to the candidate.

Content validity
Like face validity, content validity is established on a logical basis rather than by calculating validity coefficients or following other technical, statistical procedures. A predictor shows content validity when it covers a representative sample of the behaviour domain being measured. For example, a content valid test of car-driving ability would be expected to cover all of the essential activities that a competent driver should be able to carry out. A test that did not include an emergency stop and a reversing exercise would be lacking in content validity.

Construct validity
In the context of personnel selection, this involves identifying the psychological characteristics (or constructs), such as intelligence, emotional stability or manual dexterity, which underlie successful performance on the job, and then attempting to use predictors that can measure the extent to which a candidate displays the construct. Since construct validity involves relationships between predictors and characteristics that are not *directly* observable, it can be assessed only by indirect means.

Reliability
Validity, in its various forms, deals with the extent to which a test or other measuring technique measures what it sets out to measure. Another extremely important characteristic of any measurement technique is reliability. Reliability refers to the consistency with which a test (or other technique) provides results. In essence a predictor (or criterion) is reliable if it produces consistent conclusions. Equally, if the same candidate produces very different scores when she takes a test on two different occasions, the reliability for the test must be questioned. Any measuring instrument (whether predictor or criterion) used in a selection procedure must be both valid *and* reliable.

UTILITY

As shown in the previous section, the major purpose of a selection procedure is to identify relevant individual differences between candidates and to use this information to make predictions of subsequent work performance. Clearly, to achieve this end there must be a close relationship between performance on the selection instruments and work performance (i.e. criterion-related validity). Despite this essential requirement, criterion-related validity alone is not sufficient to ensure that a set of predictors are of value to an organisation. Assessing the value of a selection procedure within an organisation involves considering the *utility* of the selection procedures. The utility of a predictor refers to the extent to which the quality of people selected is improved, when the predictor is used, beyond what would have occurred if it had not been used. In other words, utility usually involves comparing the results of the current selection procedures used by the organisation with the results expected from a proposed new system.

Some new concepts
To examine utility in more detail, some new concepts must be introduced.

(*a*) *Selection ratio.* The ratio of the number of jobs to the number of applicants. A selection of 1/10 (i.e. 0.1) means that there are ten applicants for every available job.

(*b*) *Base rate of success.* The proportion of workers who reach satisfactory levels of job performance when the proposed selection procedure is not used. This provides an indication of the proportion of satisfactory employees produced without the introduction of new procedures.

The utility of any selection procedure is not dependent on the validity of the procedures alone, but is also influenced by the selection ratio and the base rate of success. In general, an organisation stands to gain most from the introduction of improved selection procedures when both the selection ratio and the base rate of success are low.

Let us examine in more detail the role that validity, selection ratio and base rate of success play in the determination of utility. Fig. 27 (*a*) shows the situation for a validity coefficient of 0.5. The shaded areas (B + C) identify people who will be hired by the organisation. Notice, however, that although all of these people achieve the minimum score on the predictor, only a proportion of them (B) also show satisfactory work performance. Similarly, although all the people in the unshaded areas (A and D) fail to achieve the cut-off score on the predictor, some of them are capable of satisfactory work performance (those in area A). Areas B and D represent *correct selection decisions* and contain people who have been

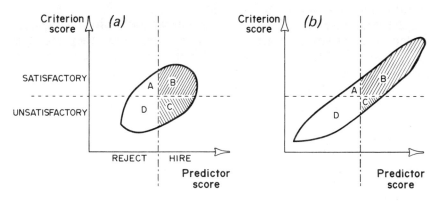

Fig. 27. *The effect of different validity coefficients: (a) validity = 0.5 coefficient; (b) validity = 0.7 coefficient.*

justifiably rejected, known as true negatives (area D). Area C contains the *false positives,* i.e. people who would be hired but produce unsatisfactory work performance. Area A contains the *false negatives,* i.e. people who would not be hired but are capable of satisfactory work performance. Areas A and C represent *errors in the selection process.*

Validity
As Fig. 27 (*b*) shows, when validity increases (to 0.7), the proportions in areas A and C decrease and the proportion of correct decisions (areas B and D) increases. Thus, as validity increases, the quality of selection decisions also increases.

Selection ratio
Clearly when the selection ratio is greater than one (i.e. there are more available jobs than applicants), the use of any selection procedure is likely to be of relatively little benefit. In this situation the organisation may be forced to accept anyone who applies for a job. In practice, even with a selection ratio of more than one, it may be still sensible for an organisation to make use of selection criteria and leave jobs empty rather than hire totally unsuitable employees. When the selection ratio is less than one (i.e. more applicants than jobs) the organisation can gain obvious benefits from using selection criteria. Consider the situation for two different selection ratios. If the selection ratio is 0.7 (i.e. seven jobs for every ten applicants), the organisation can afford to refuse jobs to people with the lowest 30 per cent of scores on the predictor. If, however, the selection ratio is 0.4, the bottom 60 per cent of applicants can be rejected.

Base rate of success
If the base rate of success in an organisation is already high, it means that existing selection procedures (whatever they are) are producing satisfactory employees and that the gains from introducing improved selection procedures are unlikely to be large. However, if the existing base rate of success is low, improved selection procedures might produce considerable gains.

Predicting utility
Given specific values for selection ratio and base rate of success, it is possible to calculate the likely benefits that will result from the operation of a new selection procedure—with a specific level of validity. These benefits might be expressed as the percentage of new starters who will be successful, the difference in average scores between workers chosen using existing or new procedures, or in various other ways. Calculating such benefits involves making certain assumptions about the statistical properties of the relevant predictor-criterion scores. It also involves statistical procedures that are beyond the scope of this book. Fortunately, it is not necessary to carry out these calculations individually, since tables have been prepared and can be used to obtain the necessary information. Taylor and Russell (1939), Lawshe *et al.* (1958) and Naylor and Shine (1965) have all prepared such tables.

Before we proceed further, one crucial point must be made concerning the personnel selection process in general. An organisation may find that, either in specific operational areas or on a more general basis, employee performance is poor. One obvious solution may be to improve the quality of future employees. In practice of course this may prove a complete waste of time and the real causes of inadequate performance may be unsatisfactory training, poor job design, low motivation, inadequate machinery, supervision or a wide range of other factors. There is no foolproof means of identifying the cause of organisational problems, but it must always be remembered that the most obvious possible cause or remedy may not be the best.

JOB PERFORMANCE, CRITERION MEASURES AND APPRAISAL

The discussion of the processes of personnel selection has shown how satisfactory selection decisions are based on strong relationships between predictors and criteria. The only specific criterion measure mentioned has been "average output per day". The average output per day produced by an employee is clearly an important measure of success, but what about other factors such as absenteeism? An average output figure that did not take absences into account would all too easily give a false impression of an employee's value to the organisation. What about less clear-cut factors such as his attitude to his co-workers, willingness to do overtime, potential for promotion to a supervisory position? The point being made is that the identification of employees who will produce high daily outputs (or any other single factor) may not be the sole requirement of an organisation's selection system.

Thus, in any organisation, there is a wide range of criteria that could be used to assess an employee's value to the company. Some possible measures are:

(a) production records (including quality and quantity of output, wastage, attainment of targets);

(b) absenteeism, lateness, disciplinary record; and

(c) ratings made by managers, supervisors, co-workers, subordinates.

The use of ratings and other methods to provide information on an employee's job performance is an established procedure within most organisations. Performance appraisal information is used for a variety of purposes, including, promotion, salary, career develop-, ment, counselling and training, as well as in the validation of personnel selection procedures. Of the available methods for obtaining appraisal data, rating scales are by far the most widely used. Guion (1965) reports that 81 per cent of the validation studies in the *Journal of Applied Psychology* between January 1950 and July 1955 used some form of rating as a criterion, and although Landy and Trumbo (1980) note a more recent study giving a figure of 72 per cent, ratings are still the most popular means for collecting such data.

Rating scales

As Fig. 28 shows, a variety of different graphical rating scales can be used to elicit performance appraisal data. Such scales vary in the extent to which they provide a satisfactory basis for performance appraisal. Like many forms of psychological measurement the key issues revolve around the problems of reliability and validity. Such scales should provide a clear indication of the meaning that can be assigned to each point on the scale (validity) so that both the rater and anyone else who needs to interpret the rating on the scale can make a valid inference. Clearly with a scale such as (a) in Fig. 28 clear and unambiguous interpretation is impossible, since the scale provides so little information. It is also important that the scale can be used consistently, either by different raters or by the same rater

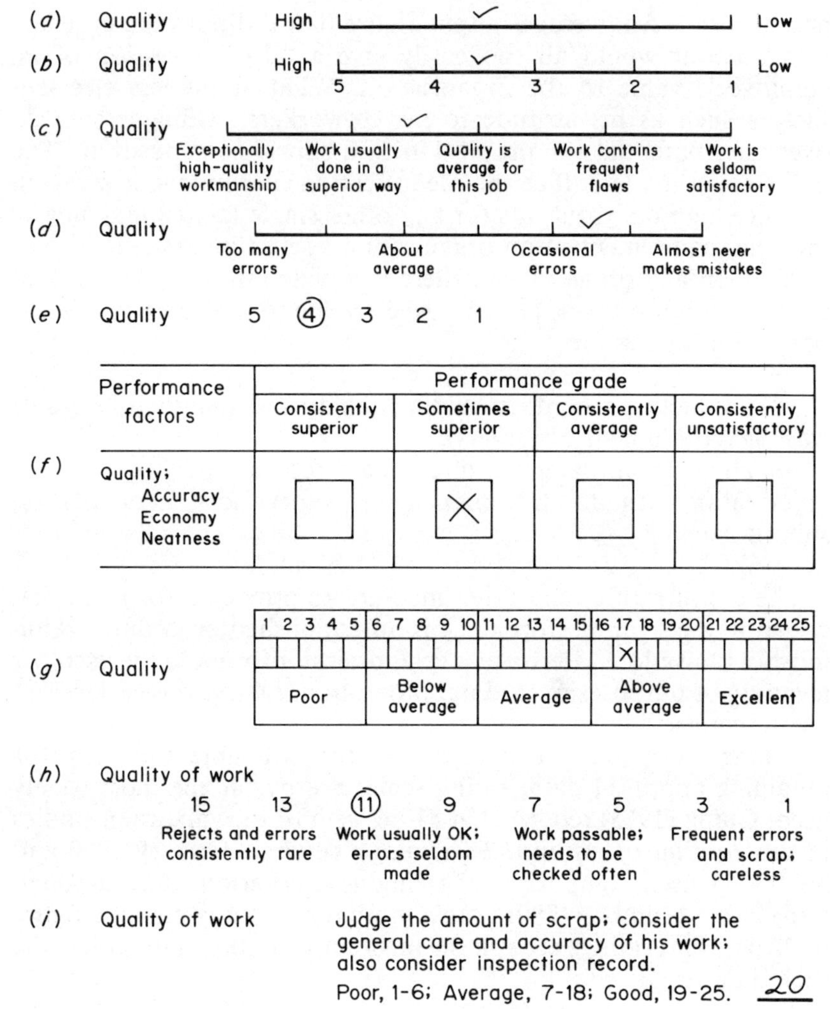

Source: Guion (1965).

Fig. 28. *Variations on a graphic rating scale—each line represents one way in which a judgment of the quality of a person's work may be given.*

on different occasions. Again a scale such as (*a*) presents problems here, since so much subjective judgment is needed that the judgments may well change from rater to rater or from trial to trial. Although a scale such as (*c*) probably provides a better basis for validity and reliability, such graphical rating scales contain many possible sources of error. These potential errors have been described by Blum and Naylor (1968). They include the following types of error.

Leniency

This relates to a characteristic of the person doing the rating. Some people appear to be "easy" raters and tend to provide a greater proportion of high scores (positive leniency). At the other extreme are the harsh or severe raters (negative leniency). Leniency can often be observed when the results of two or more judges are compared.

Halo

The halo error is, ". . . a tendency to let our assessment of an individual on one trait influence our evaluation of that person on other specific traits" (Blum and Naylor, 1968, p. 260). In other words, if we believe that someone is outstandingly good in one important area of performance, we might rate them high in all areas, regardless of their true performance. Blum and Naylor point out that this is an extremely common type of error.

Central tendency error

Many raters are very reluctant to provide ratings at the extremes of the scale that they are using and may tend to produce ratings that group around the mid-point of the scale. This may not necessarily be because the "true" distribution of ratings should be like this, but because the rater is inhibited about assigning very high or low ratings.

In addition to describing sources of error Blum and Naylor provide suggestions about how some of the errors might be avoided or minimised by the design of rating scales and the ways in which scales might be used. Their suggestions include the use of comparative methods where, instead of attempting to provide a judgment of an employee on an absolute basis, the employee is judged in relation to others. This may be done by a straightforward ranking procedure (from best to worst)—that is, by systematically comparing each employee with every other one (paired comparison) and using the resulting information to produce a rank order, or perhaps by comparing every employee with a particular one (key-man system). Another suggestion, specifically to minimise central tendency errors, requires raters to place a certain proportion of responses at certain points on the scale (e.g. on a nine-point scale at least 14 per cent of the ratings must be greater than seven or less than three).

One problem with many unsatisfactory rating scales is that the "anchors" which define the points on the scale are such broad, generalised descriptions, such as Average, Good or Excellent, that it is impossible to be sure that the terms are interpreted in the same way by everyone who uses the scales. One promising means of providing unambiguous anchor points on a scale is to use Behaviourally Anchored Rating Scales (BARS). BARS use anchors that describe specific behaviour which is critical in determining levels of job performance (Smith and Kendall, 1963). BARS are developed using a four-step procedure:

(a) With the aid of a group of "experts" (employees/ supervisors/managers) define the aspects of performance needed for successful job performance.

(b) Use a second group of "experts" to provide examples of specific behaviours associated with high, average or low performance.

(c) A third group takes the examples from step (b) and independently matches them with the aspects from step (a). This "retranslation" acts as a cross-check on the two previous steps. Examples that are not assigned correctly to the aspect for which they were written do not provide unambiguous behavioural anchors for that aspect of job performance and should not be used.

(d) The final step involves using more "experts" to assign scale values to the surviving items, which then serve as the behavioural anchors for the scale. The research evidence concerning BARS (e.g. Schwab *et al.* 1975) suggests that they produce results which are *slightly better* than *well-constructed* graphic rating scales. These results lead some people to question whether the effort involved is worth the trouble. Two points are worth bearing in mind here. First, a *well-constructed* graphic scale may require an amount of effort equal to that involved in constructing a BARS. Second, if the correct procedure is followed, a BARS is highly likely to be worthwhile and have good psychometric properties, and as Landy and Trumbo (1981) point out, "it is harder to construct a *good graphic rating scale* than it is to develop a *good behaviorally anchored scale*" (p. 129).

The Mixed Standard Scale (Blanz and Ghiselli, 1972) provides an interesting variant on the Behaviourally Anchored Rating Scale format. The Mixed Standard Scale differs from the normal BARS format in that it includes only three anchors, representing excellent, average and poor, for a particular dimension of job performance. The rater is presented with a mixture of statements representing the three levels of performance on a mixture of dimensions (*see* Fig. 29). The rater responds by indicating that the ratee's performance is "better than", "equal to" or "worse than" each statement. The fact that the performance statements do not appear in any obvious order should make the scale less subject to rater bias and error (deliberate or otherwise). Research on the Mixed Standard Scale suggests that it shows similar validity and reliability to BARS (Arvey and Hoyle, 1974; Dickinson and Zellinger, 1980).

Task A

(Excellent)	Stops vehicles for a variety of traffic and other violations.
(Average)	Concentrates on speed violations, but stops vehicles for other violations also.
(Poor)	Concentrates on one or two kinds of violations and spends too little time on the others.
(Excellent)	Utilises available equipment and solicits any available assistance to secure scene of accident quickly and effectively.
(Average)	Generally secures scene adequately before beginning accident investigation.
(Poor)	May fail adequately to secure the scene before beginning accident investigation.

N.B. On the appraisal form statements from various tasks are intermixed.

Source: Rosinger *et al.* (1982).

Fig. 29. *Items from a mixed standard scale for Ohio State Highway Patrol.*

Factors affecting appraisal

Even when systematically designed rating instruments are used, many factors that are difficult to control will exert some influence on the validity and reliability of the appraisal. Potential influences include the rater and ratee characteristics, the host organisation, the circumstances in which the appraisal is conducted and the purpose of the appraisal. Rater differences and characteristics have been investigated extensively (Latham and Wexley, 1981; Saal *et al.*, 1980). One important characteristic of the rater concerns the amount of training (in the procedures of rating). Latham and Wexley (1981) argue that rating training which involves trainee participation and practice and the provision of knowledge of results (*see* Chap. 12) is the critical factor in reducing rating errors. Fay and Latham (1982) provide an example of the benefits that training can have in reducing errors for various different types of scales. On the basis of their own study and previous work they provide suggestions about the objectives that a rating training programme should have. These include the acceptance by trainees of the following points.

(*a*) That performance-related dimensions of behaviour are often correlated. In other words, a person who is good at one thing is often good at others.

(b) That ratings which show a high proportion of positive scores are not necessarily an indication of leniency error.

(c) Ratings should not necessrily form a normal distribution (i.e. most people scoring at the mean, equal numbers above and below the mean, and few having very high or low scores).

(d) Halo error is not necessarily occurring when a ratee is given the same score on most of the scales.

Another important rater characteristic concerns the position of the rater within the organisation. Several studies have shown that differences frequently occur between ratings given by peers, supervisors, subordinates and the ratee himself. Ratings are made for a purpose and Makin and Robertson (1982) have suggested that the rater is, not unnaturally, influenced by what he may see as the possible outcome of the rating. Although the fact is not immediately apparent, rating is a social process. The ratee makes comparisons between individuals and these ratings will, directly or indirectly, influence future behaviour. Imagine, for example, how you would describe a well-liked but not very capable colleague to your close friends and then how you would rate your colleague if asked to do so for salary or promotion purposes. Not only might the position of the rater vis-à-vis the ratee be an important consideration, but there is some evidence to suggest that the host organisation might also be related to the ratings that are produced.

Zammuto et al. (1982) have shown that levels of performance ratings for people doing similar jobs in different organisations vary. Their results suggest, for example, that it might be difficult for senior managers to collate and accurately interpret ratings that originate from different sub-units within an organisation unless they have some way of taking into account the influences of differences in factors such as sub-unit, policies, tasks and psychological climate. The differences, mentioned earlier, that occur between types of raters may reflect the fact that even when well-designed appraisal instruments are used, observation of the ratee from different perspectives will produce variations in judgment. Zammuto et al. (1982) suggest that

> . . . if organisations and researchers are interested in obtaining accurate assessments of overall performance, they should employ multiple rater groups in the appraisal process. These groups should rate dimensions of performance that directly affect them. . . . The net effect would be to view the overall impact of a person's performance as opposed to parts of it, resulting in more accurate, comprehensive evaluations (p. 657).

In many organisations ratings of performance, such as those discussed above, provide the basis for a performance appraisal interview where superior and subordinate meet to discuss the subordinate's performance. Despite the fact that such interviews are commonplace, Nemeroff and Wexley (1979) point out that surprisingly little attention has been given to investigating the essential characteristics involved in such sessions. In their study Nemeroff and Wexley investigated the relationship between various characteristics of the interview and three types of outcome:

(a) satisfaction with the interview (both superior and subordinate).
(b) motivation to improve (subordinate only); and
(c) the level of satisfaction felt by the subordinate for his or her boss.

They found that "supportive appraisal behaviour" (e.g. giving praise to subordinates for things they did well, ending on a positive note, scheduling a follow-up meeting) was strongly related to all three types of outcome. Other conclusions include the finding that inviting the subordinate to participate in setting future goals was closely related to his reported motivation to improve. One of the most useful aspects of this study is that the investigators identify *specific behaviours* that the superior uses and relate them to factors such as the level of satisfaction felt by the subordinate. As Nemeroff and Wexley (1979) note: "Merely telling supervisors to 'increase their supportive appraisal behaviours' or 'invite their subordinates to participate' has little or no likelihood of modifying behaviour. By breaking down the feedback interview into behavioural components, managers can be taught the critical skills involved in conducting effective feedback interviews."

Multiple versus single criteria
When utilising data on someone's performance within an organisation one important issue to consider is whether to use a single overall measure or multiple criteria (i.e. many measures of job success). In a much-quoted and important article Dunnette (1963) makes the following points:

> Over the years our concept of *the* criterion has suggested the existence of some single all encompassing measure of job success against which other measures (predictors) might be compared . . . much selection and validation research has gone astray because of an overzealous worshipping of *the* criterion. . . . Thus, I say: junk *the* criterion! Let us cease searching for single or composite measures of job success and proceed to undertake research which accepts the world of success dimensionality as it really exists (pp. 251-2).

This issue still arouses controversy and not all personnel

psychologists share Dunnette's desire always to use multiple criteria.

It is important to point out that the use of a single criterion does not necessarily mean utilising only one measure of success; normally it involves combining the data from several measures to form a composite single criterion. By and large, in the specific context of personnel selection, most psychologists would agree with Dunnette that it is more efficient to use multiple criteria rather than a single composite. One predictor, for instance, may predict the ability of a manager to influence colleagues and subordinates, while another might predict his technical problem-solving skills. The use of a single composite criterion would not allow such detailed (and surely useful) validity data to be obtained. Despite the desirability of multiple criteria, practical considerations, including the difficulties involved in communicating with non-specialists, usually mean that only a small number of criteria are used in any validation study. For other purposes, such as job evaluation or the development of incentive payment systems, composite criteria may be more or less essential.

QUESTIONS

1. Why is job analysis information important?

2. What is meant by validity and reliability in the context of personnel selection?

3. How are behaviourally anchored rating scales constructed? What are their advantages and disadvantages?

4. What factors influence raters' behaviour? How can errors be minimised?

5. Why does Dunnette (1963) suggest that we should junk the criterion?

CHAPTER SEVEN

Personnel Selection Methods

OBJECTIVES

In the right circumstances selection procedures that use valid methods (predictors) for assessing candidates can be of considerable value. The previous chapter provided an outline of the conceptual basis for personnel selection. This chapter considers the research and development work that has been conducted in relation to specific types of predictor and examines the role that specific methods might play in the personnel selection process. By far the most widely used method is the interview, and after discussing evidence that the interview has many flaws as a selection method, the chapter looks at techniques which suggest how employment interviews might be made more effective. Another popular selection method is that of psychological tests. The next part of the chapter examines the use of such tests and other methods, i.e. work sample testing, biographical data, references, and assessment centres. Finally, the issue of fairness in selection is mentioned and the potential "adverse impact" that selection methods might have on specific groups such as women or racial/ethnic minorities.

THE INTERVIEW

Most people who apply for a job within an organisation will expect to be interviewed at some stage during the selection process. In fact the interview is by far the most widely used selection device in British industry and commerce.

Research evidence

Several published studies have reviewed the evidence available concerning the use of interviews for personnel selection. The following section outlines the research evidence, with particular reference to:

(a) the reliability and validity of interviews;
(b) factors influencing the interview process itself; and
(c) the potential value of interview training.

Reliability and validity

An important and basic requirement of any selection device is that it should enable different selectors to come to the same conclusions about candidates they are assessing. The consistency with which interviewers agree in their evaluations of the same candidate is usually referred to as a measure of inter-rater reliability. The reliability evidence concerning interviews is inconsistent (Ulrich and Trumbo, 1965) and shows that in some cases there is high inter-rater reliability, while in others reliability is low. In some recent studies quite high reliabilities have been reported (e.g. Latham *et al.*, 1980), but on balance the available evidence does not suggest that interviews in general produce consistently high reliability. Intra-individual reliability studies—to ascertain whether the interviewer makes the same assessment of the candidate on two separate occasions—often reveal quite high reliabilities. However, it is of course difficult to estimate the influence of factors such as memory in these circumstances. Clearly, if the interview is unreliable and does not provide comparable results for different raters, it is unlikely to provide valid predictions of work performance—which in many organisations is exactly what it is used for!

Studies of *the validity* of interviews suggest that interviews do not provide particularly useful predictions of subsequent performance (Wagner, 1949; Mayfield, 1964; Ulrich and Trumbo, 1965; Wright, 1969). Reilly and Chao (1982) have reviewed more recent data from studies not included in earlier reviews and found a mean validity coefficient of +0.19. They note that "this estimate is slightly more optimistic . . . than previous literature but still considerably below validities for tests" (p. 15). Also in a more recent review Arvey and Campion (1982) point out that recent research has not been as pessimistic about the validity and reliability of interviews as have earlier studies. In particular Arvey and Campion note that interviews conducted by a board or panel appear to "be a promising vehicle for enhancing reliability and validity" (p. 291). Despite the slightly more optimistic nature of recent research it is still clear that, taken as a whole, employment interviews do not produce reliable information, nor do they provide valid predictions of future job performance.

It is clear that, regardless of research evidence to the contrary, most organisations will continue to place great reliance on the interview as a selection device, and if the interview cannot be dispensed with perhaps it can be made more relevant and useful. One positive argument for the continued use of interviews rests on the idea put forward by several writers such as Miner (1969) that the interview can provide a method for gathering specific sorts of data that are difficult or impossible to collect by other means. This idea of reducing the scope of interviews has much to recommend it and there is some evidence to suggest that certain characteristics may be judged with more validity and reliability than others during interviews. Ulrich and Trumbo (1965) examined a wide range of studies and noted that "the results rather consistently indicate two areas which both contribute heavily to interview decisions and show greatest evidence of reliability. These two areas of assessment may be described roughly as personal reltions and motivation to work". Ulrich and Trumbo suggest that interviews should be limited to the investigation of these two areas and that the assessment of other factors such as aptitudes and abilities should be done by other means.

In any study that examines the interview it is often difficult to separate the validity of the interview, as a selection device, from the validity of the particular interviewer(s) or rater(s) involved in the process. Some studies have attempted to separate interviewer and interview validity but surprisingly little research has focused on the characteristics of interviewers themselves, although there are exceptions, e.g. Valenzi and Andrews (1973), and Leonard (1976). Differences in interviewer effectiveness seem likely to be a function of factors such as the particular interview processes and procedures followed and the amount and type of training that the interviewer has received.

The interview process
When one turns to the interview process itself, it soon becomes apparent that there are many factors which can be important (*see* Fig. 30), and not surprisingly therefore a great deal of research has been conducted to examine the process, what factors are important and how the process can be improved. Webster (1964) reveals the rather startling finding that interview bias appears to develop very

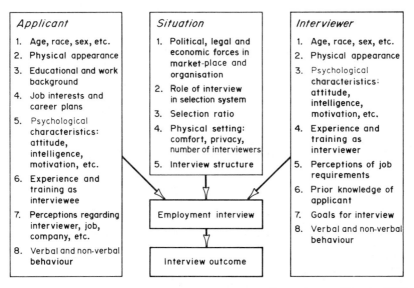

Source: Arvey and Campion (1982).

Fig. 30. *Factors involved in the employment interview.*

early on in the interview. In fact in a series of interviews limited to fifteen minutes the average decision time was four minutes! In many cases the remainder of the interview involves a selective search for information that will support this early decision. This demonstration of the importance of first impressions has been supported by other studies (e.g. Peters and Terborg, 1975), although Farr and York (1975) provide some data that conflict somewhat with the idea of first impressions being very important.

In a comprehensive review Schmitt (1976) reviewed the available research concerning the effects of specific factors such as whether information elicited early or later in the interview has the most impact, how positive and negative information is used, the effect of attitudinal and racial similarity between interviewer and interviewee, and several other factors (*see* Table VII). Schmitt's

TABLE VII. SOME OF THE RESEARCH ON THE INTERVIEW REVIEWED BY SCHMITT

Variables	Studies	Conclusions
1. Negative-positive nature of information	Springbett (1958) Bolster and Springbett (1961) Hollmann (1972)	All three studies agree that negative and positive information are processed differently. Springbett and Bolster and Springbett (1961) maintain negative information is weighted too heavily; Hollmann concludes negative information is weighted appropriately, but positive information is not weighted heavily enough.
Interviewer experience	Carlson (1967a)	Reliability of interview data was not greater for experienced interviewers, but the stress for quotas impaired the judgments of inexperienced interviewers more than it did the experienced interviewers in the sense that inexperienced interviewers were more likely to accept bad applicants.
Type of information	Carlson (1976b)	Personal history information had a greater effect on interview judgments than photographs of the interviewee. A photograph had its greatest effect on the final rating when it complemented personal history information.
2. Accuracy of interviewer as measured by number of factual questions he is able to answer	Carlson (1967a)	More accurate raters used a structured guide, were more variable in their ratings, and tended to rate lower.

Source: Abridged from Schmitt (1976).

review and the results of other work show clearly that the judgments made by interviewers may be biased or influenced in many possible ways. Many experienced interviewers make use of structured interview guides to help them to ensure that relevant information is collected, and they would argue that the use of a structured guide helps to minimise bias and distortion. The available evidence does seem to support this view.

Carlson *et al.*(1971) indicate the inadequacies of not using a structured interview guide. In their study interviewers who did not use a guide were less accurate in their subsequent recall of factual data than interviewers who used one. Often, where inter-rater reliability has been high, interviewers have worked using a structured or systematic approach (e.g. Schwab and Heneman, 1969). Although there is little direct evidence to support the value of one type of interview structure over others, there is evidence to indicate that the use of structured formats is beneficial (Schmitt, 1976; Mayfield *et al.*, 1980).

One aspect of both interviewer and interviewee behaviour which has received attention is their non-verbal conduct and the role that this plays in both the interview process and the judgments made as a result of the interview. As Forbes and Jackson (1980) point out, however, much of the research conducted has not been concerned with judgments made in real-life situations. In their study Forbes and Jackson looked at the non-verbal behaviour of candidates and how it related to interview outcome in real-life selection interviews. They uncovered different aspects of candidate non-verbal behaviour associated with "reject" and "accept" interviews. Interviews that resulted in the eventual rejection of candidates were associated with more gaze avoidance and eye wandering on the part of the candidates, whereas success interviews were associated with more eye contact. Other findings were that "accept" interviews involved more smiling, head-shaking and nodding. "Reject" interviews, on the other hand, involved less smiling and head movement.

Research by Keenan and Wedderburn (1980) has also examined the interview from the interviewees' perspective in real-life situations (graduate selection interviews in a British university). They intercepted candidates immediately after their interview and collected their views on the actual topics discussed in the interview. Topics discussed were broken down into six general categories:

(*a*) family and school background;
(*b*) university life—non-academic aspects;
(*c*) university—academic aspects;
(*d*) knowledge of job and company;

(e) extra-curricular activities; and
(f) personal circumstances and requirements.

The most popular area for discussion was knowledge of job and company—these were also the topics that provoked the most anxiety on the part of candidates. Perhaps surprisingly, topics concerned with academic aspects of university life (e.g. knowledge of subjects studied) were not discussed extensively. A possible interpretation of these results suggested by Keenan and Wedderburn (1980) is that interviewers have a preference for topics that give them an advantage over candidates in terms of superior knowledge. As Keenan and Wedderburn point out, their work on the *topics* actually discussed during real-life interviews provides some much-needed information, since they could find no other empirical studies that addressed this issue.

Interview training
The notion that experience alone can produce effective interviewers is not supported by research (Carlson, 1967), and many organisations attempt to ensure that their interviewers receive some form of systematic training. There is some evidence to confirm the value of interviewer training, but in comparison to the amount of interview training that takes place research is rather meagre; furthermore, some researchers have collected data to show that interview training has had no effect on factors such as validity (Heneman, 1975) and rater error (Vance *et al.*, 1978). By and large, however, the available evidence suggests that training which follows the same lines as the training in appraisal/rating skills suggested in Chapter 6 is useful in minimising judgmental errors—that is, training which involved practice, discussion and feedback (Wexley *et al.*, 1973; Latham *et al.*, 1975; Howard and Dailey, 1979; and Howard *et al.*, 1979). In Henemen's (1975) study, for example, where training appeared to be ineffective it involved a ninety-minute lecture. By contrast, the apparently beneficial training provided in the work of Howard and colleagues involved five days of practice, discussion, demonstration and feedback! It is perhaps not surprising that types of training which seem useful for interviewers are similar to those involved in rating training, since the underlying psychological processes concerning assessment, evaluation and appraisal are likely to be similar regardless of whether the assessment is based on an interview or some other source of evidence.

In terms of course content rather than how the training is conducted, many of the interview training courses and guidebooks available in Britain adopt a "how to interview" approach concentrating on techniques such as the types of questions to ask, how to encourage a candidate to talk and so on. Unfortunately, as Arvey and Campion (1982) point out: "There is a dearth of guidelines and suggestions concerning the improvement of interview effectiveness based on research findings. Instead many guidelines, suggestions, 'how to interview' workshops and techniques are founded on intuition, beliefs, and what seems more comfortable, rather than on research results" (p. 317). Arvey and Campion note, however, that both Schmitt (1976) and Hakel (in press) have made efforts to translate research findings into practical guidelines. Jessup and Jessup (1975) have also summarised some specific techniques for use in interviews and have attempted to show how they can be supported by research evidence.

There are many books available that give advice on how to carry out interviews. Nevertheless, whilst such books might prove helpful, the recommendations and techniques put forward are more likely to be based on the personal inclinations and experience of the writer(s) than on any systematic research evidence.

PSYCHOLOGICAL TESTS

In addition to the interview, one of the main methods for personnel selection is the use of psychological tests. Anastasi (1982) describes psychological tests in the following way:

> A psychological test is essentially an objective and standardized measure of behavior. Psychological tests are like tests in any other science, in so far as observations are made on a small but carefully chosen *sample* of an individual's behavior. . . . If a psychologist wishes to test the extent of a child's vocabulary, a clerk's ability to perform arithmetic computations, or a pilot's eye-hand co-ordination, he or she examines their performance with a representative set of words, arithmetic problems, or motor tests (pp. 22-3).

Anastasi organises her discussion of tests into three broad categories.

(*a*) *Tests of general intelligence* (*see* Chapter 3).

(*b*) *Tests of separate abilities,* including tests of specific aptitudes such as numerical, verbal or mechanical aptitude (*see* Chapter 3).

(*c*) *Personality tests,* including measures of personality traits, personal orientations, values and interests (*see* Chapter 5).

There is considerable evidence to suggest that tests can be used successfully to help with personnel selection decisions, and Ghiselli (1966, 1973) has summarised data from a large collection of research studies. He examined the predictive power of tests for a wide range of occupational groups and also considered the value of the tests used as predictors of success in training or proficiency on the actual job itself. He concluded that by and large the predictive power of tests is quite respectable, particularly where training success is concerned, although these tests did not predict actual job performance quite so well. Nevertheless, he notes that "for every job there is at least one type of test which has at least moderate validity". His results for managerial occupations are shown in Table VIII.

TABLE VIII. VALIDITY COEFFICIENTS FOR MANAGERIAL OCCUPATIONS WITH TRAINING AND PROFICIENCY AS CRITERIA

	Executives and Administrators		Foremen		All Managers	
	Train.	Prof.	Train.	Prof.	Train.	Prof.
Intellectual abilities	.27[b]	.30[e]	.33[b]	.26[e]	.30[c]	.27[f]
intelligence	.28[b]	.30[e]	.31[b]	.28[e]	.29[b]	.29[f]
arithmetic	.25[b]	.29[c]	.36[b]	.20[d]	.33[b]	.23[d]
Spatial and mechanical abilities	.25[b]	.23[e]	.36[a]	.22[e]	.28[b]	.22[e]
spatial relations	.25[b]	.22[e]	.36[a]	.21[d]	.28[b]	.21[d]
mechanical principles		.42[a]		.23[e]		.23[e]
Perceptual accuracy	.18[b]	.24[c]	.26[b]	.27[b]	.23[b]	.25[e]
number comparison		.14[a]		.37[b]		.31[b]
name comparison	.18[b]	.23[b]	.26[a]	.14[b]	.21[b]	.21[c]
cancellation		.32[b]				.22[b]
pursuit			.25[a]		.25[a]	
Motor abilities	.02[b]	.13[d]	.38[a]	.15[b]	.02[b]	.14[d]
tapping	.09[b]	.17[b]	.04[a]	.20[a]	.07[b]	.18[c]
finger dexterity	-.02[b]	.13[b]		.23[a]	-.02[b]	.14[c]
hand dexterity	-0.2[b]	.10[b]		.02[a]	-.02[b]	.09[c]
Personality traits	.53[a]	.29[e]		.16[e]	.53[a]	.22[f]
personality		.28[e]		.15[e]		.21[f]
interest	.53[a]	.30[d]		.17[c]	.53[a]	.28[d]

[a]Less than 100 cases. [b]100 to 499 cases. [c]500 to 999 cases. [d]1,000 to 4,999 cases. [e]5,000 to 9,999 cases. [f]10,000 or more cases.   Source: Ghiselli (1973).

This sort of evidence demonstrates the value that properly used psychological tests may have as part of the personnel selection process.

It is worth making special mention of the use of personality tests in personnel selection, since they present special problems when used. Tests of intelligence and aptitude are almost impossible to fake—a candidate either gets the answers right or wrong. Tests of personality, interest or values are rather different; since there are no right or wrong answers, they are merely intended to provide information about the personal characteristics of the applicant. It would not be unreasonable to suggest that, when faced with a personality or interest inventory in a selection situation, a candidate might attempt to answer the questions in a way that he feels will be desirable for the job in question. Many personality questionnaires embody what is known as a lie scale—a set of questions designed to detect distortion by the person being tested. Elliott (1981) reviewed a number of studies and reported some new data of his own. He noted that his own study follows other studies in finding that, "people undergoing selection returned higher scores on the lie scale" (p. 15). Elliott also shows that highly stressful selection situations (being sent to an assessment centre and being pressed into testing) produce higher distortion than less stressful conditions (volunteers tested at their own organisation). The results of Ghiselli (1973) do nevertheless suggest that personality tests have some modest value for selection decisions, and such inventories continue to be used for selection (Parisher *et al.*, 1979; Wysocki 1981; Bartram and Dale 1982).

Usage of tests

Much of the evidence for test validity and usage comes from studies carried out in the United States. The extent to which tests are used in British industry and commerce has been examined by Sneath, Thakur and Medjuck (1976). They sent a postal questionnaire to a sample of 495 organisations employing numbers varying from less than 500 to over 20,000. Tables IX and X illustrate the extent and purpose for which respondents used tests.

TABLE IX. CATEGORIES OF STAFF FOR WHICH TESTS WERE USED IN BRITAIN

Categories of staff	Yes, all the time (%)	Yes, sometimes (%)	No (%)
Managers	8	18	74
Technicians/supervisors	7	36	56
Clerks/secretaries	10	47	43
Skilled operators	9	28	63
Other	52	13	56

Source: Sneath, Thakur and Medjuck (1976).

TABLE X. PURPOSES FOR WHICH TESTS WERE USED IN BRITAIN

Purpose	Yes, all the time (%)	Yes, sometimes (%)	No (%)
For initial selection	7	62	31
For promotion	4	28	67
For any other purpose	11	25	64

Source: Sneath, Thakur and Medjuck (1976).

As Table X indicates, managers are the least tested group, a conclusion that is consistent with Kingston's (1971) findings on the reluctance among British middle and senior managers to be tested. Kingston revealed that out of a sample of 179 companies only 8 per cent used tests to select managers on a regular basis, although 25 per cent used them occasionally for this purpose. With the exception of the "other" category secretaries and clerks appear to be the most tested group, although many of the "tests" applied to that category consisted of a form of typing test. A typing test was consistent with the definition of test used by Sneath, Thakur and Medjuck—"an objective and standardised measure of a sample of behaviour"—but it is not normally viewed as a psychological test.

Overall their survey reveals that tests are not consistently used by organisations in their sample. Those that did report test usage made use of them "sometimes", and 80 of the 281 respondents did not use tests at all. Sneath, Thakur and Medjuck identify several problem areas concerning test usage. Problems of creditability seem important in that only 39 per cent of the respondents considered that tests were a more reliable means of obtaining data on candidates than other methods. Shortage of trained personnel to administer and interpret tests, lack of appropriate tests and costs of administration were also identified as problems.

Using tests
Most worthwhile psychological tests are available only to suitably trained and qualified personnel. This restriction of access is intended to ensure that tests are used appropriately and in the right circumstances, and although such restriction is almost certainly necessary it does inevitably make it difficult for some organisations to obtain and use tests. Despite the evidence presented earlier concerning the validity of tests, it is important to remember that in most practical selection situations the results of psychological tests are best used in conjunction with other information about candidates. Remember, for instance, that even when a test with a high level of validity is used, some candidates who obtain low test scores will nevertheless be capable of satisfactory job performance and, equally, some with high scores will not produce satisfactory job performance.

OTHER METHODS

Work sample tests
Although interviews and pencil-and-paper tests are by far the most popular selection methods, the attention of a number of researchers

and practitioners has recently turned to examining work sample tests for personnel selection. Work sample tests involve the applicant in performing a task or set of tasks that are thought (usually on the basis of job analysis) to have direct, central relevance to the job in question. The tasks performed in these tests are often sampled from the normal range of tasks performed by job-holders. Thus the candidate for a job is asked to demonstrate his or her ability by actually doing part of the job.

Robertson and Kandola (1982) and Asher and Sciarrino (1974) have reviewed the available research on work sample testing. Work sample tests can take various different forms and Robertson and Kandola used the following four category system of classification.

(*a*) *Psychomotor*. This category involves the manipulation of objects, e.g. carving something out of chalk, typing, stitching a piece of cloth using a sewing-machine.

(*b*) *Individual, situational decision-making*. Here the applicant is expected to take decisions similar to those taken in the job in question. This can be done more or less realistically by using in-basket exercises, where the applicant is presented with a collection of letters, memos, etc., and asked to deal with them, Gill (1979); or, more abstractly, by presenting the applicant with a series of hypothetical situations and asking how he or she would respond.

(*c*) *Job-related information*. Tests in this category examine the amount of information a person holds about a particular job. They are usually pencil-and-paper tests, and although not work sample tests in the simulation sense, they test the applicant's knowledge of areas thought to be directly relevant to work performance.

(*d*) *Group discussions/decision-making*. Tests of this sort involve two or more people being put together to discuss a particular topic, and their performance in the discussion is then evaluated. The tests are used widely for jobs where an individual's contribution within a group setting is an important determinant of job success.

Table XI gives the median validity coefficient for each type of work sample test. As Table XI shows, psychomotor and job-related information tests have the highest validity coefficients. Situational decision-making is the weakest of the four categories and has the lowest median.

By and large, as Table XII shows, work sample tests compare favourably with other predictors.

Although the above results show that work sample tests are undoubtedly useful, they do not provide conclusive evidence that work sample tests are better than conventional tests of intelligence

TABLE XI. SUMMARY OF VALIDITY COEFFICIENTS FOR EACH TYPE OF WORK
SAMPLE TEST

	Psychomotor	Job-related information	Situational decision-making	Group discussion
Median	0.39	0.40	0.28	0.34
No. of coefficients	78	27	53	27
Range	−0.07-0.80	0.03-0.72	−0.19-0.86	0.10-0.63

Source: Robertson and Kandola (1982).

TABLE XII. DISTRIBUTION OF VALIDITY COEFFICIENTS FOR WORK SAMPLE
TESTS AND OTHER PREDICTORS USING JOB PERFORMANCE CRITERIA

	Percentage greater than		
	0.29	0.39	0.49
(a) Work sample tests			
Psychomotor	88	69	31
Job-related information	36	27	9
Situational decision-making	50	27	8
Group discussion	80	40	30
(b) Other predictors (from Asher and Sciarrino, 1974)			
Biographical data	97	74	55
Intelligence	60	51	28
Mechanical aptitude	73	48	17
Finger dexterity	39	24	13
Personality	42	22	12
Spatial relations	16	9	3

Source: Robertson and Kandola (1982).

or personality. It is possible, for instance, that intelligence or
personality tests may have been used in situations in which they
could not reasonably be expected to have any predictive power.
Work sample tests are obviously less likely to have been used in this
arbitrary way, since they must be developed by direct reference to
the job in question. Other possible advantages and disadvantages of
work sample tests are discussed in Robertson and Kandola (1982).

Biographical data

When using predictors such as interviews, psychological tests or
work sample tests, the specific areas to be investigated in the
interview or the particular tests to be used are normally derived

from the job analysis data. The information from the job analysis provides a basis for deciding which factors (e.g. numerical ability, good personal relationships) might be important for job success. Biographical information about candidates is often used on a different basis. When a candidate applies for a job with an organisation it is likely that he will complete an application form and other documents in which he is expected to provide certain biographical information concerning factors such as his age, previous employment, personal history and education. The basic procedure for using biographical data is to collect information on a number of candidates and correlate it with subsequent performance. Items of information that predict subsequent performance can then be identified.

Items of information chosen on this basis do not necessarily have any clear relationship with the job; it has merely been demonstrated on a statistical basis that they predict future performance. At first sight this may not seem to be a problem, but consider the likely consequences of refusing to employ married women, or people from a particular area of a city, simply because the statistics demonstrate that in the past such people have not performed well at work! Potential problems such as this mean that biographical data need to be used with some caution. Nevertheless, many studies have demonstrated that biographical data can be useful in selection. Asher (1972) compared the predictive power of biographical data with other predictors such as tests of intelligence and aptitude and, as Fig. 31 shows, biographical data provide consistently superior results.

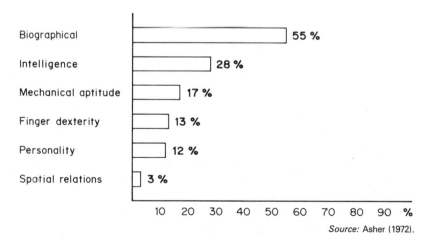

Source: Asher (1972).

Fig. 31. *A comparison of biographical data with other predictors showing the proportion of validity coefficients .50 or higher with job proficiency as the criterion.*

More recently Owens (1976) has argued in favour of an approach to biographical data that is not purely statistical and provides a better basis for their use in personnel selection. He argues that biographical information can be used to provide some understanding of how a person's life has developed and can thus help to predict his future work behaviour.

Other predictors

Other predictors that have been used with some success in personnel selection include asking the colleagues of a candidate to assess their potential for a job change or promotion. Reilly and Chao (1982) provide a review of the use of this technique. Obviously the procedure is of value only when the people concerned are already working within the organisation, and it seems likely to be open to considerable bias owing to factors such as friendship. There is also some indication that it is not popular with participants. Cederblom and Lounsbury (1980) found that 59 per cent of participants in such a system did not wish it to continue.

Applicants for employment to many organisations are often requested to provide the names of referees, though in many cases references are taken up only when an applicant is short-listed or even after a job offer has been made. Muchinsky (1979) and Reilly and Chao (1982) review the research on references and conclude that they are not of great value in the selection process. On the basis of the evidence it seems that if reference checks are used at all they should be used, as Muchinsky (1979) suggests, to identify a small proportion of people who should not be considered further.

Assessment centres

In most practical situations it is not sensible to base selection decisions on the use of one predictor only (such as the results of one test) or even on one type of predictor only. When several different predictors are used together the basic aim should be to ensure that the various predictors complement rather than duplicate each other. One successful method of selection that makes use of many different predictors is the "assessment centre" approach. Assessment centres are used frequently to evaluate people who already work within an organisation. The information gained from the assessment centre is then used to help take decisions concerning promotion and career development in general. Assessment centres make use of many different predictors, including interviews, psychological tests, in-basket exercises and group discussions. They extend for a period of, say, two to three days, although they may be as short as a day or as long as a week.

By and large assessment centres appear to produce impressive validity coefficients (Huck 1973; Kilmoski and Strickland 1977), and it has been reported that over 2,000 American companies employ this method (Parker, 1980). Kilmoski and Strickland do, however, sound a note of warning about assessment centres. Essentially they argue that these centres may not spot true ability and expertise in the job but simply be a good means of identifying people who will be well regarded by their superiors in the organisation. In other words, people who are well regarded at assessment centres may also be well thought of by their superiors (perhaps because they resemble them) and will therefore be rapidly promoted. This does not necessarily mean that they are the most competent people! Recent British research by Jones (1981) and Dulewicz and Fletcher (1982) suggests that the method produces results within situations in Britain that compare favourably with American results, and perhaps the next few years will see some growth in the use of this approach in British organisations.

FAIRNESS IN SELECTION

It should be obvious from the earlier sections in this chapter that current personnel selection procedures do not provide for perfect prediction of future performance. Equally obvious is the fact that if prediction is imperfect some people may be treated unfairly by the selection process. It has already been stressed, for example, that even when valid predictors are being used, some candidates who do not do well on the predictors (and may therefore be rejected by the organisation) will be perfectly capable of satisfactory work performance. Unless the predictor(s) criterion correlation coefficient reaches its maximum value of 1.0, there will always be false negative errors of this sort.

At first sight though, unfairness in selection may seem likely to be the lot, by pure chance, of a small minority of unlucky people. Recently, however, disquieting evidence has come to light to suggest that current personnel selection practices and procedures may often operate in a way which is systematically unfair to particular groups, such as women or ethnic minorities. One problem with test uses, for example, is the persistent finding that some racial and ethnic minorities do not perform as well as other applicants in many tests of intelligence and aptitude (*see* Chapter 3) and as a consequence they are not selected at the same rate. This difference is selection rate is usually referred to as "adverse impact". Because of factors such as this, legal requirements are exerting a significant influence on the use of tests for personnel selection in the United States. In the United Kingdom legislation is also having some influence on selection practices (Pearn, 1976). Some selection procedures seem to have more potential than others for minimising adverse impact. Robertson and Kandola (1982), for example, summarise evidence to suggest that work sample tests may produce relatively little adverse impact when designed in certain ways. On the other hand, Reilly and Chao (1982) cite evidence to suggest that both women and black people may be the subjects of adverse impact when interviews are used. Recent research on the validity and adverse impact of a large collection of different personnel selection methods is reviewed in Reilly and Chao (1982), and in Britain the Institute of Personnel Management (1978), the Training Services Agency (Pearn, 1977) and the British Psychological Society/Runnymede Trust (1980) have all produced publications designed to provide guidance and advice on the issues involved.

QUESTIONS

1. Does the interview have any future as a personnel selection method?

2. How can psychological tests be used in personnel selection? What are some of the pros and cons involved in using them?

3. What are the benefits of using multiple predictors?

4. Work sample tests may produce less "adverse-impact" than some other selection methods. Why might this be so?

CHAPTER EIGHT

Organisational Roles: The Manager, Trade Unionist and Women at Work

OBJECTIVES

If we are fully to appreciate human behaviour in organisations, it is imperative that we should understand certain roles that people play in them, the two most important of which are those of the manager and trade-union leader. This chapter examines a number of important roles. First, it looks at the role of the manager, breaking down into a number of different skills and tasks. The manager is examined as a general practitioner, as a scientist, as an entrepreneur, etc. The role of the trade unionist in an organisation is also explored. He/she is looked at as a communications channel, as a solver of management/shop-floor problems, as an improver of wages and conditions, etc. Next, the changing role of women in organisation is studied. Since more and more women are working, the role of women at work is taking on an increasing significance and their impact on the organisation is discussed in detail. Finally, there is a section on the arrangements organisations can make in order to help working women and dual-career couples in general. (Some of the material in this chapter was drawn from work written by Professor Cooper in *Psychology and Management*, Leicester: BPS, 1981, and from articles by him in the *Bulletin of the British Psychological Society*.)

THE MANAGER'S ROLE

We would have no trouble finding definitions of the role of managers or management from among the best-sellers of Drucker or other management gurus. However, the approach which appeals to the present writers is that of trying to categorise the different types of managers by acknowledging the reality that individual managers behave in quite different ways. This allows us to get a feel for the generic role of management; all the activities that should be performed if "superman-ager" existed.

Handy (1976) remarked that "the last quarter-century has seen the emergence of 'the manager' as a recognized occupational role in society." He goes on to suggest that managers seem increasingly to be playing two primary sets of roles: the manager as a person alludes to the growing professionalisation of managers, so that they are acquiring a set of skills which are, and arguably should be, independent of any organisation for which they do, or could, work. Since organisations seem to care less for the home/work interface concerns of their managers than previously (Cooper, 1981), it is in their interest to make sure they continue to make themselves marketable by further education and career-management. The manager as a GP concept, on the other hand, is based on the premise that managers are the "first recipient of problems" which require solutions or decisions. It is the role of the manager in this context to carry out four basic activities at work.

(*a*) Identify the symptoms in the situation.
(*b*) Diagnose the cause of the trouble.
(*c*) Decide how to deal with it.
(*d*) Start the treatment, or make the decision, or create the action plans.

Handy argues that all too often the symptoms are treated like diseases in the "industrial wards" of the country, and that managers who do not follow the medical model above in dealing with issues and problems, but stop at stage one, find that the illness or sources of grievance return in the same form or in disguise. Frequently we find managers who can diagnose the symptoms, such as poor morale or bad communications, but then provide solutions without knowing the cause: for example, poor communications – start in-house journal; late arrivals to work – introduce time-clocks, etc. In order to identify adequately and accurately problems or situations, it is absolutely essential to understand the needs of individual workers, be they other managers or unskilled labourers. Diagnosis not only involves understanding individual behaviour but the dynamics of groups within the organisations and the consequences of action plans that may affect groups outside.

Handy also suggests that the manager as a GP, when he is contemplating strategies for improving the health of the organisation, should consider and be aware of three sets of variables.

(*a*) The people.
(*b*) The work and the structure.
(*c*) Systems and procedures of the organisation.

In terms of "people concerns", he should be aware of individual needs, training and education potential, career development, motivation, need for counselling or support, etc., whereas in terms of the organisational structure and systems he should be aware of the nature of roles, inter-group conflict, small group behaviour, decision-making, negotiating processes, reward systems, etc. The general practitioner manager is not only expected to be aware of these factors and processes but to understand their interaction: that is, how change in one may produce change in another.

And finally, a crucial characteristic of any skilled manager should be an awareness of change and how to implement it. This requires an understanding of learning theory, the various strategies for change (counselling, behaviour modification, etc.), the dilemmas people experience at different times in their lives, identifying an "initiating" person or group, creating an awareness of change, and so on. This is part and parcel of any GP role whether in the medical field or in organisations.

To obtain a further and more amusing yet informative view of the role of the manager we turn to Mant's (1977) historical styles of management, which have contemporary application among today's managers. First, there is the *respectable buccaneer* or the British proto-manager. This is the swashbuckling Sir Francis Drake type who uses "whom he knows" and "who he is" to achieve results. The success of this style depends to a large extent on a highly developed sense of social skills and timing, but little else. He is the entrepreneur in its most extreme form.

The next managerial prototype is the *agent*. He acts on behalf of others, takes no decisions himself and has historical roots in the commercial world of nineteenth-century England. His contemporary counterpart is the "middle manager" of today, who feels, not by choice, that his power and ability to influence decisions is declining (owing to the power of the trade-union movement, greater participative decision making, etc.).

The *scientific manager* is another breed of executive who is seen in organisational jungles from time to time. He tends to make decisions based on what appear to be rational and appropriate data, but frequently ignores the "people problems" that result from his decisions or are created by them. Sheldon writing in 1923 summed it up from a historical perspective: ". . . management is no longer the wielding of the whip; it is rather the delving into experience and building upon facts" (Mant, 1977).

In contrast to the factual manager is the *managerial quisling*, or as Mant puts it, "the manager in the role of the pal". This prototypic manager stems from the human relations school of management of the 1940s and 1950s, and he is supposed to be concerned with the quality of work life and the well-being of workers. It is our view that this species of manager comes in different varieties. First, there is the *genuine quisling*, who really is concerned about the workers' health and well-being. However, this type of manager is usually so naïve about the politics of his organisation that he fails to achieve his objectives, or achieves them at the expense of other people. Second, there is the *entrepreneurial quisling*, who "appears to care" but is really using the "flavour of the month" managerial style to achieve recognition, or enhance his own image, or accomplish some political manoeuvre. He is the classical Milo Minderbinder in Heller's *Catch-22* – "it's all in the syndicate and everybody has a share".

Another managerial prototype is the *manager as a technocrat*. He is of a breed that grew up as the technology around them developed, particularly during the 1940s when Britain was looking increasingly to engineers for its salvation. This type of manager handles all issues as if they were technical problems capable of stress analysis, critical path analysis, etc. His concern for the "people component" is once again a mere "given" in the decision-making process.

Finally, there is the *manager as a constitutionalist*. This form of managerial style seemed to emerge from the Glacier Metal Company study undertaken by Brown (1965). It is a style not unlike the Tavistock approach to applied problems in industry, in that it relies heavily on contractual arrangements. That is to say, it believes fundamentally that psychological contracts between individuals or representatives of groups are essential for harmonious relationships at work. Managers are effective, according to this strategy, if they work with their subordinates and colleagues in designing contractual arrangements on most issues of importance. This reduces ambiguity and highlights the boundaries on tasks, roles and organisational units.

What Mant (1977) has done in trying to identify managerial types is to suggest implicitly that each of the caricatures of prototypic executives is ineffective, but in different ways. And although some managers utilise (consistently) one or more of these styles than others, the well-rounded and twenty-first-century manager will require a behavioural repertoire that encompass nearly the whole range, but used flexibly and appropriately. We need to educate and train managers to understand the needs of people so that they take a scientific or diagnostic approach to problems and decisions, but with a socio-technical, humanistic, and risk-taking orientation as well. To do so, one might follow the advice of many managers that "behavioural scientists are incapable of telling us anything we don't already know". This adviced was epitomised in a piece that appeared in the *Financial Times* a few years ago:

Good evening gentlemen, welcome to the X management education establishment. You will have noted, perhaps with relief, the absence of faculty or curriculum. This is a regular feature of this programme and a closely-guarded secret of its alumni, present and past. If you should require any inducement to keep this secret you may be influenced by the £500 in crisp ten-pound notes which is to be found in a brown envelope in your bedroom. This represents half the fee paid by your employers and approximate expenditure that would otherwise have been incurred with respect to teaching staff salaries and related costs. In the meantime, meals and other services will be provided and the bar will remain open at normal opening times. You will have discovered that your colleagues are drawn from similar organisations to your own and contain amongst them a wealth of practical experience in the manner of managerial roles. There is also a first-rate library at your disposal. How you decide to pass these six weeks is your own managerial decision; we trust you will enjoy it and find it beneficial. Thank you.

On the other hand, we could begin to provide managers with information that behavioural scientists have accumulated over the last thirty years of empirical and theoretical development. It is the latter approach that we have decided to take in this volume: to make available psychological knowledge that may be of some use in dealing with individual, interpersonal, group and organisation behaviour, and in creating change among individuals and organisations.

THE ROLE OF TRADE UNIONISTS

Many trade union officials carry out a variety of tasks similar to those of many managers (discussed above) working within industrial and public sector organisations. They have the job of having to deal with a variety of different people they help to organise, to understand the dynamics of group situations (committees, negotiating groups, etc.), and to understand the structure and functioning of organisations and groups within them. In addition, they require other skills, which most, although not all, managers do not use on a regular basis (e.g. negotiating and bargaining, interviewing, etc.). One of the classic studies that has helped us to understand the major duties of various trade-union officers was carried out by Clegg, Killick and Adams (1966). In their work, they identified the main constituents of the job of full-time officers, branch secretaries and shop stewards among others. Their main sources of information were union records (superannuation schemes, journals and minute books) and a set of four questionnaires: for shop stewards, full time officers (aimed mainly at the lower levels of the union hierarchies), full time branch secretaries and branch secretaries other than full time. Responses to the questionnaires were received from every important industrial area in the country, although as the authors point out the percentage geographical distribution of their sample did not correspond with the distribution of population, nor the probable distribution of trade union membership. Nevertheless, the sample provided a fair spread of respondents across both geographical areas and trade union roles.

Another feature of the study concerns the representation of

various unions in the sample. As the authors pointed out, six unions—the "Big Six"—had a total membership of slightly more than half of the total trade union membership affiliated to the Trades Union Congress. The Big Six were the Transport and General Workers Union, the Amalgamated Engineering Union, the National Union of Mineworkers, the National Union of Railwaymen and the Union of Shop, Distributive and Allied Workers. This fact is reflected in the characteristics of some of their samples. For instance, of the 226 respondents who completed the shop stewards' questionnaire, 106 were in three unions: Transport and General Workers Union (33), Amalgamated Engineering Union (50) and the National Union of General and Municipal Workers (23). Clegg, Killick and Adams point out that:

> In terms of membership, the Amalgamated Engineering Union is grossly over-represented, but this may be justifiable. Many unions have no shop stewards and the branch negotiators of other unions cover far more membership than do shop stewards. There are some sections of both the Transport and General Workers and the National Union of General and Municipal Workers which do without stewards. Consequently our union distribution may in fact be roughly representative. A distribution exactly proportionate to union membership would certainly be unrepresentative (p. 29–30).

It was found that each category of trade unionist engages in quite different activities. In other words, they each need slightly different bits of psychological knowledge and training. Whereas full-time officers have to get involved quite regularly in high-level negotiation exercises of one kind or another, this is not quite the case for branch secretaries or shop stewards (whose role in negotiations is much more circumscribed). Shop stewards, on the other hand, require greater emphasis on interpersonal skills in their dealings with local management, grievances with foremen and other first-line managers. Although the emphasis is different, the need for understanding and skill development in various psychological areas is of great importance to all trade-union representatives. Indeed, it might be argued that many industrial relations disputes, which start as local matters, develop further because of the lack of psychological insight by both local management and the shop stewards into the "real" underlying problems and their causes, and their consequent inability to deal with them at that level.

The role of the shop steward is critical, therefore, because of his unique set of boundary roles between the work group, the management and union officials. Torrington and Chapman (1979) suggest that the shop steward requires skills in at least six different and demanding tasks. First, he must have skills as a spokesman and negotiator, not only of his fellow workers but for management and "the union". Second, he is responsible for recruitment of union members among the employees. This means his approaching new employees and maintaining contacts with older ones, which requires a high level of social and interpersonal skills. Third, the shop steward is responsible for the dissemination of information, on current working practices, on union policy, on management attitudes, etc. Fourth, he must possess the skills to counsel members with difficulties and/or deal with advice to members about services available. Fifth, he must ensure, from time to time, that there is compliance with union rules in an effort to adhere to agreements or sustain union policy. Finally, and perhaps most importantly, the shop steward has to act as an important communications link between the workers, management and the union officials. Goodman and Whittingham (1969) reflect this aspect of the shop steward's role in the following:

> He will be expected to state grievances from the shop floor and, having reached an agreement with the management will be expected to carry his members with him. As such, management may have a vested interest in his strength, regarding him as both representative and advocate. Additionally, he will be expected to lead as well as reflect, shop-floor opinion. The steward's representative role may be further emphasised by participation in joint consultative committees, about which he should also disseminate information.

Although these six functions are the main ones performed by shop stewards, there are differences in emphasis among stewards, depending on what group of workers they are representing. Batstone, Boraston and Frenkel found this to be the case in their study, *Shop Stewards in Action* (1977). From this work it is clear that staff stewards saw their roles as "ensuring harmony with management" and "maintaining a communications channel with their membership", while shop-floor stewards overwhelmingly saw their roles as "protecting members, improving wages and conditions". While the balance between these various role functions can differ, the need for training in human relations skills and other aspects of human behaviour is crucial to effective trade unionism. Indeed, the Commission on Industrial Relations has suggested, in terms of the training need of shop stewards, that:

> . . . it is necessary for him (the shop steward) to combine the skills of negotiation with those involved in communicating not only with management but with his members, fellow stewards and full-time officers. He needs analytic abilities in preparing cases and dealing with problems and understanding of techniques such as work study and job evaluation" (Batstone, Boraston and Frenkel, 1977).

WOMEN AT WORK: THE PROBLEMS AND
WHAT CAN BE DONE

The role of women in society is radically changing in most Western countries (Hall and Hall, 1980). Vast numbers of women are beginning to work full-time and to aspire to climb the same "organizational ladders" as their male counterparts (Hennig and Jardim, 1978). Indeed, the latest figures from the US Department of Labor indicate that the "typical American family" with a working husband, a home-maker wife and two children now makes up only 7 per cent of all American families. In addition, whereas in 1960 31 per cent of all married women in the United States were working, as were 19 per cent of women with children under six, by 1975 the comparable figures were substantially higher at 44 and 37 per cent respectively.

A similar trend is occurring in the United Kingdom with the male labour force increasing at the rate of only 3 per cent over the last twenty-five years, whereas in the same period the number of women employed had grown by 43 per cent. In addition, in the early 1950s there were 2.7 million married women in jobs, but by 1976 that figure rose by 143 per cent to over 6.7 million. And, most interesting of all, at the start of the 1950s only a quarter of working women were married, whereas today over two-thirds of all women who are working are married.

But what does this trend mean for the health and well-being of women? Will they join the growing number of men who suffer from stress-related illnesses as a result of work? In England and Wales, for example, the death rate due to coronary heart disease in men between 35 and 44 nearly doubled between 1950 and 1973, and it has increased much more rapidly than that of older age ranges (e.g. 45 to 65). Indeed, by 1973, 41 per cent of all deaths in the age group 25 to 44 were due to cardiovascular disease (Cooper, 1981). Will women who take on full-time careers and those who take on traditionally male jobs, therefore, end up with the "male diseases of work"?

Growing body of research

More and more research work is being conducted to answer the question above and although there are medics who feel that working women are less at risk than men (*Lancet* editorial, 1979), the early studies in this field are disturbing. One of the most interesting and comprehensive investigations was recently carried out by Haynes and Feinleib (1980). Their sample was drawn from the Framingham Heart Study, which is the most comprehensive investigation of heart disease ever to have been conducted. Many of the inhabitants of Framingham, Massachusetts, had been undergoing regular medical screening for the past twenty years. The main purpose of the study was to identify the precursors to heart disease in that population. Interested to see what the impact of employment was on working women, Haynes and Feinleib collected data on the employment status and behaviour of 350 housewives, 387 working women (employed outside the home for over one-half of their adult years) and 580 men (between the ages of 45 and 64) in the Framingham Study. All 1,317 subjects in the investigation were followed for the development of coronary heart disease over an eight-year period.

Their main finding was that working women did not have a significantly higher incidence of coronary heart disease than housewives, and their rates were lower than for working men. They then analysed the data terms of married (including divorced, widowed and separated) versus single working women, and found a substantial increase in incidence of heart disease. But the most revealing of all their results appeared when they compared married working women with children beside those without children. In this case they found that "among working women, the incidence of coronary heart disease rose as the number of children increased". This was not the case, however, for women who were housewives; indeed, that group showed a slight decrease with an increasing number of children.

In addition to these results, Haynes and Feinleib found that working women as a whole "experienced more daily stress, marital dissatisfaction, and aging worries and were less likely to show overt anger than either housewives or men". Indeed, in a review of the research literature on marital adjustment in dual career marriages. Staines et al. (1978) found that of the thirteen major studies in this area, using either an American national or regional sample, at least eleven of them showed that marital adjustment was worse for dual-career wives than for non-working wives.

On the other hand, Newberry et al. (1979) examined the psychiatric status and social adjustment of a matched group of working married women and housewives drawn from a community sample. They used the Social Adjustment Scale, Gurin's Symptom Check List and the Schedule for Affective Disorders and Schizophrenia. They found that although there was no difference between the two groups on overall psychiatric symptoms, depressive symptoms, diagnosable psychiatric disorders or treatment for an emotional problem in the past year, married working women did differ from housewives in their attitudes towards work and the home. Indeed, they found that housewives suffered from greater "work impairment", feelings of inadequacy, disinterest and overall work maladjustment than working wives. On the other hand, working wives were found to be more impaired, disinterested and inadequate in respect of their housework as compared to their work.

Although there is some scattered evidence, as above, that working women may not be "at risk" of stress-related illness or other negative social consequences, the data are beginning to mount to the contrary, particularly for working women who are married with a family. In a study of psychiatric disorders among professional women, Welner et al. (1979) found, for example, that women GPs had a significantly higher rate of psychiatric depression than a control, and that women with children were found to have significantly more career disruption than those without children. In addition, Davidson and Cooper (1980a) found that married female executives with children were under greater stress than single or divorced working women. Indeed, Hall and Hall (1980) suggest that the main source of stress among two-career couples stems from the fact that the number of demands on the partners exceeds the time and energy to deal with them. Families, in this context, add a further series of potential problem areas, particularly when organisations are doing very little, if anything, to help the dual-career family, and specifically the wife who is expected to play "mother" and "worker".

Aside from these findings, some startling results are beginning to emerge from the total Framingham sample in regard to Type A coronary-prone behaviour and women. Two distinguished cardiologists, Friedman and Rosenman (1974), showed a significant relationship between behavioural patterns of people and their prevalence to stress-related illness, particularly coronary heart disease. Type A behaviour is characterised by "extremes of competitiveness, striving for achievement, aggressiveness, haste, impatience, restless, hyperalterness, explosiveness of speech, tenseness of facial muscles, feelings of being under pressure of time and under the challenge of responsibility". Type B behaviour, on the other hand, is characterised by the relative absence of the behaviour associated with Type A individuals. On the basis of large-scale prospective research work, Rosenman et al. (1960) found that this Type A behaviour pattern in all groups of people is a significant precursor to coronary heart disease and other stress-related illnesses: Type A men between the ages of 39 and 49 and 50 and 59 had 6.5 and 1.9 times (respectively) the incidence of coronary heart disease as Type B men.

In this context, one interesting finding that is beginning to emerge from the Framingham Study is that working women who score high on Type A are *twice* as likely to develop coronary heart disease as their male Type As. Indeed, in a recent study in Britain carried out by one of the authors (Davidson and Cooper, 1980*b*), it was found that senior female executives had significantly higher Type A behaviour scores than male executives, which in terms of these Framingham results may mean that female professional women may be at greater risk of actual coronaries than the mythical "high-flying" male executive.

The next question that must be asked is, "Why do working women suffer more than their male colleagues?" The answer is a simple one: most working women are expected, without much support from their husbands, to fulfil the roles of both home-maker and career person simultaneously (Hall and Hall, 1980). Although many husbands of working women *intellectually* accept and encourage their wives in their careers, few either psychologically or practically (e.g. by taking on traditional housewife chores) support them. When one considers that most males come from homes where their role model was a "mother at home", the fact that they still expect their working wives to carry out the traditional household duties is not surprising.

In addition, most work organisations have not adequately planned for the increasing desire of women both to work and have a family. It is this social myopia that is putting enormous pressure on working women.

Setting aside all moral arguments, it is in the long-term economic interest of work organisations to begin to accommodate the needs of the increasing army of women at work, particularly the married ones with families. There are a number of strategies available to private and public sector organisations to help alleviate some of the unnecessary burdens of working women.

WHAT ORGANISATIONS CAN DO

In his recent books Cooper (1981, 1982) highlights the kinds of strategies that might help to minimise the problems of working women and dual-career couples in general. Such strategies should provide a firm foundation by means of which the alleviation of home/work interface stresses and strains can be accomplished.

Flexible working arrangements
There is a wide range of flexible working arrangements that

organisations can provide their male and female employees which can help them to accommodate to changing family patterns. *Flexitime* is obviously one good example. In order that a dual wife or husband can meet the psychological responsibilities associated with their children's education, or indeed free themselves of guilt, many parents feel that they must take their children to school and/or pick them up. This is very difficult to accomplish under the current 9 to 5 (or later) arrangement, and would be made much easier under flexitime conditions – as long as it was applicable for both husband and wife. Flexitime is useful not only during the work week, so why should it not be extended to "school vacation" times? Many dual-career parents are concerned about arrangements for their children during the summer months when they are at home. There are several ways of coping with this problem: allowing the dual wife or husband to have a lighter load during these months; allowing them to build up a backlog of working time during other months to relieve them during these ones; providing facilities on site during the summer months for young children (perhaps by the use of university students training in the field of primary education); or some combination of all of these.

Another more flexible working arrangement could be achieved by introducing more *part-time work* in a variety of different forms: limiting the number of days a week by allowing individuals to work three- or four-day, 40-hour weeks. This last suggestion is growing in popularity and if dual husband and wife were able to work on this basis they could, by careful planning, easily manage their domestic work arrangements between them. In 1972 an American Management Association survey estimated that between 700 and 1,000 firms of over 100,000 employees in toto were on a four-day, 40-hour week in the United States. By 1975, the number of firms grew to 3,000, covering over 1 million workers. Indeed, many firms are moving to a three-day, 38-hour week without decline in productivity and job satisfaction (Foster *et al.*, 1979).

Allied to many of these suggestions is the notion that organisations provide crèche or nursery facilities in the work-place. There is an increasing growth of these in many of the "advanced thinking" organisations. Many educationalists and psychologists have thought this to be a good idea, since it provides the mother or father with the opportunity of seeing their children some time during working hours. A less satisfactory solution would be community-based nurseries, but these may be necessary for those who work for small companies or who are self-employed. The benefits that organisations could derive from the introduction of the *industrial kibbutzim* seems so obvious that it is surprising that more companies have not followed suit.

Working at home

With the advent of the microprocessor revolution, it should become increasingly easier for dual husbands and wives in certain types of jobs to work at home. The need for a central work-place should decrease quite dramatically over the next decade or two. Already, employees can take home a computer terminal or indeed a minicomputer itself to carry out many of the tasks that they were once able to do only in a centralised work environment. In order to allow such practice, work organisations will have to rid themselves of their deep-rooted, nefarious suspicion of their fellow workers—namely, that the latter will always take every opportunity to exploit their employers and work as little as possible, and that only by overseeing them will the work get done! Indeed, it is this very control that has made the process of work unsatisfying and has encouraged the compartmentalisation of work and home life to the detriment of the former. As C. Wright Mills (1959) has suggested: "Each day men sell little pieces of themselves in order to try and buy them back each night and weekend with little pieces of fun".

Some organisations may one day realise that they may not need a centralised work-place at all. For the time being, however, work organisations ought to explore the variety of jobs that could easily be done at home and provide their employees with the necessary degree of flexibility to enable them to work there. At the very least, it is worth an experiment.

Smoothing the way for women

Many women, who have played the traditional family "caring" role, need particular help if they are to change the pattern of their marriage and fulfil a more dual role. One problem these women may face, after many years away from work, is lack of confidence and the feeling that they are out of date (or, in fact, actually are out of date). It is in the interest of employers and the wider community to provide opportunities for these sorts of women to be brought up to date with current developments. This might best be done by professional associations, or indeed by work organisations providing updating courses for ex-employees who have temporarily left employment to raise a family. As Fogarty *et al.* (1971) have suggested: "The important thing in the interests of both employers and of young mothers themselves is to minimize the interruption to a highly qualified woman's career and to keep her as closely in touch as possible with her particular world of work.'' Any help the industrial organisation can give its former employees in maintaining their skills may pay off greatly in the future, not only in terms of "good will" but in reducing costs of retraining or initial training of replacement staff. As far as the question of confidence is concerned, this can be achieved during the updating activity or by specialised courses prior to retraining or updating, depending on the time-gap between the termination of full employment and the return to work.

Maternity and paternity leave

It is obvious that what many women at work need, if they are preparing to have a family, is some sense of security about their job. In this respect it seems only sensible to have some reasonable maternity leave with a guaranteed right to return to work after it, and with some financial security during the leave period. Most countries in the European Common Market have guarantees against dismissal during pregnancy, a guarantee of paid maternity leave (usually between eight and twelve weeks and up to six months in many Eastern European countries) and guarantees of the right to return to work either immediately following the paid maternity leave period or unpaid leave after some prearranged return period (in some cases up to two or three years later). Different countries have different arrangements in this respect.

Paternity leave is also particularly important in the changing circumstances of the family. Few organisations provide this contemporary innovation, but many will have to consider it in the near future if they want to deal more systematically with what may end up, if ignored, as an uncontrolled absenteeism problem in the years ahead. Dual-careeer families will increasingly need the flexibility of short-leave periods, and provision of leave for both men and women should help to ease the problem.

QUESTIONS

1. What are the characteristics of the role of the manager?
2. What are the major duties of trade-union officers?
3. What are the main problems of women at work?
4. What can organisations do to help women at work?

CHAPTER NINE

Stress

OBJECTIVES

Stress at work is costing industry a great deal of money. It has been estimated that over 1 per cent of our GNP is spent in coping with job-generated stress manifestations. This chapter looks at the ways in which an organisation can create stress for its employees, how much it is costing industry and what can be done to minimise the adverse effects. It discusses the manager's role, relationships at work, career development, and home/work stresses.

ORGANISATIONAL STRESS ON MANAGERS

Work in organisations provides a large section of the population with life-sustaining income and job satisfaction. It also exerts its own pressures and stresses which ultimately can have negative consequences – in respect of the achieving of goals of organisations as well as of meeting the needs of the individuals working within them. Before we examine the various forms and sources of managerial pressure and stress at work, it may be useful to define these two central concepts. "Pressure" is an external or internal force acting on an individual to perform in a particular way or achieve a particular end result. It can be a source of some discomfort and some anxiety, but at the same time it can be exciting, challenging and growth-producing. "Stress", on the other hand, has only negative outcomes for the individual concerned because (a) the individual feels that he or she will not be able (in the long term) to cope, and therefore (b) will find it necessary to deal with it in a defensive and maladaptive way. Pressure is a tolerable, manageable condition, includes some positive attributes, and is characterised by activity and productive coping; stress is a regressive and counter-productive condition, can produce extreme and usually undifferentiated anxiety, and is characterised by defensive coping. Why is understanding the nature and sources of managerial stress important? Why should we be concerned about it? Primarily because a manager's mental and physical health may be adversely affected by such stresses.

Coronary heart disease is declining in the United States for the first time this century, according to recent statistics from the World Health Organisation. In the United Kingdom, however, it is still rising, with an increase of 6 per cent in male deaths in England and Wales in the period 1970–9 and 12.5 per cent in Northern Ireland; and Scotland, after a small increase, now heads the world league table of deaths caused by heart disease. What accounts for the dramatic drop in coronary artery and other stress-related illnesses in the United States? Why is British experience still moving in the opposite direction? The evidence points overwhelmingly to improvements in American dietary habits, and to companies being concerned about their employees.

Nor is this the only result of action taken by individuals in the United States for the sake of their own health. Among the several factors which, over the last ten to fifteen years, have obviously helped strengthen immunity to stress and its numerous nefarious manifestations, is this: more and more organisations in North America are providing health and counselling facilities for their employees. This is not so much because appalling statistics in past decades, showing younger and younger employees succumbing to stress-related illnesses, have awakened the corporate conscience; rather it is because organisations have recognised the economic cost of not protecting their workers from the potentially harmful effects of stress in the work-place. This cost is widespread: it includes the expense of days lost to illness, lost opportunities and, more recently, a massive increase in claims for worker compensation based on stress at work. In California, for example, the courts have been awarding employees damages because of "cumulative trauma or stress", particularly where employers have done nothing to minimise the pressures of the work-place. Indeed, the largest industrial insurer in California, Industrial Indemnity Company, says that at the start, in 1971, the reserves for "cumulative trauma" claims were only 5.5 per cent of all new indemnity claim reserves. By 1976 they had jumped to nearly 17 per cent, and these claims are now estimated at over 20 per cent.

A "cumulative trauma" claim is pressed by an employee when he contends that a major illness or disability he has suffered is the cumulative result of minor job stresses and strains stretching back over a period of years. The precedent for such a claim and all subsequent cases was based on the Carter versus General Motors case heard in the Michigan Supreme Court, which found that James Carter, a machine operator, had suffered an emotional breakdown resulting from job pressure. The courts in the United States are sustaining such compensation claims on evidence that certain organisations seem to be doing very little to minimise the pressure and health consequences of jobs which are intrinsically stressful.

In order to do something positive about sources of stress on managers at work, it is important to be able to identify them. The success of any effort to minimise stress and maximise job satisfaction will depend on accurate diagnosis, for different stresses will require different action. Any approach in the management of stress in an organisation that relied on one particular technique (eg, OD or job enrichment or TM), without taking into account the differences within work groups or divisions, would be doomed to failure. A recognition of the possible sources of management stress, therefore, may help us to suggest ways of minimising its negative consequences.

Research work (Cooper and Payne, 1978; Cooper, 1981; Cooper and Davidson, 1982) into managerial stressors reveals that there are a number of generalisable precursors to ill health and job dissatisfaction. Fig. 32 is an attempt to represent these diagrammatically;

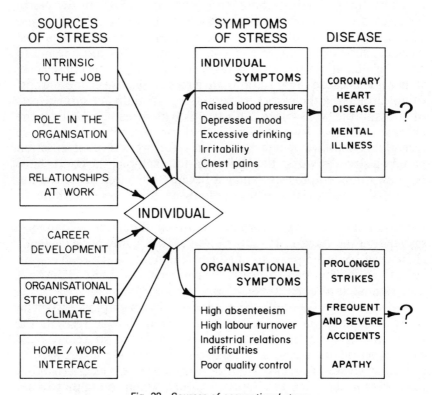

Fig. 32. *Sources of occupational stress.*

below they will be dealt with in a natural progression from those related to the job, organisation and individual. (Some of the research literature reviewed here has been drawn from Cooper's article, "Occupational Sources of Stress", *Journal of Occupational Psychology*, 49 (1976), 11–28.)

Intrinsic to the job of management
Factors intrinsic to the "job of management" were a first and vital

focus of study for early researchers in the field (Stewart, 1976) and in "shop-floor" (as opposed to management) studies are still the main preoccupation. Stress can be caused by too much or too little work, time pressures and deadlines, having too many decisions to make (Sofer, 1970), working conditions, excessive travel, long hours, having to cope with changes at work and the expenses (monetary and career) of making mistakes (Kearns, 1973). It can be seen that every job description includes factors which for some individuals at some point in time will be a source of pressure.

One of the main sources of stress on managers is their tendency to work long hours and to take on too much work. Research into work overload has been given substantial empirical attention. French and Caplan (1973) have differentiated overload in terms of *quantitative* and *qualitative*. Quantitative refers to having "too much to do", while qualitative means work that is "too difficult". Miller (1960) has theorised that overload in most systems leads to breakdown, whether we are dealing with single biological cells or managers in organisations. In an early study, French and Caplan (1970) found that objective quantitative overload was strongly linked to cigarette smoking (an important risk factor or symptom of CHD). Persons with more phone calls, office visits and meetings per given unit of work time were found to smoke significantly more cigarettes than a person with fewer such engagements. In a study of 100 young coronary patients, Russek and Zohman (1958) found that 25 per cent had been working at two jobs and an additional 45 per cent had worked at jobs which required (owing to work overload) sixty or more hours per week. They add that although prolonged emotional strain preceded the attack in 91 per cent of the cases, similar stress was observed in only 20 per cent of the controls. Breslow and Buell (1960) have also reported findings that support a relationship between hours of work and death from coronary disease. In an investigation of mortality rates of men in California, they observed that workers in light industry under the age of forty-five, who are on the job more than forty-eight hours a week, have twice the risk of death from CHD compared with similar workers working forty or less hours a week. Another substantial investigation on quantitative work-load was carried out by Margolis *et al.* (1974) on a representative national American sample of 1,496 employed persons of sixteen years of age or older. They found that overload was significantly related to a number of symptoms or indicators of stress, namely:

(*a*) escapist drinking;
(*b*) absenteeism from work;
(*c*) low motivation to work;

(*d*) lowered self-esteem;

(*e*) an absence of suggestions to employers.

The results of these and other studies (Cooper and Marshall, 1978; Marshall and Cooper, 1979) are relatively consistent and indicate that this factor is indeed a potential source of managerial stress that adversely affects both health and job satisfaction.

There is also some evidence that qualitative overload is a source of stress for managers. French *et al.* (1965) looked at qualitative work overload in a large university. They used questionnaires, interviews and medical examinations to obtain data on risk factors associated with CHD for 122 university administrators and professors. They found that one symptom of stress, low self-esteem, was related to work overload, but that this was different for the two occupational groupings. Qualitative overload was not significantly linked to low self-esteem among the administrators but was significantly correlated for the professors. The greater the quality of work expected of the professor, the lower his self-esteem. French and Caplan (1973) summarise this research by suggesting that both qualitative and quantitative overload produce at least nine different symptoms of psychological and physical strain: job dissatisfaction, job tension, lower self-esteem, threat, embarrassment, high cholesterol levels, increased heart rate, skin resistance and more smoking. In analysing this data, however, one cannot ignore the vital interactive relationship of the job and manager; objective work overload, for example, should not be viewed in isolation but in relation to the manager's capacities and personality.

Such caution is sanctioned by much of the American and some British literature, which shows that overload is not always externally imposed. Many managers (perhaps certain personality types more than others) react to overload by working longer hours. For example, in reports on an American study (Uris, 1972) it was found that 45 per cent of the executives investigated worked all day, in the evenings and at the week-ends, and that a further 37 per cent kept week-ends free but worked extra hours in the evenings. In many companies this type of behaviour has become a norm to which everyone feels they must adhere.

Manager's role in the organisation

Another major source of managerial stress is associated with a person's role at work. A great deal of research in this area has concentrated on role ambiguity and role conflict, since the seminal investigations of the Survey Research Center of the University of Michigan (Kahn *et al.*, 1964). Role ambiguity exists where a manager has inadequate information about his work role – that is, where there is *"lack of clarity* about the work objectives associated with the role, about work colleagues' expectation of the work role and about the scope and responsibility of the job". Kahn *et al.* found in their study that men who suffered from role ambiguity experienced lower job satisfaction, high job-related tension, greater futility and lower self-confidence. French and Caplan (1970) found, at one of NASA's bases in a sample of 205 volunteer engineers, scientists and administrators, that role ambiguity was significantly related to low job satisfaction and to feelings of job-related threat to one's mental and physical well-being. This also related to indicators of physiological strain such as increased blood pressure and pulse rate. Margolis *et al.* (1974) also found a number of significant relationships between symptoms or indicators of physical and mental ill health and role ambiguity, in their representative national sample (n = 1,496). The stress indicators related to role ambiguity were:

(*a*) depressed mood;
(*b*) lowered self-esteem;
(*c*) life dissatisfaction;
(*d*) job dissatisfaction;
(*e*) low motivation to work; and
(*f*) intention to leave the job.

Role conflict exists when the "individual in a particular work role is torn by conflicting job demands or doing things he/she really does not want to do or does not think are part of the job specification" (Khan *et al.*, 1964). The most frequent manifestation of this is when a manager is caught between two groups of people who demand different kinds of behaviour or expect that the job should entail different functions. Khan *et al.* found that men who suffered more role conflict had lower job satisfaction and higher job-related tension. It is interesting to note, however, that they also found that the greater the power or authority of the people "sending" the conflicting role messages, the more did role conflict produce job dissatisfaction. This was related to physiological strain as well, as the NASA study (French and Caplan, 1970) illustrates. French and Caplan telemetered and recorded the heart rate of twenty-two men for a two-hour period while they were at work in their offices. They found that the mean heart rate for an individual was strongly related to his report of the role conflict.

A larger and medically more sophisticated study by Shirom *et al.* (1973) obtained similar results. Their research is of particular interest, as it tries to look simultaneously at a wide variety of potential work stresses. They collected data on 762 male kibbutz members aged thirty and above, drawn from thirteen kibbutzim throughout Israel. They examined the relationships between CHD, abnormal electrocardiographic readings, CHD risk factors (systolic blood pressure, pulse rate, serum cholesterol levels, etc.) and potential sources of job stress (work overload, role ambiguity, role conflict, lack of physical activity). Their data was broken down by occupational groups: agricultural workers, factory groups, craftsmen and managers. It was found that there was a significant relationship between role conflict and CHD (specifically, abnormal electrocardiographic readings), but for the managers only. In fact, as we moved down the ladder from occupations requiring great physical exertions (e.g. agriculture) to those requiring the least (e.g. managerial), the greater was the relationship between role ambiguity/conflict and abnormal electrocardiographic findings. It was also found that as we go from occupations involving excessive physical activities to those with less such activity, CHD increased significantly. Drawing together this data, it might be hypothesised that those in managerial and professional occupations are more likely to suffer occupational stress from role-related stress and other interpersonal dynamics and less from the physical conditions of work.

Another aspect of role conflict was examined by Mettlin and Woelfel (1974). They measured three aspects of interpersonal influence – discrepancy between influences, level of influence and number of influences – in a study of the educational and occupational aspirations of high school students. Using the Langner Stress Symptom questionnaire as their index of stress, they found that the more extensive and diverse an individual's impersonal communications network, the more stress symptoms he showed. A manager's role which is at a boundary – i.e. between departments or between the company and the outside world – is, by definition, one of extensive communication nets and of high role conflict. Kahn *et al.* (1964) suggest that such a position is potentially highly stressful. Margolis and Kroes (1974) found, for instance, that foremen (high role conflict-prone job) are seven times more likely to develop ulcers as shop-floor workers.

Another important potential source of stress associated with a manager's role is "responsibility for people". One can differentiate here between "responsibility for people" and "responsibility for things" (equipment, budgets, etc.). Wardwell *et al.* (1964) found that responsibility for people was significantly more likely to lead to CHD than responsibility for things. Increased responsibility for people frequently means that one has to spend more time interacting with others, attending meetings and, in consequence, as in the NASA study (French and Caplan, 1970), more time in trying to meet deadline pressures and schedules.

Having too little responsibility (Brook, 1973), lack of participation in decision-making, lack of managerial support, having to
keep up with increased standards of performance and coping with
rapid technological change are other potential stressors mentioned
repeatedly in the literature but with little supportive research
evidence. Variations between organisational structures will determine the differential distribution of these factors across differing
occupational groups. Kay (1974) does suggest, however, that
(independent of employing organisations) some pressures are to be
found more at middle than at other management levels. He depicts
today's middle manager as being particularly hard pressed by:

(a) pay compression, as the salaries of new recruits increase;
(b) job insecurity – they are particularly vulnerable to redundancy
or involuntary early retirement;
(c) having little real authority at their high levels of responsibility;
and
(d) feeling "boxed" in.

Relationships at work

A third major potential source of managerial stress has to do with
the nature of relationships with one's boss, subordinates and
colleagues. Behavioural scientists have long suggested that good
relationships between members of a work group are a central factor
in individual and organisational health (Cooper, 1981). Nevertheless, very little research work has been done in this area either to
support or disprove the hypothesis. French and Caplan (1973)
define poor relations as "those which include low trust, low
supportiveness and low interest in listening to and trying to deal
with problems that confront the organizational member". The most
notable studies in this area are by Kahn *et al.* (1964), French and
Caplan (1970) and Buck (1972). Both the Kahn *et al.* and French
and Caplan studies came to roughly the same conclusions: that
mistrust of persons one worked with was positively related to high
role ambiguity, which led to inadequate communications between
people and to "psychological strain in the form of low job satisfaction and to feelings of job-related threat to one's well-being".

Relationships with boss

Buck (1972) focused on the attitude and relationship of workers and
managers to their immediate boss, using Fleishman's leadership
questionnaire on consideration and initiating structure. The
consideration factor was associated with behaviour indicative of
friendship, mutual trust, respect and a certain warmth between boss

and subordinate. He found that those managers who felt that their boss was low on "consideration" said they experienced more job pressure. Managers who were under pressure reported that their boss did not mete out criticism in a helpful way, played favourites with subordinates, "pulled rank" and took advantage of them whenever they had a chance. Buck concludes that the "considerate behaviour of superiors appears to have contributed significantly inversely to feelings of job pressure".

Relationships with subordinates

Officially, one of the most critical functions of a manager is his supervision of other people's work. It has long been accepted that an "inability to delegate" might be a problem, but now a new potential source of stress is being introduced in the manager's interpersonal skills – he must learn to "manage by participation". Donaldson and Gowler (1975) point to the factors that may make today's zealous emphasis on participation a cause of resentment, anxiety and stress for the manager concerned:

(a) Mismatch of formal and actual power.

(b) The manager may well resent the erosion of his formal role and authority (and the loss of status and rewards).

(c) He may be subject to irreconcilable pressures, e.g. to be both productive and participative.

(d) His subordinates may refuse to participate.

Particularly for those with technological and scientific backgrounds (a "things orientation"), relationships with subordinates can be a low priority (seen as "trivial", "petty", time-consuming and an impediment to doing the job well), and one would expect their interactions to be more a source of stress than those of "people-oriented" managers.

Relationships with colleagues

Besides the obvious factors of office politics and colleagues' rivalry, we find another element here: stress can be caused not only by the pressure of poor relationships but by its opposite: a lack of adequate social support in difficult situations (Lazarus, 1966). At highly competitive managerial levels, it is likely that problem sharing will be inhibited by the fear of those concerned of appearing weak, and much of the (American) literature particularly mentions the isolated life of the top executive as an added source of strain.

Morris (1975) encompasses this whole area of relationships in one model – what he calls the "cross of relationships". While he acknowledges the differences between relationships on two continua – one axis extends from colleagues to users, and the other intersecting axis from senior to junior managers – he considers that the focal manager must bring all four into "dynamic balance" in order to be able to deal with the stress of his position. Morris's suggestion seems "only sensible" when we see how much of his work time the manager spends with other people. In a research programme to find out exactly what managers do, Minzberg (1973) showed just how much of their time is spent in interaction. In an intensive study of a small sample of chief executives he found that in a large organisation a mere 22 per cent of time was spent in desk work sessions, the rest being taken up by telephone calls (6 per cent), scheduled meetings (59 per cent), unscheduled meetings (10 per cent) and other activities (3 per cent). In small organisations basic desk work played a larger part (52 per cent), but nearly 40 per cent was still devoted to face-to-face contacts of one kind or another.

CAREER DEVELOPMENTS

Two major clusters of potential managerial stressors can be identified in this area:

(a) lack of job security – fear of redundancy, obsolesence or early retirement, etc.;

(b) status incongruity – under- or over-promotion, frustration at having reached one's career ceiling, etc.

For many managers their career progression is of overriding importance – by promotion they earn not only money but status and the new job challenges for which they strive. Typically, in the early years at work, this striving and aptitude to come to terms quickly with a rapidly changing environment is fostered and suitably rewarded by the company. Career progression is, perhaps, a problem by its very nature. For example, Sofer (1970) found that many of his sample believed that "luck" plays a major role.

At middle age, and usually middle management levels, career becomes more problematic and most executives find their progress slowed, if not actually stopped. Job opportunities become fewer, those jobs that are available take longer to master, past (mistaken?) decisions cannot be revoked, old knowledge and methods become obsolete, energies may be flagging or sapped by demands from the family, and there is the "press" of fresh young recruits to face in competition. Both Levinson (1973) and Constandse (1972) – the latter refers to this phase as "the male menopause" – depict the manager as suffering fears of the above mentioned and disappointments in "silent isolation" from his family and work colleagues. The fear of demotion or obsolescence can be strong for those who know they have reached their "career ceiling", and most will inevitably suffer some erosion of status before they finally retire. Goffman (1952) extrapolating from a technique employed in the con-game "cooling the mark-out" suggests that the company should bear some responsibility for taking the sting out of this (felt) failure experience.

From the company perspective, on the other hand, McMurray (1973) puts the case for not promoting a manager to a higher position if there is doubt that he can fill it. In a syndrome he labels "the executive neurosis", he describes the over-promoted manager as grossly overworking to keep down a top job and at the same time hiding his insecurity, and he points to the consequences for his work performance and the company. Age is no longer revered as it was − it is becoming a "young man's world". The rapidity with which society is developing (technologically, economically and socially) is likely to mean that individuals will now need to change career during their working life (as companies and products have to do). Such trends breed uncertainty and research suggests that older workers look for stability (Sleeper, 1975). Unless managers adapt their expectations to suit new circumstances, "career development" stress, especially in later life, is likely to become an increasingly common experience.

ORGANISATIONAL STRUCTURE AND CLIMATE

A fifth potential source of managerial stress is simply "being in the organisation" and the threat to an individual's freedom, autonomy and identity that this situation poses. Problem areas such as little or no participation in the decision-making process, no sense of belonging, lack of effective consultation, poor communications, restrictions on behaviour, and office politics are some of those with the most impact here. An increasing number of research investigations are being conducted in this area, particularly into the effect of the employee participation in the work-place. The research development is contemporaneous with a growing movement in North America and in the EEC countries of worker participation programmes, involving autonomous work groups, worker directors, and a greater sharing of the decision-making process throughout the organisation (*see* Chapter 10).

In the NASA study (French and Caplan, 1970), for example, it was found that managers and other professional workers who reported greater opportunities for participation in decision-making reported significantly greater job satisfaction, low job-related feelings of threat and higher feelings of self-esteem. Buck (1972) found that both managers and workers who felt most "under pressure", reported that their bosses "always ruled with an iron hand and rarely tried out new ideas or allowed participation in decision-making". Managers who were under stress also reported that their bosses never let the persons under them do their work in the way they thought best. Margolis *et al.* (1974) found that non-participation at work, among a national representative sample of over 1,400 workers, was the most consistent and significant predictor or indicator of strain and job-related stress. They found that non-participation was significantly related to the following health risk factors: overall poor physical health, escapist drinking, depression, low self-esteem, low life satisfaction, low job satisfaction, low motivation to work, intention to leave job and absenteeism from work. Kasl (1973) also found that low job satisfaction was related to non-participation in decision-making, inability to provide feedback to supervisors and lack of recognition for good performance; and that poor mental health was linked to close supervision and no autonomy at work (Quinn *et al.*, 1971). Neff (1968) has highlighted the importance of lack of participation and involvement by suggesting that "mental health at work is to a large extent a function of the degree to which output is under the control of the individual worker".

To summarise, the research above seems to indicate that greater participation leads to lower staff turnover and high productivity, and that when participation is absent, lower job satisfaction and higher levels of physical and mental health risks may result.

HOME/WORK INTERFACE STRESSES

The sixth "source" of managerial stress is more of a "catch-all" for all those interfaces between life outside and life inside the organisation that might put pressure on the manager: family problems, life crises, financial difficulties, conflict of personal beliefs with those of the company and the conflict of company with family demands (Cooper, 1981). The area which has received most research interest here is that of the manager's relationship with his or her spouse and family. The manager has two main problems *vis-à-vis* his family:

(*a*) The first is that of "time management" and "commitment-management". Not only does his busy life leave him few resources with which to cope with other people's needs, but in order to do his job well the manager usually also needs support from others to cope with the "background" details of house management, etc., to

relieve stress when possible, and to maintain contact with the
outside world.

(b) The second, often a result of the first, is the spill-over of crises
or stresses in one system which affect the other.

As these two are inseparable we shall go on to discuss them
together.

Marriage patterns

The "arrangement" the manager comes to with his or her spouse
will be of vital importance to both problem areas. Pahl and Pahl
(1971) found in their middle-class sample that the majority of wives
saw their role in relation to their husband's job as a supportive,
domestic one; all said that they derived their sense of security from
their husbands. Barber (1976), interviewing five directors' wives,
finds similar attitudes. Gowler and Legge (1975) have dubbed this
bond "the hidden contract", in which the wife agrees to act as a
"support team" so that her husband can fill the demanding job to
which he aspires. Handy (1978) supports the idea that this is
"typical" and that it is the path to career success for the manager
concerned. Basing his findings on individual psychometric data he
describes a number of possible marriage-role combinations. In his
sample of top British executives (in mid-career) and their wives he
found that the most frequent pattern (about half the twenty-two
couples interviewed) was the "thrusting male-caring female". This
combination he depicts as highly role segregated, with the emphasis
on "separation", "silence" and complementary activities.
Historically both the company and the manager have reaped the
benefits of maintaining the segregation of work and home implicit
in this pattern. The company thus legitimates its demand for a
constant work performance from its employee, no matter what his
home situation, and the manager is free to pursue his career but
keeps a "safe haven" to which he can return to relax and
recuperate. The second and most frequent combination was
"involved-involved" – a dual-career pattern, with the emphasis on
complete sharing. This combination, while potentially extremely
fulfilling for both parties, requires energy inputs which might well
prove so excessive that none of the roles involved is fulfilled
successfully. It is unlikely that the patterns described above will be
negotiated explicitly or that they will in the long term be "in
balance". Major factors in their continuing evolution will be the
work and family demands at particular life stages. A recent report
(Beatie et al., 1974), for example, highlights the difficult situation
of the young executive who, in order to build up his career, must
devote a great deal of time and energy to his job just when his young

house-bound wife, with small children, is also making pressing demands. The report suggests that the executive fights to maintain the distance between his wife and the organisation, so that she will not be in a position to evaluate the choices he has to make. Paradoxically he does so at a time when he is most in need of sympathy and understanding.

Mobility

At an individual level the effects of mobility on the manager's wife and family have also been studied (Cooper, 1981). Researchers agree that, whether she is willing to move or not, the wife bears the brunt of relocations, and they conclude that most husbands do not appreciate what this involves. American writers point to signs that wives are suffering and becoming less co-operative. Immundo (1974) hypothesises that increasing divorce rates are seen as the upwardly aspiring manager races ahead of his socially unskilled, "stay-at-home" wife. Seidenberg (1973) comments on the rise in the ratio of female-to-male alcoholics in the United States – from 1:5 in 1962 to 1:2 in 1973 – and asks the question, "Do corporate wives have souls?" Descriptive accounts of the frustrations and loneliness of being a "corporate wife" in the United States and Britain proliferate. Increasing teenage delinquency and violence are also laid at the door of the mobile manager and the society he has created.

Constant moving can have profound effects on the life-style of the people concerned, particularly on their relationships with others. Staying only two years or so in one place, mobile families do not have time to develop close ties with the local community. Immundo (1974) talks of the "mobility syndrome", a way of behaving geared to developing only temporary relationships.

Pahl and Pahl (1971) suggest that the British reaction is, characteristically, more reserved and that many mobiles retreat into their nuclear family. Managers, particularly, do not become involved in local affairs owing both to lack of time and to an appreciation that they are only "short-stay" inhabitants. Their wives find participation easier (especially in a mobile rather than in a static area) and a recent survey (Middle Class Housing Estate Study, 1975) suggested that, for some, involvement is a necessity to compensate for their husband's ambitions and career involvement which keep him away from home. From the company's point of view, the way in which a wife does adjust to her new environment can affect her husband's work performance. Guest and Williams (1973) illustrate this with an example of a major international company which, on surveying 1,800 executives in seventy countries, concluded that the two most important influences of overall satisfaction with the overseas assignment were the job itself and, more importantly, the adjustment of the executives' wives to the foreign environment.

THE INDIVIDUAL MANAGER

Sources of pressure at work evoke different reactions from different managers. Some are better able to cope with these stressors than others; they adapt their behaviour in a way that meets the environmental challenge. On the other hand, some managers are psychologically predisposed to stress – that is, they are unable to cope with or adapt to the stress-provoking situations. Many factors may contribute to these differences: personality, motivation, being able or ill-equipped to deal with problems in a particular area of expertise, fluctuations in abilities (particularly with age), insight into one's own motivations and weaknesses, etc. It would be useful to examine, therefore, those characteristics of the individual that research evidence indicates make him predisposed to stress. Most of the research in this area has focused on personality and behavioural differences between high- and low-stressed individuals.

The major research approach to individual stress differences began with the work of Friedman and Rosenman (Friedman, 1969; Rosenman et al., 1964, 1966) in the early 1960s and developed later showing a relationship between behavioural patterns and the prevalence of CHD. They found that individuals manifesting certain behavioural traits were significantly more at risk to CHD. These individuals were later referred to as the "coronary prone behaviour pattern Type A" as distinct from Type B (low risk of CHD). Type A was found to be the overt behavioural syndrome or style of living characterised by "extremes of competitiveness, striving for achievement, aggressiveness, haste, impatience, restlessness, hyperalertness, explosiveness of speech, tenseness of facial musculature and feelings of being under pressure of time and under the challenge of responsibility". It was suggested that "people having this particular behavioral pattern were often so deeply involved and committed to their work that other aspects of their lives were relatively neglected" (Jenkins, 1971). In the early studies persons were designated as Type A or Type B on the basis of clinical judgments of doctors and psychologists or peer ratings. These studies found higher incidence of CHD among Type A than Type B. Many of the inherent methodological weaknesses of this approach were overcome by the classic Western Collaborative Group Study (Rosenman et al., 1964, 1966). It was a prospective (as opposed to the earlier retrospective studies) national sample of over 3,400 men free of CHD. All these men were rated Type A or B by psychiatrists after intensive interviews, without knowledge of any biological data about them and without the individuals' being seen by a heart specialist. Diagnosis was made by an electrocardiographer and an independent medical practitioner, who were not informed about the subjects' behavioral patterns. They found the following result: after two to five years from the start of the study Type A men in the age groups of 39–49 and 50–59 had 6.5 and 1.9 times, respectively, the incidence of CHD than Type B men. They also had a large number of stress risk factors (e.g. high serum cholesterol levels, elevated β-lipoproteins, etc.). After four to five years of the follow-up observation in the study, the *same* relationship of behavioural pattern and incidence of CHD was found. In terms of the clinical manifestations of CHD, individuals exhibiting Type A behavioural patterns had significantly more incidence of acute myocardial infarction and angina pectoris. Rosenman *et al.* (1967) also found that the risk of recurrent and fatal myocardial infarction was significantly related to Type A characteristics.

An increasingly large number of studies have been carried out which support the relationship between Type A behaviour and ill health (Caplan Cobb and French, 1975). From a management perspective the most significant work was carried out by Howard *et al.* (1976). Twelve different companies examined 236 managers for Type A behaviour and for a number of the known risk factors of CHD (blood pressure, cholesterol, triglycerides, uric acid, smoking and fitness). Those managers exhibiting extreme Type A behaviour showed significantly higher blood pressure (systolic and diastolic) and higher cholesterol and triglyceride levels. A higher percentage of these managers were cigarette smokers, and in each age group studied Type A managers were less interested in exercise (although differences in cardio-respiratory fitness were found only in the oldest age group). The authors conclude that Type A managers were found to be higher in a number of risk factors known to be associated with CHD than Type B managers.

THE MANAGEMENT OF STRESS

Cooper and Davidson (1982) have argued that understanding the sources of managerial pressure, as we have tried to do here, is only the first step in stress reduction. Next, we must begin to explore "when" and "how" to intervene. There are a number of initial changes that can be introduced in organisational life to help ease stress at work. For example:

(*a*) to re-create the social, psychological and organisational environment in the work-place in order to encourage greater autonomy and participation by managers in *their* jobs;

(*b*) to begin to build the bridges between the work-place and the home, by providing opportunities for the manager's spouse to understand better the manager's job, to express views about the consequences of the manager's work on family life and for the spouse to be involved in the decision-making process of work that affects all members of the family unit;

(*c*) to utilise the well-developed catalogue of social and interactive skill training programmes to help clarify role and interpersonal relationship difficulties within organisations; and more fundamentally,

(*d*) to create an organisational climate to encourage rather than discourage communication, openness and trust, so that individual managers are able to express their inability to cope, their work-related fears and are able to ask for help if needed.

QUESTIONS

1. What are some of the major causes of stress among managers?

2. What are some of the personality characteristics of managers who are vulnerable to stress?

3. How can we change the organisational structure to minimise stress?

4. How can we help the individual to cope with the problems of organisational stress?

CHAPTER TEN

The Quality of Working Life

OBJECTIVES

Throughout the developed world, companies and organisations are increasingly allowing their employees to participate in the decision-making processes of their job. This is happening at boardroom level and, more importantly, on the shop-floor. This chapter explores what is happening in a number of countries which are encouraging "Quality of Work Life" (QWL) experiments. We look specifically at the EEC countries, and also at some of the more advanced countries in this field, notably Sweden, the United States and Japan.

REDESIGNING JOBS AND WORK

Beric Wright (1975) has aptly summarised the dilemma of "man" in organisations when he contends that "the responsibility for maintaining health should be a reflection of the basic relationship between the individual and the organisation for which he works; it is in the best interests of both parties that reasonable steps are taken to live and work sensibly and not too demandingly". In this respect we have heard a great deal in the last couple of years about the need to democratise or humanise the work-place in industry, to improve the quality of working life by providing the industrial worker with greater participation in the decisions involving his work. This can be achieved by including employees on boards of companies and involving them in the long-term policy-making issues of the organisations, or by increasing their participation in the decision-making processes of their work group by allowing them greater freedom in deciding how to organise and conduct their own jobs. These two approaches to industrial democracy – which, it might be added, are not mutually exclusive – have been termed by Strauss and Rosenstein (1970) as *distant* and *immediate* participation respectively. In this chapter the intention is to consider the work that has been done in the field of *immediate* participation, for it is the opinion of the authors that, at least in the initial stages of the "participative revolution" (Preston and Post, 1974), these developments are likely to have the most impact on increasing people's job satisfaction, performance and improving the industrial relations climate generally.

A substantial number of immediate participation programmes have been introduced throughout Europe and other countries under differing labels over the last decade: autonomous work groups, job enrichment schemes, work restructuring, etc. Each of these approaches is attempting to meet any one of a combination of the following objectives that have been put forward by Herrick and Maccoby (1975) as the four principles of humanisation at work:

(*a*) *Security* – employees need to be free from fear and anxiety concerning health and safety, income and future employment.

(*b*) *Equity* – employees should be compensated commensurately with their contribution to the value of the service or product.

(*c*) *Individuation* – employees should have maximum autonomy in determining the rhythm of their work and in planning how it should be done.

(*d*) *Democracy* – employees should, whenever possible, manage themselves, be involved in the decision-making process that affects their work and accept greater responsibility in the work of the organisation.

The experiments in the humanisation of the immediate work environment vary enormously from those which emphasise "participative decision-making" to those that attempt to nurture "work autonomy"; from those which have been thoroughly conceived and planned to those which have developed out of political crises and expediency; from those which have been systematically monitored to those which have been uncritically praised, etc. Since we in Great Britain and in the European Community at large are likely to move increasingly towards greater participation in industry for a variety of political and socio-psychological reasons (e.g. EEC's Fifth Directive), it might be worthwhile exploring some of the examples and results of the recent work undertaken to humanise the workplace in different countries, so that we may be able to plan and organise more effective programmes in the future. We shall be exploring first the developments in some EEC countries, and then we shall look further afield and examine those in Sweden, the United States and Japan – where new initiatives in participation and quality of working life have already been extensively used.

EUROPEAN ECONOMIC COMMUNITY

Many companies within the EEC have begun to experiment with "quality of working life" programmes. Indeed, many of the Community countries have introduced legislation to set up governmental agencies to encourage such development. Although there are a growing number of participation programmes being initiated and in progress, the systematic documentation of them in most EEC countries has not kept up with this growth. What we shall attempt to do here, therefore, is to provide a "thumb-nail" sketch of one or two of the better documented examples in order to impart some flavour of their approach and give an assessment of their effect.

United Kingdom

In a report during the 1970s on job and work redesign experiments in the United Kingdom, the Work Research Unit claimed to have traced 111 industrial examples: schemes relating to job rotation, job enlargement, job enrichment and autonomous work groups. The industries in which these programmes most frequently occur are the chemical, food and drink, manufacturing, engineering, electrical, paper and printing, and electronics. Of these 111 experiments in British firms, only slightly over a dozen seem to be documented or to show sufficient objective economic and human results for drawing any firm lessons. Like Sweden, the United States and Japan, Britain has a longer history of work humanisation efforts than is generally realised. The work of the Tavistock Institute of Human Relations in the early 1950s (e.g. Trist and Bamforth, 1951), in terms of the application of socio-technical system concepts, is the most notable example of early quality working life research and practice. But it is only recently that the development of these and other British approaches to work humanisation has been systematically encouraged, mainly through the Department of Employment, which set up the Work Research Unit for this purpose in 1974 at the recommendation of the TUC, the CBI and the Government. The stated overall objective of the WRU is:

> . . . the stimulation of changes in the ways in which work is organised in industry and commerce. . . . In practice this often means introducing such things as: allowing some degree of discretion and responsibility; giving scope for learning and development; introducing challenge and variety in the job; and by giving the individual an opportunity to make an identifiable contribution to the end product (Butteriss, 1975).

One of the best-documented and well-designed programmes in a British company was one carried out by Shell UK Ltd at their Stanlow Refinery (Hill, 1972). This took place in their micro-wax department, where until the work system redesign, morale was very low, costs were high and maintenance poor. A major restructuring of job tasks was then introduced whereby the employees worked as a team to complete *all* of the job tasks as opposed to only *part* of them. The workers were given more decision-making power about their jobs and in respect of running the plant generally. As a consequence the company attained more commitment and increased morale. On objective criteria, sickness and absenteeism were down 50 per cent, off-plant wax testing was reduced by 75 per cent, output increased by between 30 per cent and 100 per cent in various units, and occasionally significant reprocessing costs were saved. Another recent example was that of Ferranti's avionics plant in Edinburgh between 1968 and 1972. There they introduced group cell technology, with teams of four workers controlling six machines to deal with 300–400 different components. Each group cell was left to organise the job tasks and methods of production. It was found that the time taken to reset tools dropped by 60 per cent, production time for each component was cut by 30 per cent, and delay in getting parts, and quality, improved steadily (Clutterbuck, 1973).

Although the bulk of the British experiments in this field are production or assembly orientated, there are also some notable white-collar ones as well. For example, ICI in 1967 introduced greater autonomy and responsibility for their sales representatives in order to increase sales efforts. Sales representatives were given discretion on reports, complaint refunds and some pricing policies, etc. A job reaction survey showed a significant increase in job satisfaction and also an 18.6 per cent increase in sales (a control group of salesmen showed a drop in sales of 5 per cent) (Paul and Robertson, 1970).

Denmark
Denmark is moving, as have other Scandinavian countries, on both "immediate" and "distant" participation fronts simultaneously – in the late 1960s on shop-floor humanisation and in 1973 on company law associated with boardroom participation. In 1969, representatives of various trade unions, employers' organisations and the staff (managers and workers) of a select number of companies were encouraged by the Danish Productivity Fund to tour the United States and assess the work system redesign programmes there. On the basis of this experience, a number of these companies formed their own pilot experiments in new forms of work organisations along the lines of autonomous work groups. The three most notable examples are: Foss Electric Co., Sadoin and Hohmblad, and Colon Emballage (Taylor, 1975).

Foss Electric is a small manufacturer of dairy product testing equipment. In 1969 it introduced semi-autonomous work groups for natural parts of the production process. These groups planned and manufactured their segment of the operation, were paid on a flat rate, had flexible working hours, recruited staff and had a say in designing the immediate socio-technical system. It was found that labour turnover dropped in one year by 10 per cent and quality errors were reduced by 35 per cent. Not as much information about results is available about the Sadoin and Hohmblad (paint manufacturers) experiment, but that firm introduced a major change in its structure by creating interlocking managerial groups throughout the organisation. Jenkins (1974) reports that production improved as a result of solving more quickly and efficiently the production problems generated.

The final examples of Danish efforts at work humanisation took place in a small corrugated board plant, Colon Emballage, in southern Jutland in 1970. Autonomous work groups of between seven and eight workers were formed to decide on work roles, the wage system (shifted from piece rates to uniform flat rates), etc. – though they were restricted on production scheduling. It was found that production rose 8 per cent and the employees expressed greater satisfaction with their work.

The Netherlands

Since the early 1960s the Netherlands have been involved in work humanisation programmes, stemming mainly from the activities of the Philips Company but also from work system design experiments in the Dutch steel industry, post office and railways. As Butteriss (1975) points out, much of the stimulus to these attempts to improve the quality of working life in Dutch companies and government/quasi-government agencies was due to the problems of the time such as "graduate unemployment, failure of the government to adjust the quality of labour supply to the demand requirements, the discrepancy between the high quality labour force and the low quality jobs with resulting absenteeism, turnover, etc.". By far the most extensive and interesting examples of work redesign and participation programmes come from Philips (manufacturers of electrical appliances and other equipment), mainly in their assembly operations, but there is also an example from among the clerical workers. Most of these experiments took place during the 1960s in different assembly departments. For instance, autonomous work groups were set up in the bulb assembly and finishing departments where thirty individual jobs were combined into groups of four with a certain rotation. It was found (den Hertog, 1974) that production costs were reduced by 20 per cent, rejects were halved, and output increased. Worker satisfaction was not any higher, but workers indicated a strong preference for the current job design in contrast to the old.

In the black-and-white television factory they had the same sort of results with the autonomous work groups introduced there between 1969 and 1972. They formed seven-person work groups with twenty-minute work cycles and multiple job tasks (e.g. quality control, work distribution, material ordering, etc.). The 1972 evaluation programme in this department revealed that there was significantly lower absenteeism, lower waiting time for materials, better co-ordination and improved training, and that component costs were reduced by 10 per cent. Moreover, unlike the bulb department, greater job satisfaction was expressed there as well.

Also worthy of note was the white-collar experiment in the order department of Philips. There, the department was reorganised by product: three operational lines became three product lines. Within each product line every employee learnt all the tasks and rotated them; and each unit decided on their work leader who, in conjunction with his team, was responsible for delivery of a complete product. They found that productivity doubled and the majority of employees expressed a preference for the new system, although some indicated that the supervision was "too close".

France

It was not until the early 1970s that the French Government introduced legislation setting up the Agence National pour L'Amélioration des Conditions du Travail, whose main task was to provide information, carry out research and assist companies to improve the quality of working life (e.g. reorganisation of work and working hours, improving the physical environment of companies, encouraging employee participation and methods of assessing, and changing working conditions). This agency is trying to collate information on employee participation schemes and to encourage more systematic data collection on the consequences of the different approaches. Presently there are only a few well-documented cases in France, but there are two in particular that we might briefly explore here which best illustrate the current work in France (Jenkins, 1974).

Guillet SA, a woodworking machinery manufacturer in Auxerre, introduced semi-autonomous work groups of between seven and ten persons covering the manufacturing process of their machinery. Each of these work groups assembled nearly an entire piece of equipment by themselves. The programme was carried out in 1969 and covered nearly 800 employees. The most positive outcomes for the company were the increased sales and substantially enhanced job satisfaction.

Another example was that of a nylon-spinning plant of 100 workers. The employees introduced a work redesign scheme (with the co-operation of management) in which each worker carried out a larger number of skills including maintenance (replaced five jobs with two) and in which the work group took on the decision-making responsibility in the areas of quality control, staffing and work assignments. The experiment was carried out between 1969 and 1972 with the following encouraging positive results: absenteeism was reduced by two-thirds of traditional levels, no grievances or strikes were initiated and labour turnover was significantly reduced, indeed workers refused transfers to other plants (Taylor, 1975).

West Germany

Although West Germany has been the model of Western European countries for worker participation at boardroom level, or what is termed "co-determination of employees in the economic enter-prise" (*Mitbestimmung*), it has progressed very slowly indeed in shop-floor participation. It was not until the Federal Government carried out a research programme into job satisfaction in the early 1970s, which indicated that the low paid were the least satisfied with their job (e.g. income, security of employment, participation, etc.) and their career prospects, that any quality of worklife experiments were encouraged. It was in the middle of 1974 that the Federal Ministry of Labour and Social Affairs planned a programme for Research for the Humanisation of Work, which was similar in objectives to the French version. Its "brief" was to collate information on issues related to stress at work, worker partici-pation, work and job design, etc., and to stimulate further research. There is very little work reported on German experiments of employee participation, mainly because this is not particularly strongly supported by the German federation of Trade Unions (DGB), as Mire (1975) has emphasised: ". . . the DGB continues to pay lip service to the demands for direct representation of the workplace, but only as part of its broader demand for worker participation at the top. . . . Most efforts of the trade unions are directed at this aspect of their legislative programme rather than at bringing about worker participation at the plant level". Indeed, there is only one well-reported case of employee participation, and that is the work at the Singer Company of Germany (Ruehl, 1974). At Singer they introduced autonomous assembly work groups of electric and electronic equipment, precision parts and house appliances – these were described by the company as assembly islands. Unfortunately, no information is available on the objective consequences of these innovations, so we are left with very little evaluative data.

The Germans are very much aware of the need to develop their programme to improve the quality of working life and participation generally, even though to date their record in this area is far from progressive. This was particularly highlighted when Chancellor Brandt in the early 1970s set up a working party of five employers' representatives, five trade unionists and seven academics to consider new approaches to the organisation of work life.

Italy

The Italian Government has only recently set up an agency to explore the quality of working life issues, namely the Instituto di Studi di Lavoro. It has some of the same objectives as government institutes that have been established in other countries. Italy, like other EEC countries, has not been at the forefront of employee participation schemes, with the exception of a very few large companies, particularly Olivetti and Fiat. The most widely known example of work redesign in Italy took place at Olivetti's Ivres plant in the parts workshop and two assembly departments. There, Olivetti abolished the "long assembly line" on two product lines and introduced what it called "integrated assembly units" or "assembled islands". These are composed of a group of thirty people whose job is to assemble, inspect and maintain the whole product. The entire output needed is produced by a number of identical integrated units. A detailed account of Olivetti's work redesign programme can be found in Butera (1975), including an assessment of its success. Briefly, the following changes were evident from the work system change programme:

(a) Increase in the speed of the product through-put and decrease in-process time to less than one-third of the time of the line system.

(b) Quality of product improved significantly, and lower wastage.

(c) Increased job satisfaction and worker motivation under the new schemes.

(d) Per capita costs had increased and also training costs.

(e) There was a greater flexibility in the system for allocating human resources in the plant.

Summary of EEC countries

The Council of Europe has acknowledged the importance of work humanisation programmes in member countries by passing Resolution 565 which states: ". . . in view of changing worker attitudes and aspirations, that some working conditions have an adverse effect on health and attitudes, therefore, there is a belief that some work should be dramatically changed to take into account worker attitudes". The Resolution recommends the following objectives:

(a) The removal of soul-destroying jobs, as social progress depends on the interest workers take in jobs.

(b) That government authorities together with employees and work organisations promote the humanisation of working conditions.

(c) More opportunities should be given to participate in the methods and conditions of work.

(*d*) Assembly work should be eliminated and consideration given to job enlargement, job enrichment and autonomous work groups.

(*e*) Pay structures should be re-examined in the light of these proposals (Butteriss, 1975).

DEVELOPMENTS IN OTHER COUNTRIES

There are a number of other countries outside the EEC that have been extensively involved in quality of working life projects over the last decade, notably Sweden, the United States and Japan.

Sweden

There are literally hundreds of examples of serious systematic efforts at work redesign and participation in Sweden (Agervold, 1975). Although many of these have not been published in English or have not been fully evaluated by objective criteria, Sweden has certainly been at the forefront of recent ventures in this field. Much of the work done there was initially prompted by the country's need to "overcome an inability to recruit Swedish workers to Swedish factory work (particularly in the 1960s) and to respond to union demands for better quality of working life" (Elden and Taylor, 1983). One of the best-documented Swedish examples is, contrary to general expectations about Volvo, the Saab engine assembly line (at the Sodertalje truck and bus plant). The process of moving towards autonomous work groups began in 1969 with the expansion of the works council, the formation of development groups and of small team production groups of between seven to eight workers, in which job tasks were decided by foremen and workers in collaboration. By 1974, the plant had ninety development groups and 200 production groups, where decisions about work organisations were jointly reached. In the first year of the change programme, capital costs were higher and absenteeism/turnover were about the same as previously, but significantly more labour was attracted into the plant (and a more flexible work system was materialising). By the third year, labour turnover was reduced from 70 per cent to 20 per cent, unplanned stoppages were down from 6 per cent to 2 per cent, production had increased, costs were 5 per cent below budget and absenteeism was markedly improved (Norstedt and Aguren, 1974). Another interesting Swedish example, which involved a comparative analysis of two different forms of work restructuring, was carried out in Granges AB, a die-casting foundry near Stockholm. The plant introduced in one unit a job enrichment scheme and, in another, autonomous work groups (Jenkins, 1974). It was found that labour turnover rose from 60 per cent to 69 per cent and productivity dropped by 7 per cent in the former case, but productivity rose 20 per cent for the self-managed work group with turnover dropping from 60 per cent to 18 per cent. (In addition, absenteeism dropped 5 per cent and quality spoilage dropped 2 per cent in the latter case.)

There are many other encouraging examples of successful quality of working life cases from Sweden, as it builds up an impressive catalogue of work environment changes which are the model for other countries. Indeed, the Swedish Government enacted legislation in 1971 to set up the Work Environment Fund to sponsor more research and work in this field.

The United States

There are a large number of industrial cases of work humanisation projects in the United States, some dating back to the late 1940s (Coch and French, 1948) and 1950s (Morse and Reimer, 1956). Most of these examples are found in small plants of up to 250 employees and involve predominantly assembly or production operations. Many of these can be found in O'Toole's classic book, *Work in America* (1973).

An example of the kind of programme carried out in the United States is best illustrated by the Corning Glass and Texas Instruments experiments. At the Corning Glass factory in Medfield, Massachusetts, they introduced autonomous work groups in their electric hotplate assembly department. Groups of six workers assembled an entire electric hotplate and had the freedom to schedule work any way they chose. Abseenteeism dropped from 8 per cent to 1 per cent, rejects dropped from 23 per cent to 1 per cent, and expressed job satisfaction increased. A similar experiment was carried out among 120 maintenance workers in the Dallas plant of Texas Instruments. The maintenance workers were organised into nineteen member cleaning teams, with each member having a say in planning problem solving, goal setting and scheduling. It was found that turnover dropped from 100 per cent to 10 per cent and cost savings were $103,000 in two years between 1967 and 1969.

There are also some examples of quality of working life experiments outside an industrial context in the United States – for instance, in government departments. An example of this was a programme carried out by the Operations Division of the Ohio Department of Highways. It established three experimental construction crews with differing degrees of self-determination of work schedules and division of labour, and compared them to three crews who maintained the traditional assignments of duties and work schedules. It was found (Powell and Schacter, 1975) that as participation increased, so did morale and job satisfaction (but not productivity).

Japan

A recent report by the International Labour Office entitled "Improvements in the Quality of Working Life in Three Japanese Industries" provides us with detailed explanations of why Japan is successful in three of its most important industries: electrical/electronic, automobile manufacturing and shipbuilding. The report was compiled by Japanese industrialists and trade-union leaders in each of these industries, who formed study groups to assess the reasons for their growth and how they overcame the problems that have plagued their counterparts in the West. Their observations of Japanese management and the trade unionists is particularly interesting for us in the United Kingdom, in two of the industries — namely, electrical/electronic and automobile manufacturing.

How successful have the Japanese been?
For fifteen years from 1955 to the beginning of the 1980s, Japan's GNP had increased approximately twenty-five times in *nominal* and over six times in *real* terms, the main growth being in manufacturing industries, with production increasing over eleven times in that period. If we look at the electrical machinery and appliance industries, we can see just how far ahead Japan is moving. In 1977, the annual sales figures per employee for three of the largest manufacturers of electrical machinery were as follows: Hitachi £42,390; General Electric £26,630; and for Siemens £20,382. In the electrical appliance industry: Matsushita £87,549; North American £33,137; Thorn EMI £12,798. In the manufacturing industry, the differences are even more dramatic. Comparing Toyota and Nissan in terms of annual sales per employee with the figures for Ford, General Motors, Benz and Fiat, they are staggering: Toyota £111,426; Nissan £92,289; Ford £46,087; General Motors £40,254; Benz £30,635; Fiat £18,413.

Why are they successful?
The International Labour Office report characterises the success of Japanese industry in the following global way:

> Among the most important (factors) are timely and continuous application of technological innovations, aggressive capital formation and investment policies, financial systems led by major banking institutions, thorough marketing research and product development, continuous refinement of production techniques, quality control and resource utilisation, careful cultivation of both domestic and foreign markets, effective and flexible management structure and decision making, and a highly trained, motivated and flexible labour force.

The report particularly emphasises their success in managing people, in taking into account the needs, skills and concerns of their employees. A key concept in this regard is *ikigai*, which is defined by the Japanese as a set of psychological needs among workers for a fulfilling, involving and self-actualising job.

After the Second World War the Japanese worker turned away from the individual acquisition of material goods and towards pursuing satisfaction of non-material needs such as recognition, participation in the decision-making processes and reward based on merit. This latter need was picked up by management and transformed into a system of encouraging and rewarding "willing, able, but hitherto less privileged individuals" in the work-force. In other words, the Japanese class system was vigorously attacked, "depriving the overprivileged of their unjustified advantages in job promotion and compensation".

Another major development was the "small group participatory" schemes are frequently used in the production process, such as autonomous work groups (a group of workers making a whole product themselves), job enlargement (extending the range of a job) and, most important of all, "quality circles" (i.e. voluntary groups of workers who assist engineers to improve the quality and standards of the products).

All these innovations are aided by a process of collective bargaining that is unheard of in the British enterprise-based unions. For example, in the electrical machinery industry, there is a single enterprise-based union for each company, with collective bargaining and labour agreements negotiated and carried out at a level of the individual company. The workers are members of the company's union, and not the trade's union. The enterprises's union can then affiliate to the industry's trade union, in this case Denki Roren, which do not get involved with the collective bargaining in a particular organisation but leave that task to the enterprise-based union and management.

There are an enormous number of quality of work life projects in process at the moment in Japan (Takezawa, 1974), and they are likely to increase in the future. In a recent Japanese Government survey of the 700 influential national leaders from the unions, industry and the institutions of higher education, it was concluded that wages and salaries would be less important in the 1980s than job satisfaction and working conditions – a factor that was particularly strongly supported by the trade-union officials.

WHAT HAVE WE LEARNED FROM THIS WORK?

After surveying briefly some examples of work humanisation and employee participation schemes in various countries, it is important to attempt to answer a number of more general questions raised by them. First, why were these programmes undertaken in the first place – that is, what did they hope to achieve? Second, how successful were they in achieving their objectives? Third, and finally, what are some of the problems raised by the implementation of such innovations in industry and how might they be improved in the future?

Reasons for implementation of QWL experiments

If we examine in detail most of the published work in this field (e.g. Davis and Cherns, 1975; Cooper and Mumford, 1979), we can begin to answer the first question we have set for ourselves about the objectives of quality of work life experiments – that is, what organisations hope they will achieve. A survey of the best-documented and most quantifiable of the available studies reveals that firms give a wide range of reasons for doing this kind of work: recruitment difficulties, high costs, poor quality, low productivity, demarcation disputes, high labour turnover, automation, introduction of new technology, etc. By far the two most common reasons given are low productivity and high absenteeism and labour turnover. These two together represent something of the order of 50 per cent of the overt stated reasons why organisations are undertaking these change programmes. The next category of expressed overt problems is comprised of industrial relations difficulties (e.g. poor worker-management communication) and lack of worker job satisfaction, which together represent roughly 25 per cent of the problems needing resolution. Of the remaining 25 per cent, the following are given as reasons for introducing change (in order of frequency of expression): experimentation of new work designs, poor quality, to encourage participation, unnecessarily high costs, inability to recruit, introduction of new equipment, productivity deals, etc.

It can also be seen that most of these innovations apply to manufacturing or assembly type operations with few white-collar, clerical or middle management programmes. This supports Taylor's (1975) survey of the 100 best documented international cases of work restructuring, in which he found that most of them were in assembly operations (33 per cent), semi-skilled machine tending (23 per cent) and process operating (21 per cent); while only 9 per cent of them were among white-collar workers, and maintenance tasks were a poor fifth at 3 per cent.

How successful are these quality of working life experiments?

There are several reasons why it is unwise of us to draw any firm conclusions, capable of generalisation, about the efficacy of the quality of working life and participation projects that are available to date. First, it may be the case that we are hearing about only the successful interventions, while the ones that are less successful or of marginal benefit are buried under piles of reports or forgotten altogether. Second, that not enough reported work has objective criteria measures by which we can confidently judge it. Third, not enough of the work in this area is comparative – that is, where one approach, such as absenteeism reduction, is compared to another or two other possible approaches.

Nevertheless, given these *caveats* there still is convincing evidence that many of the participative and work humanisation projects (which meet some of the criteria discussed above) have had positive individual and organisational consequences. The empirical work associated with these types of experiments was summarised by French and Caplan (1973). They found that the more participative and involving a particular work-place, the lower the psychological strain (e.g. higher job satisfaction); the lower the role ambiguity; the higher the individuals utilised their potential skills; the better the working relations with boss, subordinates and colleagues; the more positive are employees' attitudes towards work; and the higher production is with the accompanying decline in absenteeism and labour turnover.

Problems associated with work humanisation

In spite of the fact that we have reason to believe that quality of work life experiments have many beneficial outcomes, there are a number of problems associated with their implementation. The following are only the tip of the proverbial iceberg of potential problem areas:

(*a*) Difficulties associated with the consequent changing roles of management and workers occasioned by these interventions.

(*b*) Problems of designing and re-creating training programmes to meet the specific needs of the different varieties of work humanisation projects.

(*c*) Coping with the fears of first-line supervisors.

(*d*) Dealing with the resistance of the unions which may feel threatened that some of these approaches may affect the number of jobs and manning levels.

(*e*) Increasing costs during the initial phase of these interventions.

(*f*) Organisations may have to pay more for workers taking increased responsibility.

What we must keep in mind in introducing job/work redesign are four guidelines (French and Caplan, 1973):

(*a*) The participation or change programme should not be *illusory* – that is, it should not be used as a manipulation tool (for example, when management asks employees for advice and then ignores it).

(*b*) The decisions on which participation are based *should not be trivial* to the people concerned (e.g. management asking workers to decide on the colour of the paper to be used for the company's newsletter).

(*c*) Those aspects of the work environment on which participation are based should be *relevant* to the needs of the workers.

(*d*) The decisions in which people participate should be perceived as being *legitimately* theirs to make.

QUESTIONS

1. What is the difference between distant and immediate participation?

2. In your view, which countries have carried out the most effective quality of work life experiments?

3. How successful have the Japanese been in the quality of work life field?

4. What have we learned from all the quality of work life experiments?

PART FOUR

Learning, Development and Behaviour Change in Organisations

CHAPTER ELEVEN

Human Learning, Memory and Skilled Performance

OBJECTIVES

This section of the book is concerned with the process of individual change, development and growth, particularly within organisational settings. Some of the central and most important issues relate to the nature of human learning and the models and conceptual frameworks that can be used to provide fundamental insights into how and what people learn. This chapter briefly outlines three major approaches to human learning: behaviourist, cognitive and humanistic. The cognitive approach is then explored in some detail, while the other two approaches are dealt with in Chapters 13 and 14. The processes of attention and perception are considered first. An explanation of the structure of human memory systems into immediate, short and long term and of the factors involved in storage is then presented, followed by a consideration of how and why we forget learned material. The chapter concludes with an examination of the psychological factors underlying skilled performance and argues that these factors are the same whatever the learned human ability – be it that of a successful salesman, cricketer or computer programmer.

THE DIFFERENT APPROACHES TO THE STUDY OF LEARNING

The study of learning has been one of the central concerns of psychology since the nineteenth century. This justifiably reflects the enormous importance that learning has in human development and society. All of the great achievements of the human race (and the great disasters) could not have occurred if we did not possess an ability to learn from experience which, as far as we know, surpasses that of all other species. Like many other fields of psychological enquiry, learning has not been studied from one perspective only. Different methods and techniques have been adopted and different theoretical frameworks have been used to attempt to explain the phenomena involved. Three major approaches can be identified: *behaviourist*, *cognitive* and *humanistic*.

Early researchers into learning tackled the problem directly and attempted to use introspection (asking people to monitor and describe their own thought processes). Introspection has the advantage of simplicity and directness, but it is fairly obvious that the reports and findings based on this method of enquiry can be affected by selective perception, faulty recall and many other unwanted and difficult-to-control factors. Although it is not possible to observe mental processes directly, it is possible to observe behaviour and to focus attention on the stimuli and responses involved in the learning process. The behaviouristic approach stresses that learning or any other psychological process can be studied scientifically only by concentrating on factors that can be observed directly. In the view of the extreme behaviourists, internal mental processes, thinking, emotions, etc., that cannot be directly observed are not legitimate areas for scientific study and are treated as a black box which is not worth attempting to examine.

By contrast, the cognitive approach rejects the behaviouristic notions and does attempt to study internal mental processes, but with the aid of more elaborate and sophisticated experimental methods than those of early introspectionists. Cognitive means pertaining to mental and intellectual processes – to "cognise" means to "know", and cognitive research is principally concerned with studying the mental processes involved when people obtain and develop knowledge and skill.

Although the behaviourist and cognitive approaches to learning have different perspectives and focus on different aspects of learning, they do share some common ground in that they rely on the use of controlled experiments and the systematic, often very detailed, examination of specific elements involved in learning.

Humanistic psychology takes a very different position. Often referred to as the "third force" in psychology (Behaviourism and Psychoanalysis being the other two), humanistic psychology advocates a more individualistic and personal approach to learning (e.g. Rogers, 1951). It stresses the uniqueness of each human being and the importance that factors such as emotion and self-concept have in the process of learning and development. Although it has a great deal to say about the development of the whole person and the conditions under which learning can be successful, humanistic psychology does not present any clear and specific views about the actual processes involved in learning. Because of this and because humanistic views of learning are so closely interwoven with views of the development of the whole personality, the work of the humanistic psychologists and its implications as relating to behaviour in organisations are considered in Chapter 14 rather than here.

A definition of learning

Regardless of their perspective, most psychologists would accept a definition of learning in these terms: a relatively permanent change in the potential to behave, gained as a result of experience. It is worth examining some of the elements of that definition in more detail. First, the change is *relatively* permanent. The implication here is that although learning may occur and enable someone to solve new problems, recall historical facts, telephone numbers and so on, it is also possible that forgetting might take place and that the facts or methods for problem solution can no longer be recalled. Some learning is much more resistant to decay than others. Most of us, for example, learned to ride a bike when we were quite young, and even though we may not have practised the skill for some time, we could still do so. The above definition of learning refers also to the *potential* to behave. It is important here to distinguish between learning and performance or behaviour. We cannot observe learning directly, we can only observe the behaviour that someone is capable of and infer, from that behaviour, that they have learned. Let us say that a student preparing for an examination has revised very thoroughly and knows the subject concerned very well, but because of the stress and nervous tension he experiences when he actually takes the examination, his performance in it is extremely poor. In an instance such as this, learning had taken place, since the student understood the material and *had* the potential to perform well, but because of the debilitating effects of anxiety did not do so. Thus, although a person's behaviour provides, in general, a good indication of the learning that has taken place, the influence of factors such as anxiety or a lack of motivation can mean that learning is not always reflected accurately in behaviour.

Behaviourism
The explanation of learning provided by the behaviourists is considered in detail in Chapter 13, along with an examination of the use of behaviourist principles to modify organisational behaviour. It is important to remember, when considering any work on the subject, that learning is not reserved only for experiences that take place in formal educational or occupational settings. Learning takes place constantly and what we learn and how we learn it have a profound and deep connection with many other aspects of our psychology. In that sense, learning cannot be considered as a separate and isolated phenomenon, and although much of the work of behaviourists is centred on conditioning and learning, their principles and ideas represent a view of the whole of human psychology with conditioning and learning being the main factors involved (other than maturation) in the development of *all* aspects of human behaviour.

Behaviourists suggest that learning is a somewhat arbitrary process in which various responses are tried out on a trial-and-error basis. The ones that are reinforced (rewards) are strengthened and others become less likely to occur again. This may fit our understanding of how a rat learns the correct response in an experiment, but can such an approach really be used to explain more complex forms of learning and to explain all types of learning in all situations? Opponents of the behaviourist view consider that behaviourist ideas cannot be used to explain all forms of learning. One of the major early pieces of evidence against the behaviourist approach was collected by the German psychologist Wolfgang Köhler. In some famous experiments Köhler placed chimpanzees in an enclosed play area with food out of their reach but with various potential tools such as poles or boxes within it. The chimps rapidly learned how to use the "tools" to stand on or to rake the food towards them. At times, they even "pole-vaulted" with the poles! The important point, however, is not that they used the tools but the manner in which their learning appeared to take place. Learning did not appear to develop as a result of trial and error and reinforcement, but occurred in sudden flashes of "insight". A chimp would pace around the enclosure for some time and then, quite suddenly, grab a stick, stand on a box and knock down a banana dangling out of normal reach above the enclosure. In other words, the learning did not occur when a more or less arbitrary response was eventually reinforced after a series of trials and errors. The chimp did not need trial and error. Through sudden insight it knew what to do. An even more important aspect of Köhler's work derived from his placing the chimps in novel situations. It was then that they showed that their earlier learning could transfer and help them to solve new problems very quickly, without their having slowly to build up new stimulus, response, reinforcement chains.

The most fundamental difference between Köhler and the behaviourist position was Köhler's belief that learning represents a change in what the learner *knows* rather than what *he* does. The emphasis on knowledge and internal mental processes led to Köhler and other like-minded earlier researchers such as Tolman (1948) being described as cognitive theorists.

Cognitive theory
Contemporary cognitive theory is less concerned than was Köhler with attacking behaviourism, but more interested in developing its own theories and methods of enquiry. Modern cognitive theorists have not developed a unified theory of learning and information processing, but they do share a common approach which emphasises the importance of internal psychological processes. The remainder of this chapter explores the processes of learning, memory and skilled performance from a cognitive perspective.

The essence of the cognitive approach involves an attempt to get to grips with the internal psychological processes that take place during learning. A helpful starting-point for this endeavour is to consider the way in which people process, store and recall information in an attempt to envisage the psychological processes that intervene between inputs (or stimuli) which impinge on the sense organs and the outputs (or behaviour) of a person. Fig. 33 shows a six-stage process. The behaviourist approach to learning (as Chapter 14 shows) concentrates on the stimulus, response and

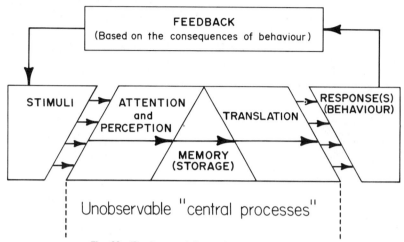

Fig. 33. *The human information processing system.*

feedback (or reinforcement) stages of this processing system. The centre of attention for cognitive approaches to learning are the unobservable *central processes* involved in attention, storage and translation. Clearly it is not possible to make direct observation of the information processing and thinking that takes place, as it occurs. However, it is possible, by careful experimental techniques, to draw some inferences about how the processing involved takes place. Some experiments to illustrate how this can be done will be discussed at appropriate points below. A close examination of how feedback can be used to improve learning is reserved for Chapter 12. Meanwhile some characteristics of the central processes involved in learning will be examined.

ATTENTION

In many ways attention is the most important phase in the learning process. If we do not allocate attention to something we cannot possibly learn about it. One of the most important features of human attention is that attending (or perceiving) is not simply a mechanistic process whereby the external world is reproduced exactly in our mind; on the contrary, a variety of psychological factors organise, interpret and to some extent distort incoming information. Visual illusions can provide striking examples of the subjective and interpretive nature of perception (*see* Fig. 34). Most illusions occur because organising principles that normally help us to interpret our experiences are misleading or confusing in some situations. Although illusions provide dramatic examples of the role

Fig. 34. *An ambiguous figure that can be seen as either a vase or as two faces.*

of subjective and personal organising principles at work, it is important to remember that such principles are continually influencing our experience of the outside world. We do not experience an exact replica of the outside world, but each of us reconstructs or "creates" his or her own personal version of it.

As well as being subjective, our attending and perceiving processes are also selective. We do not attend to everything that is going on around us but select (consciously and unconsciously) the things that we will notice. William James (1890) provided a vivid description of the selective allocation of attention: "Millions of items of the outward order are presented to my senses which never properly enter my experience. Why? Because they have no interest for me. My experience is what I agree to attend to. Only those items which I notice shape my mind – without selective interest experience is an utter chaos."

Broadbent (1958) proposed a theory of attention which suggested that human information processing is basically a single-channel system. Put simply the theory suggests that we can concentrate on only one thing at a time and that information on the unattended channel is filtered or "blocked out". This theory was consistent with early experimental evidence. However, an important experiment by Cherry (1953) demonstrated that the "non-attended" messages are not completely blocked. In that experiment people were presented with two different streams of information. By using headphones one stream can be presented to each ear and the subject can be told to *shadow* (i.e. repeat aloud) the messages coming to one ear. Messages to the other ear, according to the original theory, would then be blocked completely. The experimental results showed, however, that if highly relevant or meaningful information (e.g. the subject's name) was presented on the "non-attended" channel, subjects did notice it. This research amounts to an experimental demonstration of the "cocktail party syndrome". This occurs when we are (supposedly) completely involved in a conversation at a party, yet when our name is mentioned in another conversation within earshot we notice it. Other aspects of everyday experience also suggest that we are capable of concentrating on two things at once (driving a car and talking, for example).

Experimental demonstrations of people shadowing speech and playing the piano simultaneously (Allport *et al.*, 1972) or shadowing speech and typing meaningful material (Shaffer, 1975), support this view. Some authors (e.g. Allport *et al.*, 1971) propose that evidence of this sort demonstrates that human information processing is best represented as a multi-channel system which, under certain conditions, processes streams of inputs in parallel. Others (e.g. Ostry *et al.*, 1976) take a view that is more similar to Broadbent's original model, whereby only one channel operates at once and attention is switched very rapidly from one stream of information to another. Regardless of which view is the most appropriate, it seems clear that available processing capacity is limited and that the allocation of attention involves distributing available capacity across the tasks at hand. At any given time some tasks may be allocated the vast majority of available capacity and others very little or none at all. This capacity is used not only to process inputs (stimuli) but for central processing (e.g for recalling material from memory), for outputs (e.g. co-ordinating the movements involved in a manual task), or for processing feedback about the consequences of action. Learning takes place when material to which attention has been allocated is stored or memorised for a period of time.

STORAGE/MEMORY

The available evidence suggests that we have three kinds of memory: immediate memory, short-term memory (STM) and long-term memory (LTM).

Immediate and short-term memory

Short-term memory (STM) has a rapid decay, limited capacity storage system that is capable of holding only a small amount of information for a few seconds or so. To keep information in STM for any length of time it is necessary to pay attention to it continually, perhaps by rehearsal (repeating it over and over again). In a sense STM is the "working memory" and items of information move into and out of it depending on the direction of attention and the current task(s) at hand. STM is operating when, for example, someone takes an order for a round of drinks and has to try to remember the order until he comes to repeat it at the bar. Once given, the order can be displaced by new material entering STM.

The storage capacity of human STM is limited to about seven items (Miller, 1956) – an item being a single "chunk" of information. Thus we can remember seven names more or less as easily as seven random letters of the alphabet, although there will be many more letters in the names. Try, for example, to remember the words listed below. Look at them now, before reading any further.

knew	each
man	young
the	the
and	boy
well	other
extremely	old

It is a difficult task, but if the words are rearranged to make a sentence – *The young boy and the old man knew each other extremely well* – the task becomes quite simple! By "chunking" the words together the load on memory is reduced considerably.

As noted earlier, although psychological processes cannot be studied directly it is possible to carry out experiments that enable us to draw inferences about various aspects of human psychology. Much of the research on memory is carried out on this basis and some experiments by Sperling (1960) provide a good illustration of how it is possible to draw inferences about internal psychological states without being able to study them directly. In his experiments Sperling showed his subjects three rows of four letters for very brief periods. Most people would not be able to recall all of the letters displayed – seven (i.e. the capacity of STM) would be an average score. Sperling required his subjects to recall specific rows from the display of letters, but they were not told in advance which row they had to recall. A split second after the display was terminated a musical tone sounded to indicate which row the subjects should report. The results of Sperling's research showed that as long as the tone sounded within half a second or so of the end of the display, the subjects' recall was excellent. Recall as good as this showed clearly that for half a second or so all of the items must have been available for potential recall, indicating the existence of an immediate memory (half a second or so) with a larger span than STM.

Long-term memory
We do not normally say that something has been learned until the material can be recalled reliably after a period of, say, a day or a week. When this happens the information has been recalled from long-term memory (LTM). This means that at some stage in the learning process material must be transferred from STM to our long-term store.

It is often suggested that the limited capacity of STM is one of the greatest barriers to effective transfer to LTM since this represents a "bottle-neck" in the information processing system corresponding to the limitations in our capacity to attend to several things at once, discussed earlier. It is clear then that by the time information becomes available for transfer to LTM it is likely that a great deal of other information which could have been processed has, in fact, been lost. An implication of this is evidenced by the fact that, even when people are presented with identical material, the learning which takes place is likely to be different for each person involved. Individual differences in ability to process material, and preferences and prejudices about which aspects of the material are most important, lead to quite different learning. In contrast to immediate memory and STM, the capacity of LTM is extremely large.

Forgetting in LTM is also much slower than STM, and items of information can sometimes be recalled after many years.

Relatively little is known in detail about information transfer into long-term storage systems, but it is clear that for learning to take place effectively some very long-term storage systems must operate effectively. From the point of view of learning, two particular aspects related to the operation of long-term storage are worth examining. These are organisation and elaboration.

Organisation

The idea of organising or chunking information to aid STM has already been mentioned. Mandler (1966) has demonstrated the importance of organisation for learning and long-term storage. He examined how well people were able to recall a set of words. One group of people were asked to study the words in preparation for a subsequent test of recall. Another group were asked to sort the words into categories – using categories of their own choice; they were not told that they would be asked to recall the information later. In a subsequent test of recall both groups recalled about the same amount of information. Mandler and Pearlstone (1966) also showed that words arranged according to a classification system devised by the learner were more readily recalled than words arranged in a predetermined sequence that the learner had to comprehend and follow. These results suggest that the very act of organising material is in itself an aid to learning, and that learning might be particularly efficient if the learner is involved in developing the system of organisation that is used. This principle is used in many teaching situations; for example, when a group is divided into syndicates, asked to discuss course material and present a summary of their views. Involving the learner in developing the category system is not, however, crucial for successful learning. Bower et al. (1969), for example, have shown that learners can be helped to recall more efficiently when provided with material organised systematically.

When new material is learnt it is not transferred to an empty memory system. There will already be an enormous amount of existing stored material and the new learning must be integrated with the learner's existing store. Often this takes place more or less unwittingly. Bousfield (1953), for example, has shown that if learners are presented with a mixed-up list of words, those in the same category are recalled together, indicating that the words have been systematically rearranged and organised on the basis of existing category systems. For effective learning to take place, information must be coded and categorised in a way that will both aid transfer to long-term storage and assist in subsequent recall.

Elaboration

In a series of classic studies in the 1920s and 1930s Bartlett (1932) demonstrated that when material is retrieved from long-term storage a considerable amount of reconstruction and elaboration takes place and that stored information is only rarely recalled accurately. In Bartlett's studies it became clear that people remembered in a very selective way. Certain aspects of information that were difficult for people to integrate into their existing storage systems were omitted altogether, while other more familiar aspects were enhanced or "sharpened" and given much greater prominence. Bartlett emphasised the organisation that people imposed on information as they tried to recall or reconstruct it. Often recall was dependent to a large extent on how well the information matched the existing information held by the learner rather than on what he had actually seen or heard. One of the most striking aspects of this work was the fact that people were often unaware of their inventions or inaccuracies. A demonstration of this is provided in an experiment conducted by Sulin and Dooling (1974). Two groups of people were presented with a short passage describing some aspects of the life of a girl. The only difference between the groups was that group 1 was told that the girl's name was Carol Harris, while group 2 was told that she was Helen Keller. One week later the groups were asked whether the passage had included the statement that the girl was deaf, dumb and blind. Only 5 per cent of group 1 said yes, in contrast to 50 per cent of group 2. In fact this information was not included in the original passage – but presumably most people in group 2 knew that Helen Keller was actually deaf, dumb and blind and convinced themselves that they had been told as much.

This tendency, which we display to amend material so that it fits our preconceptions can clearly lead to considerable inaccuracies in recall. Nevertheless, it is an important and in some ways helpful aspect of our memory systems. An experiment by Owens *et al.* (1979) illustrates this. They presented two groups with a story of a female patient, Nancy, who consults a medical practitioner. One group – the "theme" group – was led to believe that Nancy might be pregnant. The "neutral" group was not given this information. In all other respects the groups were given the same story. When the groups were tested for recall it was found that, as might be expected, the theme group reported more items than the neutral group that *had not been* in the original story but that they had inferred or "invented". Surprisingly, however, the theme group also recalled, accurately, more items that *had been* in the original story than did the neutral group. This suggests that when people are presented with a theme or framework that can be used to interpret new material they will both learn more effectively *and* concoct more false elaborations.

Forgetting

From a practical point of view, one of the unfortunate features of human memory is that it is not perfect – we forget! Systematic research into forgetting has provided various theories of how and why it takes place. The theory that fits with most people's intuitive ideas of what causes forgetting is *decay theory* (e.g. Brown, 1958). There are various different decay theories but the common view shared by all of them is that memory traces are laid down when we allocate attention to perceptual events. With the passage of time the trace, and hence our memory of the perceptual event, decays.

Although decay theories have a certain common-sense appeal, the evidence supporting them is not great. An alternative to decay theory, which is supported by considerable experimental evidence, is *interference theory*. Interference theory suggests that recall is imperfect because things that we have learned both before and after a specific event will interfere with our recall of that event. An early demonstration of the possible importance of interference was provided in a famous experiment by Jenkins and Dallenbach (1924), who investigated the effect that different types of intervening activity had on people's ability to recall learned material. They found that when a period of sleep intervened between learning and recall, recall was much better than when a period of activity intervened. Their results suggest that forgetting is not a function of the passage of time alone, but that the nature of intervening activity influences recall. Presumably, the relative inactivity of sleep provides less interference than a period of wakefulness when other more recent perceptual and learning experiences can inhibit memory and recall. Interestingly, there is some evidence to suggest that more forgetting occurs when one is dreaming (a period of time when the brain is relatively active) than during non-dreaming sleep (Ekstrand, 1972).

The interference that affects memory and recall can take two main forms: retroactive and proactive. Retroactive interference is produced by material that has been learned after the acquisition of the target material, as demonstrated in the sleep experience mentioned above. Proactive interference takes place when material learned before the target material interferes with recall. Many studies have demonstrated interference effects (*see* e.g. Underwood, 1957). A typical experiment to demonstrate it would take the following form:

(*a*) Two groups learn the same material.

(*b*) One group (experimental) learns a second set of material. The other group (control) spends the same amount of time doing an unrelated second task.

(*c*) Both groups are tested for recall.

Retroactive interference is demonstrated if the experimental group recalls less of the first set of material than the control group.

It seems possible that both decay and interference have some influence on recall although, on the basis of the available evidence, interference effects seem more important. Other phenomena such as repression (a psychological block or unwillingness to recall traumatic or unpleasant events) and consolidation (the need for a period free from very traumatic or exciting events, immediately after learning when memories are first laid down) also seem to play a part in forgetting.

Improving learning and memory

Various techniques and principles can be used to aid the learning and memorising processes. These include the controlled and systematic use of feedback to the learner, the use of specific procedures to aid organisation in memory and strategies for influencing motivation. Because of their importance within the practical training context, these and other aids to learning are discussed in Chapter 12.

TRANSLATION: CONTROLLING AND GUIDING BEHAVIOUR

As we have seen, material stored in the memory does not consist of isolated bits of information. It is organised and there are complex interconnections with and associations between material that is stored. Furthermore, it is not merely facts or beliefs that are held in storage but often quite complex processing systems, rules and strategies that can be used to guide thinking and behaviour. These frameworks are referred to by various different names such as *plans* (Miller *et al.*, 1960) *schemata* (the Greek plural of *schema*) (Bartlett, 1932; Neisser, 1976) or *scripts* (Schrank and Abelson, 1977). They represent large, often complex bodies of knowledge that control the way we think and act. For example, as we develop the ability to play a game such as chess the complexity and level of organisation of our processing systems develop. The experienced chess player who has a wide repertoire of existing, well-organised strategies for playing chess can rapidly assimilate the positions of the pieces on a board, interpret them in terms of his existing knowledge of the game and rapidly recall stored information about possible moves or strategies (e.g. a king-side attack). As de Groot (1965) has shown, for a novice or less expert player the situation is quite different. Each new item of information is difficult to deal with and cannot be related quickly and easily to existing, stored material, and no special purpose-learned systems are available for use. This often results, during the early stages of learning, in confusion and a simple lack of ability to process and respond to incoming information. As learning develops, storage systems become increasingly more organised and elaborate, learned special-purpose systems develop and responses become increasingly rapid and appropriate. This is true whether the learning is about how to play chess, drive a car, interview a candidate for promotion or sell computers.

The distinctions between a cognitive skill such as selling a computer, speaking a foreign language or playing chess, and a psychomotor skill such as typing, operating machinery or driving a car are still unclear, but many theorists believe that there are great similarities involved in the way they are learnt. Fitts and Posner (1967) suggested a general set of stages through which skill learning progresses, and many psychologists (e.g. Anderson, 1980) accept that any sort of skill is learnt by progression through these same stages. The stages involved are: *cognitive*, *associative* and *autonomous*. In the cognitive stage we learn knowledge and attempt to conceptualise and understand the task confronting us (e.g. memorise the position of the gears); in the associative stage we begin to co-ordinate the various elements involved in performance with each other; and in the autonomous stage the procedure becomes more and more automated and rapid.

Learning, organisation and processing systems

In a series of classic experiments Bryan and Harter (1899) showed how learning involves the development of processing systems that are capable of dealing with increasingly difficult tasks. They studied telegraph operators learning Morse code and showed that learning took place in stages. The learning curve (*see* Fig. 35) has a number of flat *plateaux*, followed and preceded by rapid increases. This occurs as the learners become capable of dealing with more and more complex units. At first, for example, single letters are analysed, then syllables, words, and so on. As each level is mastered (e.g. syllables), learning can improve rapidly until another plateau is reached. This same effect can be observed in many examples. An experienced driver will go through the various stages involved in starting a car and moving away smoothly and without error. To her the unit involved is "start up and move". A learner will be attempting to deal with each unit in isolation (insert keys, check gears, switch on . . .). The processing systems are not well organised or capable of controlling large units of behaviour.

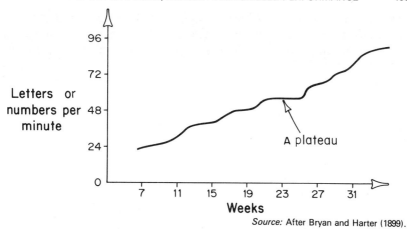

Source: After Bryan and Harter (1899).

Fig. 35. *A typical apprentice telegrapher's learning curve.*

Most theorists consider it is useful to think of processing systems as being organised into some sort of hierarchy. At the lowest level there are systems concerned with fundamental activities such as walking, breathing, standing. At the next level there are fairly specific systems, most of which result from learning and are capable of recognising and using specific sorts of information for controlling behaviour, e.g. playing chess, solving a mathematics problem or translating from one language to another. At the highest level is what Legge and Barber (1976) describe as a "super-channel". The super-channel is extremely adaptive and flexible. "It is in this channel that problem-solving is accommodated – at least when it is accomplished at the level of conscious awareness. The special purpose channels below are limited in the situations that they can deal with, though extremely efficient in handling problems within their competence" (Legge and Barber, 1976, p. 131). Thus, when novel and apparently unfamiliar information arrives the highest level, general purpose systems will attempt to deal with it. It may become clear that the input is not, in fact, novel or unfamiliar and that it is the sort of input that has been dealt with many times before. If this is the case the appropriate intermediate level system will be called on to deal with it.

In very general terms the amount of attention (i.e. processing capacity) required by a process depends on how well learned and practised the process is. Thus novel, truly unfamiliar inputs that need to be dealt with by high-level, general purpose processing systems require a great deal of processing capacity, whereas some fundamental activities such as walking or breathing need very little processing capacity – in fact it is sometimes suggested that some "automatic" activities (e.g. walking or breathing) require no processing capacity at all. Many people, for example, can drive a car, eat and talk simultaneously. But what would happen if the steering were adjusted so that the wheels turned in the opposite direction? The "automatic" manoeuvres would not work and most people would not have the spare capacity available to talk and eat, all their attention being used up by the demands of an unfamiliar task.

Once learned skills have become more or less automatic (i.e. reach the autonomous stage) a striking side-effect can be produced, caused by the fact that once the relevant processing systems have been triggered and begun to operate they will continue automatically, regardless of the intentions of the person concerned! We read advertisements at the side of the road whether or not we intend to do so; the presence of words in our field of view is enough to trigger more or less automatic reading-processing systems. An experimental demonstration of this can be provided by the so-called Stroop effect (Stroop, 1935). To demonstrate it subjects are shown a list of groups of letters (not actual words) written in different colours. They are then asked to state the colour of each group of letters. This task is easy. If, however, the groups of letters used are words, specifically the names of colours, and if the words used are *not* the names of the colours in which they are printed (*see* Fig. 36), the task is far from simple. What happens here is an automatic response to read the word – but then this is not the same as the

LIST A	LIST B
APSTE	RED
LCNRL	BLUE
QBULN	BLACK
PBXCM	WHITE
TPRSC	BLUE
PRNOS	WHITE
KJHLY	YELLOW
XBPYS	BLUE
FGNSI	BLACK
VRGPO	RED
FDRCP	YELLOW
RLTSA	WHITE

A list of "nonsense words". Words are written in different colours (e.g. red, black, white, blue, yellow).

A list of colour names. Names are written in different colours but the names and colours in which they are written do not correspond.

Fig. 36. *The Stroop effect. The task is to read down list A and list B and call out the colours in which the words are written. A is easy, B is very difficult.*

colour in which it is printed. The result is considerable confusion and difficulty.

A HIERARCHY OF LEARNING

This chapter began by comparing the cognitive and behaviourist approaches to the learning process. These approaches are different in many ways. In particular they have adopted different units, levels and methods of analysis and have focused on different phenomena. In many ways they are quite incompatible and there is a basic and underlying disagreement about whether internal psychological processes should be investigated and studied or not. In other ways the two approaches, although never entirely compatible, may be used in conjunction with each other to provide some understanding of how learning and change might occur. As Chapters 12 and 13 show, both approaches can be of some value for understanding and changing organisational behaviour.

Gagné (1977) has developed a view of learning that incorporates a hierarchy of intellectual skills (*see* Table XIII). (Gagné's views are described in more detail in the next chapter.) At the bottom of this hierarchy is the type of learning based on simple stimulus response connections. At the top, complex problem-solving skills involving the use and generation of rules. In very general terms it seems that the behaviourist research findings and underlying principles are most useful when we are dealing with learning at the lower levels of Gagné's hierarchy. Learning of the sort described by the upper levels of the hierarchy seems to be more readily explored and understood with the aid of cognitive ideas. This viewpoint represents a considerable over-simplification of the complexity of human learning, but it does at least offer support for the opinion that, whilst neither behaviourism nor cognitive theory offers an entirely appropriate view that is useful in all circumstances, they are not entirely inappropriate and useless either!

Individual differences in learning

The chapter has provided an overview of some of the characteristics of human learning that are common to everyone. It is important to remember that despite these common factors there are also important individual differences in the way people learn. These differences are related to factors such as personality, motivation and cognitive style and relevant material is presented in other chapters in this book. Entwistle (1981) also provides an extensive review of individual differences in learning strategy and style.

TABLE XIII. A HIERARCHY OF LEARNING

Type of learning	Example	
BASIC LEARNING	Stimulus-response associations and chains	
INTELLECTUAL SKILLS		
Discriminations	Being able to make distinctions between stimulus objects or events	Discriminations between the French sounds of "u" and "ou"
Concrete concepts	Classification by observation, e.g. red circular	Names the root, leaf and stem of representative plants
Defined concepts	Classification by definition, e.g. mass, square roots	Defines the concept of "family"
Rules	Use of relation or association to govern action	Demonstrates the use of rules to solve problems involving positive and negative numbers
Higher order rules (Problem-solving)	Generation of new rules, e.g. by combining existing rules	Generates by synthesising applicable rules a short written paragraph describing someone's reactions in a situation of fear

Source: Adapted from Gagné and Briggs (1974) and Gagné (1977).

QUESTIONS

1. What are the main features of the cognitive approach to human learning, memory and skill, and how does it differ from behaviourist and humanistic approaches?

2. What psychological factors influence perception and memory?

3. Why do people forget?

4. How can ideas such as strategies or processing systems be used to describe the psychological processes underlying skilled performance?

CHAPTER TWELVE

Training and Development in Organisations

OBJECTIVES

This chapter is concerned with the processes and activities of planned training and development that occur in organisations. An outline of the training process is presented and the following major stages are identified: assessment of need; the analysis of tasks and specification of aims and objectives; the selection and management of methods and conditions for successful learning; and finally, the validation and evaluation of training/development programmes. Each stage is discussed with reference to relevant research, theory and practice, with the intention of providing a coherent and practical overview.

THE TRAINING PROCESS

People in organisations develop and change as time passes. Some of this development occurs in a rather unsystematic fashion and takes place as people learn from each other and learn how to integrate themselves into the organisation. Other development and change take place, in a more controlled and planned fashion, when programmes of planned training and development are organised in attempts to improve the knowledge and skills that people have. In most modern organisations such programmes represent an important component in their success and have significant cost/benefit implications. Fig. 37 represents an outline of the major elements involved in the training and development process, and during the remainder of this chapter each of the elements will be described in some detail.

As Fig. 37 shows, the training and development process moves from an assessment of need through the development of programmes to validation and evaluation of what has taken place. It is important to recognise that, although Fig. 37 presents the elements involved in an orderly sequence, in practice there are many links and interactions between these elements, and often parts of various elements will be taking place in parallel or in a different order from the one shown.

Although this chapter covers the major factors involved in the training process itself, other chapters present material of considerable importance to the training process including, in particular, the psychological basis of learning, memory and skill (Chapter 11), job analysis and personnel selection (Chapters 6 and 7).

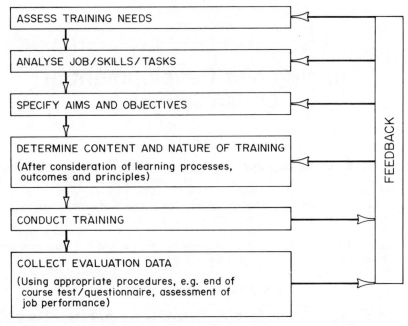

Fig. 37. *The training process.*

Assessing needs

Before setting in motion any systematic training or development within any organisation, those responsible should satisfy themselves that such activity is going to produce worthwhile results and is therefore necessary. On occasions, in some organisations, it is clear that programmes of training and development can take on a more or less independent "life of their own" and various activities will take place regardless of any clear and established need for them. Without adequate systems for staff training and development, an organisation cannot function effectively, but as Davies (1972) points out, both too little and too much training can cause problems. Davies notes that the penalties of too little training might include:

(*a*) unnecessary "on the job" learning;
(*b*) production shortfalls;
(*c*) errors and wastage;
(*d*) unsafe working practices; and
(*e*) dissatisfaction with the work itself.

On the other hand, too much training might result in:

(*a*) wasteful, excessively long courses;

(*b*) unnecessary instructors, equipment and accommodation;

(*c*) unnecessary failure of trainees; and

(*d*) job dissatisfaction resulting from "overtrained" employees not being able to use all their skills.

Thus a systematic assessment of training needs is a necessary first step in the development of any programme.

Boydell (1973) suggests that the assessment of training needs can be addressed at three different levels of analysis: *organisational*, *occupational* and *individual*.

At the organisational level, the first step in the assessment of need is to examine and identify the aims and objects of the organisation. These can often be identified in general terms by examining plans and statements of policy and by discussion with senior personnel in the organisation. Very broadly, organisational training needs exist when there is, or is likely to be, some sort of barrier hindering the achievement of organisational aims and objectives (either now or at some predicted future occasion). Symptoms might include output problems caused by bottle-necks in production, excessive errors or wastage, stress and related problems caused by lack of ability in some people or overload on other fully trained individuals. It is important to stress, however, that such problems represent training needs only if the barrier to the achievement of aims and objectives might be best removed by training rather than some other activity. Production problems, for example, might well be solved more effectively by redesigning the job or equipment, improving recruitment and selection procedures, or providing job aids.

Occupational analysis is concerned with the identification of the specific occupational areas within the organisation where training is needed to meet organisational needs. The particular skills, knowledge and attitudes that need to be developed are usually discovered with the aid of the techniques of job, skills and task analysis (*see below*). Individual analysis involves identifying which individual people should be trained.

Job, skills and task analyses

To bring about any form of training it is important to have a clear understanding of the target behaviour that is to be developed, and in most organisational settings this means a clear grasp of the main job components or activities that are involved. The closely related techniques of job analysis, skills analysis and task analysis have an important role here.

Job analysis

A great deal of job analysis is carried out in organisations in order to produce job descriptions. Such descriptions include information about the conditions of work, salary, physical surroundings, etc., but provide only a general description of the tasks involved in the job and of the skills required; as such they are of very limited value in a training context. Some of the methods for job analysis can be useful for training purposes – for example, the Position Analysis Questionnaire (PAQ) of McCormick *et al.* (*see* Chapter 6). However, even techniques such as the PAQ provide information that, although comprehensive, is often not detailed enough to allow for the construction of specific exercises and programmes of planned training.

Skills analysis
This term is usually reserved for procedures and methods of analysis similar to the technique described by Seymour (1966). Essentially such techniques call for detailed analysis of the skilled physical movements involved in manual operations, and although they are useful in some training situations, their range of application is limited.

Task analysis
This is probably the most important form of analysis for training purposes. The technique focuses on the objectives or outcomes of the tasks that people perform and provides an extremely flexible and useful method for analysis. The main unit of analysis is the *operation*. An operation is defined by Annett *et al.* (1971) as follows: "Any unit of behaviour, no matter how long or short its duration and no matter how simple or complex its structure which can be defined in terms of its objective."

One of the important features of the procedures developed by Annett *et al.* is that tasks are analysed and broken down into increasingly specific operations in a hierarchical fashion. Because of this approach to analysis the technique is known as Hierarchical Task Analysis (HTA). The starting point for HTA involves a general description of the main operation(s) involved in the job or job components being analysed. These operations are then divided into sub-operations and, in turn, the sub-operations themselves may be subdivided. Consider an example of a task that many of us have had to contend with, that of "knock-flat" furniture. Fig. 38 shows how this may be described in task analysis terms.

The analysis begins with a fairly high-level description of the main operation involved, i.e. assemble table, which is then subdivided into further operations at increasingly specific levels of analysis. It is important to remember that an operation is a very flexible unit, and at the beginning of the process the analyst will not

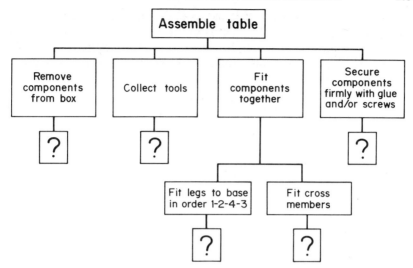

Fig. 38. *Part of a task analysis for the assembly of a "knock-flat" table.*

have any fixed ideas about how many operations are involved nor about the number of levels of analysis that will be needed. An analysis conducted in this way could continue to break down the operations involved until they are describing very tiny units of behaviour, and obviously at some point it is necessary to be able to decide that the analysis has reached a sufficiently specific level of detail. Two factors may be taken into account to help with this decision. The first of these is the probability that an untrained person would fail to carry out the operation successfully (P). The second is the cost to the system that would be incurred if the operation was carried out inadequately (C). Each operation in the analysis is examined with these two factors in mind in order to determine whether the operation needs to be divided further.

An operation needs to be analysed in more detail if the product of P × C is unacceptably high. The rationale for this is fairly straightforward. *If the probability of failure is high*, the operation will probably need to be described in more detail before the analysis can be used as a basis for developing training, unless the cost of failure is minimal. If *the cost of failure* (C) *for a particular operation is high*, more detail will be needed, unless the operation is easy for even an untrained person to perform. In other words, difficult operations with important cost consequences need to be analysed further until P × C becomes acceptably low. Additional information about the analytical techniques and recording procedures for HTA may be found in Annett *et al.* (1971), Duncan (1972) and Shepherd (1976), and a useful introduction to the technique is given in Stammers and Patrick (1975).

Much of the original work using HTA has been conducted on jobs that do not involve substantial executive or managerial activities. Some recent work, however, has demonstrated that HTA can be applied with some success to managerial positions (*see* Johnson, 1979).

Defining aims and objectives

Training and development activities are designed to bring about changes in people's behaviour and the success of such endeavours is determined by how effectively these changes are instituted. Developing a clear grasp of the operations involved in the relevant jobs by the use of techniques such as HTA is an essential step in the process. Before training begins, however, the results of such analyses need to be used in order to provide a clear statement of the outcomes or targets of training. As Mager (1962) puts it: "If you don't know where you're heading you'll probably end up someplace else."

A useful distinction can be made between the *aims* and the *objectives* of training. Aims involve general statements of intent: examples might be that a programme sets out to provide participants with "a grasp of the basic principles of management accountancy" or "an awareness of the relevance of industrial psychology to the management process". By contrast, objectives are much more specific and precise. In their most explicit form, objectives are sometimes expressed in the following, three-component form:

(*a*) The terminal behaviour. A statement of what the trainee should be able to *do* at the end of training. Because of this emphasis on terminal behaviour objectives expressed in this way are often referred to as *behavioural* objectives.

(*b*) The conditions under which the behaviour is to be exhibited.

(*c*) The standard performance of the behaviour.

This method of expressing objectives is derived from work carried out in the field of programmed instructions (*see* Chapter 13).

It is important to recognise that objectives specify what the person will be able to do *at the end* of training; they do not describe what will happen *during* training. The statement that participants will gain experience of various personnel selection interviewing techniques would not be acceptable as an objective. It says what will happen on the course but not what the outcomes will be.

In many practical training situations a full description of the expected outcomes of training is not provided in the form described above. Sometimes competence at the end of training is assessed by the use of various tests, or job simulation exercises. The behaviour that will produce satisfactory performance on these exercises represents the targets for the programme of training. Regardless of whether behavioural objectives or other methods are used to define these targets, it is important that the desired outcomes of training are clear at an early stage so that programmes can be designed to enable trainees to reach the targets. Of course, in some circumstances it is legitimate for the objectives of a programme to be relatively general and not expressed in the precise way described above. For example, many experimential learning exercises such as T-groups (*see* Chapter 14) are conducted within organisations and have quite general aims concerned with the psychological awareness and growth of participants. To attempt to express precise objectives for such experiences would be completely counter to their purpose, since the learning that takes place for each individual is of a highly personal and often emotional nature and each person acquires different things from such experiences.

Types of learning capability

The type of learning that takes place as a result of training and development programmes is quite varied and it is traditional to make distinctions between the development of knowledge, skills and attitudes. According to this distinction, knowledge is concerned with the recall and understanding of facts and other items of information. Skills are usually used with reference to the "psychomotor" movements involved in practical activities such as operating equipment or machinery. Attitudes refer primarily to the emotional or "affective" feelings and views that a person has, although attitudes also have other components (*see* Chapter 4). For example, a person might be able to operate a drilling-machine (skill) and might also be aware that certain safety procedures should be observed (knowledge) but feel that observing such procedures was time-wasting and unnecessary (attitude). This very simple distinction between knowledge, skills and attitudes is a useful starting-point for identifying different types of learning but is inadequate in many ways. For example, the distinction between knowledge and skill is not as clear as it might at first seem. At first sight the job of a car mechanic might seem to be largely skill-based and that of a medical practitioner largely knowledge-based. Consider what happens, however, when the car mechanic is confronted with a car that is making a peculiar noise. The mechanic will make use of various fault-finding strategies in an attempt to establish what is causing the noise. These strategies are based on the application of various rules for finding faults, probably developed from direct experience and training. In much the same way, the medical practitioner will attempt to diagnose the cause of a patient's symptoms. Both of them are exhibiting a form of skill, but the skill in question is not dependent on co-ordinated physical movements, though the mechanic may need these as well; rather, it is an intellectual skill involving the use of rules and analysis to guide behaviour.

The categories of different types of learning developed by Gagné (1977) (*see also* Chapter 11) provide a much more comprehensive description than the knowledge/skills/attitudes distinction. Gagné identifies the following five types of learning, which he calls *capabilities*.

(*a*) *Basic learning*. Stimulus-response associations and chains. This represents the formation of simple associations between stimuli and responses such as those that occur during classical conditioning (*see* Chapter 13).

(*b*) *Intellectual skills*. Divided into the following hierarchy:

(*i*) discriminations – being able to make distinctions between stimulus objects or events;

(*ii*) concrete concepts – classification of members of a class, by observation, e.g. red, circular;

(*iii*) defined concepts – classification by definition, e.g. mass, square roots;

(*iv*) rules – use of a relation or association to govern action; and

(*v*) higher order rules – generation of new rules, e.g. by combining existing rules.

(*c*) *Cognitive strategy*. Skills by which internal cognitive processes such as attention and learning are regulated (e.g. learning how to learn or learning general strategies for solving problems).

(*d*) *Verbal information*. Ability to state specific information.

(*e*) *Motor skills*. Organised motor acts.

(*f*) *Attitude*.

(The psychological processes involved in attention, memory, etc., that underlie the types of skills and strategies identified by Gagné are explored in some detail in Chapter 11. Attitudes are also dealt with in depth in Chapter 4.)

The benefit to be gained from identifying learning capabilities involved in a training programme is that it can often provide guidance on the methods or sequences of training that might be most useful. Consider the development of an intellectual skill, for example. Gagné argues that, like other skills, they are developed in a sequential fashion. Each type of skill (e.g. the ability to define a concept) is a prerequisite for the next level of skill (e.g. the use of rules). Thus, skills can be developed most effectively if training in each level is provided in the appropriate order. Fig. 39 gives a hierarchical analysis of the component parts involved in the skill of parking a car parallel to the kerb. Guidance about training methods

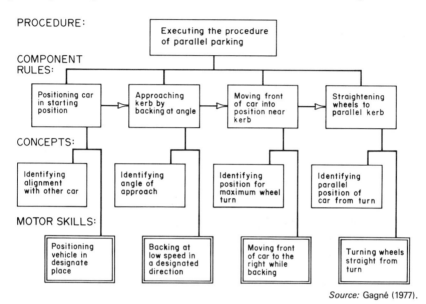

Source: Gagné (1977).

Fig. 39. *A hierarchical analysis of the rules, concepts and motor skills in the parallel parking procedure.*

and sequence can thus be arrived at by using the results of a task analysis to identify the learning outcomes that are desired and, after determining the type of learning capability involved, deciding on the sequence for instruction. Gagné (1962) has expressed it as follows: "The basic principles of training design consists of: (a) identifying the component tasks of a final performance; (b) insuring that each of the component tasks is fully achieved; and (c) arranging the total learning situation in a sequence which will insure optimal mediation effects from one component to another" (p. 88).

Another system for categorising types of learning has been developed by the Industrial Training Research Unit (ITRU). Its work has been designed specifically to provide guidance on the type of training method that is appropriate, for the type of learning involved. The learning types involved in the ITRU system can be summarised by the word CRAMP.

(*a*) *Comprehension.* Knowing why, how and when things happen.

(*b*) *Reflex skills*. Skilled physical movement and perceptual capacities.

(*c*) *Attitude*.

(*d*) *Memorisation*. Committing information to memory.

(*e*) *Procedural*. Following a procedure, e.g. operating a petrol-pump.

Once the type of learning has been identified, the CRAMP algorithm (*see* Fig. 40) can be used systematically to identify the training method(s) or the conditions for learning that might be appropriate.

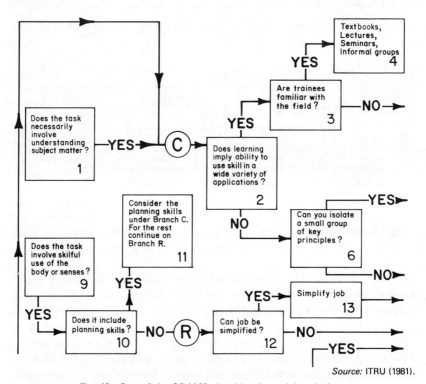

Source: ITRU (1981).

Fig. 40. *Part of the CRAMP algorithm for training design.*

Methods and conditions for training

One of the more frequent problems which arises with training programmes is that the method of instruction which is to be used is the first decision that is taken. It should be obvious from the previous pages that methods should be chosen or developed as a consequence of the desired targets of training and not the other way round. An enormous range of possible training methods is available. Campbell *et al.* (1970), for example, identify twenty-two different methods that are applicable to management training. The ITRU CRAMP booklet provides information on over thirty different training methods. Some illustrative methods are listed below.

Textbooks	Programmed instruction
Company training manuals	Lectures
Individual projects/case studies	Seminars
On-the-job coaching	Demonstration and practice
Seminars	Group projects/case studies
Closed circuit television	Films
Job rotation	Computer-aided instruction

To discuss training methods as if they were separate and clearly defined techniques is inappropriate, since even the most widely used and well-known methods such as lectures, case studies, demonstration and practice show wide variation in use depending on factors such as instructors and trainees involved and the task being learnt. Methods are adapted and combined in an almost infinite variety of ways. The use of closed circuit television (CCTV) as a training method provides a good illustration. CCTV is often used to provide trainees with feedback on their own behaviour so that, with the aid of a trainer, they can observe their own behaviour and assess their strength and weaknesses. Recently, however, a number of researchers using social learning theory (Bandura, 1977) as a basis have shown that such training might be carried out more effectively by using films or CCTV to present model behaviour that the trainees should attempt to emulate (Latham and Saari, 1979). Thus, although both approaches use CCTV as "the method", because of developments in underlying ideas about how learning takes place the two approaches are quite different. From the training and development viewpoint, understanding of the general process involved in learning and some grasp of the theoretical background (*see* Chapter 11) is likely to provide a much more useful framework than detailed examination of specific methods.

Conditions and principles of learning

The conditions for training concern both internal conditions relating to the trainees, such as the existence of previous learned capabilities and external conditions that might be controlled more directly by the trainer, for instance the spacing between periods of practice and the provision of feedback to trainees. Several factors related to the conditions of learning are often referred to in connection with the so-called "principles of learning". These

principles have emerged from the enormous amount of psychological research and theory devoted to the subject and are widely
accepted as factors that are of importance during learning. The
principles of learning relate to:

(a) *feedback or knowledge results*, which concerns the nature and
extent of information provided to trainees as a result of their
behaviour;

(b) *part or whole methods*, i.e. whether the task(s) or job should
be taught as a whole or in parts;

(c) *the distribution of practice*, which means the length of training
sessions and the gaps between them;

(d) *the transfer of learning*, i.e. the extent to which previous
training will benefit performance or learning in a different setting,
as for example when a different but related job is attempted; and

(e) *reinforcement*, which concerns the use of rewards/
punishment, etc., to "shape" learning.

The importance of these factors in training settings is clear and
accepted widely. However, although the "principles" indicated
certain factors to be considered, there are relatively few generalised
rules for training design that can be derived from research and
theory on these factors. Much of the relevant research is based on
situations far removed from those likely to be involved in real-life
training.

Feedback involves a flow of information back to the trainee.
Sometimes this feedback is *intrinsic* to the task itself and will be
present whenever the task is conducted. Other, *extrinsic*, feedback
can be used during training to provide the trainee with information
that is not normally available. One of the tasks of a trainer is to help
the trainee to focus on the aspects of intrinsic feedback that are
available (e.g. the "feel" from clutch and accelerator pedal as the
car pulls away, or the response that a client makes during a sales
meeting) and to make use of these so that performance gradually
becomes more self-directed and autonomous. For human learning a
particularly important form of feedback involves "knowledge of
results". A company director, for example, who received no
knowledge of the results of his sales policies, would find it
impossible to learn and improve policy-making, just as a tennis-
player who could not see where the ball went would not improve. It
is important when providing learners with feedback to give them
information that is useful. For example, the simple response "That
is wrong, try again" does not give the learner any clue about why it
was wrong or how much error was involved.

Some research, however, suggests that there is a limit to the amount of detail that should be included when providing feedback. An experiment by Rogers (1974), for example, used three increasingly precise conditions of feedback and found that learning was better when more precise feedback was given. However, the addition of a fourth, even more precise condition, did not necessarily improve matters, especially if trainees were not given extra time to process the new information. This suggests that there is a limit to the amount of detail which is useful when providing feedback. In general terms feedback during training should attempt to provide trainees with information appropriate to their level of learning. Feedback should concentrate on the aspects of the task that are important for overall success. One problem with the provision for extrinsic feedback is that the trainees can become dependent on it and, when it is removed, performance may deteriorate. This seems to be particularly true if the feedback is removed early on in learning.

The use of *part or whole methods* is made particularly difficult in practice by the problems involved in deciding what tasks represent parts and what represent wholes. It is clear, however, that the extent to which task elements are interdependent (highly interdependent tasks are best learned as a whole), complex and organised is important. Stammers and Patrick (1975) provide an algorithm that can be used to take decisions about part or whole training depending on these factors.

Bass and Vaughan (1966) point out that *distributed practice* appears to be of more consistent benefit for motor skill learning than verbal or more complex learning, and that as the difficulty and amount of material to be learned increases, distributed practice becomes more valuable. It seems reasonable that for most tasks long periods of massed learning are unlikely to be beneficial, although perhaps where motor activity is not involved (as in a lecture) there is more opportunity for trainees to control their own periods of attention and relaxation. Placed at points that are sensible from the point of view of the material being learned, breaks will probably do no harm and may produce some benefit.

Research on *transfer* has focused heavily on motor tasks and simple forms of verbal learning. Some general principles derived from this work have been presented by Holding (1965). Again, however, for management training the available research is of little direct help; although recently Leifer and Newstrom (1980) and Michalak (1981) have examined the transfer problems involved when trainees move from the training setting into the job situation. Factors such as the interest and involvement of superiors and continued reinforcement of learning seem to be important.

The use of *reinforcement* in learning is one of the most well-established principles of learning and its use is discussed extensively in the next chapter.

Motivation

It seems self-evident that a trainee who is highly motivated will learn more effectively than one who is not and it may also seem obvious that one should attempt to develop trainee motivation as much as possible. The position is not, however, as straightforward as this. Most attempts to encourage motivation in trainees involve manipulating levels of drive and/or anxiety (e.g. fear of failure), and the relationship between drive/anxiety and performance is not straightforward (*see* Fig. 41). Levels of drive that are too low *or* too

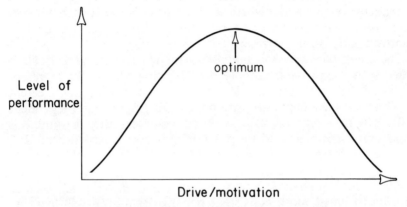

Fig. 41. *The relationship between motivation and performance.*

high produce poor performance. Put simply, too little drive may result in a lack of interest and involvement in learning, while too much drive may result in "trying too hard", such that breakdown in attentional control and other important components in the learning process will occur. This inverted "U" curve relating drive and performance helps to emphasise an important point concerning motivation and training. This is that for any situation and person there is an optimum level of drive. Another important point is that motivational problems can arise during initial learning or at later stages and can result in a failure to learn in the first place, or an inability to demonstrate learning when needed (e.g. at work under stress or during a test — *see* Sarason, 1975).

The methods and tactics used to control trainee motivation will depend on the particular circumstances, people and training outcomes involved, but some general points can be made. As with feedback, when considering the control of motivation it is useful to distinguish between intrinsic motivation (related to the task itself) and extrinsic motivation (independent of the task, e.g. extra payment on successful completion of training).

Ausubel has suggested how *intrinsic* motivation might be useful for uninterested trainees:

> Frequently the best way to treat an unmotivated student is to ignore his motivational state for the time being, and to concentrate on teaching him as effectively as possible. Some degree of learning will ensue in any case, despite the lack of motivation; and from the initial satisfaction of learning he will, hopefully, develop the motivation to learn more (quoted in Gagné, 1977, p. 289).

In essence, using intrinsic motivation to assist in the learning process involves getting trainees interested in the material itself, perhaps by ensuring that they are aware of its relevance or importance, or, as Ausubel suggests, by teaching well and trusting that trainees' interest will grow naturally.

The use of *extrinsic* motivation is common in many training and educational situations and an important consideration is that the level of motivation induced by the extrinsic reward (or punishment) is near optimum and not excessively high or low. Extreme levels of reward for success or penalties for failure may lead to a breakdown in learning competence. Finally, as expectancy theories of motivation (*see* Chapter 5) suggest, the rewards offered must be seen by the trainees as describable and the effort involved in learning must be seen as likely to produce desired rewards.

Events and processes
The conditions of learning discussed above, such as methods, feedback, practice and the control of motivation, make up what Gagné describes as the *events of learning*. These events can either be internal (psychological) or external (outside the person) and it is these events that form the basis of successful or unsuccessful training. The outline of human learning and memory provided in Chapter 11 indicates the processes involved when learning takes place. Gagné (1977) has shown how the psychological *processes* involved when learning takes place can be linked with the *events* of learning, and Fig. 42 relates his ideas to the learning processes discussed in the previous chapter. Fig. 42 suggests, for example, that before any learning begins, it is important to attempt to activate trainee motivation and subsequently, when the trainee is in a position to make some attempt to demonstrate learning, feedback should be provided.

It must be emphasised that although the work of Gagné, ITRU and others can provide guidance on the sequencing and methods of instruction that might be helpful, the transition from a specification of what is to be learned to the implementation of a successful

Learning phases and psychological processes	Events of instruction
(Apprehending phase) PERCEIVING/ATTENDING	• Activate motivation • Inform learner of objectives • Direct attention to relevant points
(Acquisition and retention phase) MEMORY/STORAGE	• Stimulate recall and aid memory/storage • Provide learning guidance
(Recall phase) TRANSLATION/RETRIEVAL	• Enhance retention
(Performance phase) RESPONDING	• Elicit performance
(Feedback phase) FEEDBACK	• Provide feedback

Fig. 42. *The relationship between learning phases, psychological processes and instructional events.*

programme is not a simple matter. Such schemes and ideas provide only a partial picture of the issues involved and a considerable amount of ingenuity and even inspired guesswork are still needed on the part of the training designer/practitioner. One of the important issues concerns the relationship between the trainer or "change agent" and the trainee. The relationship is important, regardless of the learning outcomes that are being sought and the techniques and methods that are adopted. A theoretical basis (Cooper's, 1976, dualistic theory of management education) for understanding and improving this relationship is examined in Chapter 14.

VALIDATION AND EVALUATION

It has already been emphasised that the development of successful programmes of training and development is a difficult and uncertain process and frequently programmes will need to be modified or redesigned as a result of experience. Techniques for the validation and evaluation of training provide a means of examining the success of programmes and identifying areas where change is needed. Examining the *validity* of a training programme involves assessing the extent to which trainees have reached the objectives of the training and can be established properly only by examining trainees' capabilities after training. Goldstein (1978) identifies different types of validity that training programmes might show. For example, if trainees reach the objectives at the end of the course assessment, this demonstrates internal or training validity. But external or performance validity is achieved only when it can be demonstrated that trainees' work performance is up to the desired standard.

The *evaluation* of training is usually taken to be a much broader concept than validation, dealing with the overall benefits of a training programme (often including validity). Warr *et al.* (1970) identify four major types of evaluation data: reaction, outcome, context and input.

Reaction evaluation involves gaining and using information about trainees' reactions. Many training designers collect this sort of information, sometimes without asking for it! It is undoubtedly useful to collect trainees' comments, but unfortunately in many cases this is the only information that is collected (*see* e.g. Cantalanello and Kirkpatrick, 1968).

Outcome evaluation involves examining the validity of the training by collecting information about the extent to which learning objectives have been met (i.e. validity) and/or the amount of change that has occurred, usually with the aid of pre- and post-course measures. Most training is designed to bring about changes in the way people behave at work and ideally outcome data should be collected to examine trainees' performance not only at the end of training (i.e. internal validity) but back in the work situation (external validity). In many circumstances the learning that takes place during a course does not transfer satisfactorily to the work situation. An external validity study using appropriate criteria to measure work behaviour is the only way to check whether or not this is occurring. Unfortunately such studies are not conducted as a matter of routine. A study by Campbell *et al.* (1970) showed that of a total of seventy-three management training programmes studied, only twenty-one made use of external criteria.

As well as deciding whether a training course is meeting its objectives or not it is important to examine the relevance and value of the objectives even if they are being met. Warr *et al.* (1970) describe this as context evaluation. It provides an answer to the question, in this context (organisation) what training should we be doing?

Finally, input evaluation involves obtaining and using information about possible training resources so that a choice can be made between alternative "inputs" (methods, media, training personnel, etc.) that might be used. Extensive discussion of the role of validation and evaluation in training is provided in Hamblin (1974).

ASSESSING TRAINABILITY

Input evaluation and the other forms of evaluation mentioned above can often be of considerable value in improving the design of courses and the extent to which the courses are successful for the trainees concerned. Redesigning courses so that they are suitable for the trainees concerned represents one major method for improving or maintaining the quality of training in an organisation. As well as taking trainees into account when designing training, it is often both possible and desirable for the organisation to have some control over the choice of trainees.

In many respects the problems and procedures involved in selecting people for training are the same as those involved when selecting people for employment (*see* Chapter 7). One important difference, however, is that when people are selected for training, an attempt is made to assess the extent to which they can *learn* and benefit from the training being offered. The technique of trainability testing (Robertson and Downs, 1979; Downs, 1982) is particularly useful here. Basically, a trainability test is a form of work sample test (*see* Chapter 7). Work sample tests involve applicants in performing a small set of tasks that are thought (usually on the basis of job analysis) to have direct relevance to the job in question. Often the tasks in these tests are sampled from the normal range of activities covered by the job. Trainability tests differ from normal work sample tests in that in a trainability test the applicant is expected to *learn* how to do the tasks involved during the test session. The extent to which the candidate does learn, and the resulting level of task performance, are assessed during the test. Considerable research and development work on these tests, initiated by Downs, has demonstrated that they can be extremely useful in training contexts, both as a selection instrument and as a means of providing potential trainees with a "taste" of the tasks in question. Trainability testing has been most widely used for manual tasks, but seems to have potential value for a wide range of occupational groups (Robertson and Downs, 1979; Gill, 1979).

Behaviour modification
Training and development activities are designed to enable people to change their behaviour at work by providing them with new learned capabilities. Sometimes it seems appropriate to bring about behaviour change that does not rely on new learned capabilities but merely attempts to encourage people to change their patterns of behaviour in a direction which might be more compatible with organisational effectiveness. Behaviour modification of this sort has been the subject of a considerable amount of research and development work during recent years and is discussed in the following chapter.

QUESTIONS

1. What are the main stages in the training process?

2. How can an understanding of Gagné's categories of learning capabilities help in the design and implementation of training?

3. What are the principles of learning? How can they be used in training design and implementation?

4. Why is it important to validate and evaluate training programmes? How can this be done?

CHAPTER THIRTEEN

Behaviour Analysis and Modification

OBJECTIVES

There are two broad classes of psychological theories that can be used to understand and influence people's behaviour in organisations: those which emphasise the role of internal thinking (cognitive) processes, such as the expectancy theories of motivation (*see* Chapter 5); and those which emphasise the role of external factors, such as rewards and reinforcement (operant theory). This chapter begins by outlining the principles that underline the operant approach and explains the role of conditioning in human behaviour. The influence of reinforcement schedules, the reinforcement hierarchy, punishment and other factors that are important within the content of organisational behaviour are also examined. Applications of operant principles to instructional techniques such as programmed learning are reviewed, and the use of operant techniques in Organisational Behaviour Modification (OB Mod) and the five main stages of OB Mod (identify the critical behaviours, measure them, conduct a functional analysis, intervene, evaluate) are discussed. Operant techniques are based on the idea that behaviour is controlled exclusively by direct, external reinforcement. Social learning theory extends this idea by showing how behaviour can be influenced by factors other than direct, observable reinforcement, including the expectations that develop from observing other people being reinforced and the processes of self-reinforcement. Recent applied research showing how social learning theory can be used to enhance the ideas of operant conditioning is discussed, and examples from various organisational settings are given.

CONDITIONING AND BEHAVIOUR

In a recent article Davis and Luthans (1980) make the following comment:

> There is today a jungle of theories that attempt to explain human behavior in organizations. Unfortunately, many of the theoretical explanations have seemed to stray from behavior as the unit of analysis in organizational *behavior*. There is a widespread tendency for both scholars and practitioners to treat such hypothetical constructs as motivation, satisfaction and leadership as ends in themselves. We think it is time to re-emphasize the point that *behaviors* are the empirical reality, not the labels attached to the attempted explanation of the behaviors (p. 281).

The viewpoint that Davis and Luthans are proposing is derived from the ideas of behaviourist psychology (e.g. Skinner, 1974). Behaviourist ideas have a long and influential history within fundamental psychology and in many areas of applied psychological research and practice. In rudimentary terms the behaviourist view argues that a satisfactory and useful science of psychology must be based on the observation and analysis of external, *observable behaviour*. Behaviourists argue that to focus attention on internal psychological processes which cannot be directly observed is both unscientific and unlikely to provide a coherent and systematic understanding of human behaviour. Thus, internal psychological states, processes, emotions, feelings and many other aspects of human subjective experience are rejected as topics for study in favour of an examination of behaviour, the external conditions in which the behaviour is exhibited and the observable consequences of behaviour. For some this represents a limited and restricting view of human psychology, but for behaviourists it represents a philosophically clear and practical view from which to develop an understanding of behaviour. As this chapter demonstrates, the research of the behaviourists has produced a variety of interesting ideas, many of which have been applied with enthusiasm and some success in organisational settings.

The application of behaviourist ideas within organisations is explored later in this chapter, but first an outline of the major research findings and key concepts of behaviourism will be provided, since a grasp of the fundamentals of behaviourism is an essential prerequisite to understanding how such ideas can be used to analyse and modify organisational behaviour. Two main types of conditioning provide the basis of the behaviourist approach: classical (respondent) conditioning and instrumental (operant) conditioning.

Classical conditioning

Classical conditioning is a simple but important form of learning first identified by the Russian physiologist Pavlov. As a physiologist, Pavlov was studying the digestive and nervous system of dogs. He did in fact win a Nobel Prize in 1904 for this work, but it was a chance discovery resulting from this original research that earned him lasting fame. Like all dogs, the ones in Pavlov's laboratory would salivate when food was placed in their mouths. Pavlov noticed, however, that once the dogs had been in the laboratory for some time, the sight of their food dish arriving, or even the approaching footsteps of the attendant who fed them, would be enough to cause salivation. Pavlov recognised that the salivation which occurred in response to the dish or attendant's footsteps involved some form of very basic learning on the part of the animals. After his initial observations, Pavlov went on to investigate the phenomenon in a controlled, experimental setting. He arranged for the amount of saliva produced by the dogs to be measured. Then he sounded a tone slightly before food was placed in the animals' mouths. After several trials it was found that the tone by itself would produce salivation and therefore the dogs had been *conditioned* to respond to the tone.

The general form of classical conditioning involves an unconditioned stimulus (UCS), such as food, which produces an automatic unconditioned response (UCR), such as salivation. Conditioning occurs when the unconditioned stimulus becomes associated with a conditioned stimulus (CS), such as a bell. Anyone who has seen the film *Jaws* will have experienced this. From the early stages of the film onwards, the approach of the killer shark is linked with some deep, throbbing music; very quickly the music alone is capable of provoking a strong emotional response and heightening of nervous tension. In fact, classical conditioning is an extremely widespread phenomenon and it is clear that Pavlov had discovered something of considerable importance and generality. Although we can only guess at the scope and variety of phenomena that can be explained in terms of classical conditioning, such conditioning is often closely involved in our emotional or "gut" reaction to the various experiences. Many people experience strong emotional reactions to certain situations, often because in the past these have been paired with particularly vivid, painful or pleasant experiences. Consider the response evoked in many people to the words "The boss wishes to see you!" The American psychologist J. B. Watson, a prominent figure in early behaviourist research, demonstrated how emotional reactions may be classically conditioned in humans (Watson and Rayner, 1920). As a UCS Watson used a sudden, very loud noise, the UCR to which in young children is crying and trembling. As a subject in an experiment Watson used a child named Albert. At the beginning of the experiment, whenever Albert was presented with a small white rat (the CS), he would try to play with it. When the loud noise (UCS) and rat (CS) had been paired several times, Albert developed a very strong aversive reaction to the rat and would whimper and recoil when it came into sight.

As an illustration of the effects of classical conditioning, you might consider the effect that the report of this rather unpleasant experiment has had on your views of some behaviourist research methods and of J. B. Watson in particular! A wide variety of human emotional reactions can often be explained in terms of classical conditioning and it is clearly not a form of learning confined to laboratory animals only. The idea that certain basic learning phenomena such as classical conditioning can be used to explain the behaviour of a range of organisms from laboratory rats, pigeons or dogs to humans is one of the mainstays of the behaviourist tradition. The behaviourists began their work in the hope that by studying simple forms of learning in simple animals, it should be possible to uncover the basic laws and principles of learning. These could then be generalised and used to explain human learning and behaviour.

Operant conditioning

The most famous contemporary behaviourist, B. F. Skinner, is often described as the most influential psychologist of this century. Skinner distinguishes between two types of behaviour, *respondent* and *operant*. Respondent behaviour refers to the kind of behaviour shown during classical conditioning when a stimulus triggers a more or less natural reaction such as the salivation produced by Pavlov's dogs or other automatic responses like excitement, fear and sexual arousal. Operant behaviour (behaviour that operates on the environment) deals with the forms of behaviour that are not the result of simple, automatic responses. Most human behaviour in fact is operant behaviour – going to work, driving a car, solving a mathematical problem, playing tennis, are all examples of operant behaviour. According to Skinner, such behaviour is learned and strengthened by a process of operant conditioning.

The major elements involved in operant conditioning are the *stimulus*, the *response* and *reinforcement* or reward. As an example of the operant conditioning process at work consider an executive who is asked to speak at a management meeting. The stimulus is the request for the executive to speak. The executive responds by giving certain views and this response may be reinforced (rewarded) by nods and smiles from a senior manager. The effect of reinforcement is to increase the likelihood that the executive will respond with the same or similar views at future meetings. The learning involved is sometimes described as instrumental conditioning because the response of the person or other organism involved is "instrumental" in obtaining the reinforcement.

Although the example given above involves human behaviour, much of the work on operant conditioning has been carried out with laboratory animals such as rats and pigeons. In some classic experiments, mostly with rats and pigeons, Skinner was able to show that by providing them with reinforcement (usually food) at appropriate points, animals could be taught to exhibit a wide range of behaviour. Many of the experiments were conducted with the aid of an operant chamber or "Skinner box" (*see* Fig. 43). Reinforcement is provided when the animal in the box exhibits certain operant behaviour (e.g. pressing the lever, or pecking a certain region of the box).

Operant techniques, unlike classical conditioning, can be used to produce behaviour that is not normally part of the organism's repertoire. For example, pigeons have been taught to play ping-

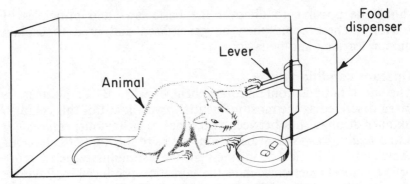

Fig. 43. *An operant chamber (Skinner box).*

pong and "Priscilla the Fastidious Pig" was taught to turn on the radio, eat breakfast at table, drop dirty clothes in a washing hamper, vacuum the floor and select her sponsoring company's food in preference to brand X (Breland and Breland, 1951). According to Skinner, the same fundamental processes of operant conditioning are involved regardless of whether we are concerned with a pigeon learning how to obtain food in an operant chamber, a child learning to talk and write, or a subordinate learning how to deal with a difficult manager. Operant behaviours (pecking in the right spot, pronouncing a difficult word correctly or saying the appropriate thing at a committee meeting) produce reinforcement (food, the praise of parents or the manager), and as a consequence the behaviour that produced the reinforcement is learned and strengthened. The process of operant conditioning is often described with the aid of a three-term framework: Antecedents (A), Behaviour (B) and Consequence (C). Antecedents refer to the conditions or stimuli that precede the behaviour, and consequences refer to the reinforcing or punishing outcomes that the behaviour produces.

With animals, reinforcement often takes the form of food; but for humans, reinforcement may take a wide variety of forms, smiles, gifts, money, complimentary words, and a wide range of other things may provide reinforcement for behaviour. Broadly, reinforcement is anything which *follows* operant behaviour and *increases* the probability that the behaviour will recur. In many circumstances, of course, during our daily lives we administer reinforcement to others in a fairly unsystematic and uncontrolled fashion. Smiles, nods, praise, etc., are all given with little thought for the consequences on the operant behaviour of others or the learning that we are unwittingly encouraging. A common example occurs when parents say no to a child's request for something and at first resist even when the child cries and makes them feel mean and unfair. Eventually, when they can stand it no longer, they give in and comply with the child's request – thus unwittingly reinforcing the child's crying.

The behaviourist research into operant learning has proved to be a rich source of information about certain types of learning experience; many of the basic principles have been applied in a wide range of organisational and other contexts. Over the next few pages some of the more important principles derived from behaviourist research are discussed.

Extinction

So far we have looked at the effect that reinforcement has on strengthening behaviour. What happens when reinforcement is not produced as a result of behaviour? When reinforcement is withdrawn or perhaps never given at all, the operant behaviour associated with it will gradually cease to occur. In technical terms, it is extinguished. Learned behaviour will continue only if the person is being reinforced. For many things we learn during formal education, at work and in everyday life, reinforcement is so frequent and common that we do not notice it. Nevertheless, as Zohar and Fussfield (1981) point out, when operant techniques are used to change employees' behaviour in organisations, the new behaviour will sometimes extinguish quite rapidly if reinforcement is removed.

Schedules of reinforcement

Sometimes reinforcement takes place on a *continuous* basis. An employee who is rewarded every time a satisfactory piece of work is produced is being reinforced on a continuous basis. Most reinforcement at work and in everyday life, however, occurs on a *partial* basis: parents rarely praise their children every time they exhibit good manners, good work often goes unnoticed by superiors, people do not always laugh uproariously at our jokes! In general, behaviour that is based on a partial reinforcement schedule is much more persistent and likely to continue even when reinforcement is removed. This is true despite the fact that on partial reinforcement schedules *less* reinforcement is provided. In fact the general rule is that the *lower* the percentage of correct responses that are rewarded, the *more* persistent the behaviour will be. An experiment reported by Lewis and Duncan (1956) helps to explain this apparent paradox. In the experiment people were allowed to gamble, using slot-machines. The machines were "rigged" so that some paid out on every trial (i.e. continuous reinforcement). Other machines paid out on a partial basis (as real slot-machines do). In the second part of the experiment everyone played on a second machine – rigged so that it would never pay out. People who had been trained on the partial schedules were much more resistant to extinction and they continued to play long after people on a continuous schedule had stopped. In fact the overall results conformed well with the idea mentioned above, that the lower the percentage of responses rewarded, the more resistant to extinction is the behaviour concerned, demonstrating the powerful effect of partial reinforcement schedules compared with continuous reinforcement.

Partial reinforcement may be given on either an *interval* or *ratio* schedule. Interval reinforcement occurs when a specified amount of time has passed. The next response that occurs will then produce reinforcement. For example, a telephone salesperson might be told to take a break by the supervisor as soon as the last call in any forty-five-minute period is completed. Ratio reinforcement is based, not on the passage of time, but on the number of responses that have occurred (e.g. a worker is given a break after every fifty components he has produced). Schedules of reinforcement can also be either *fixed* or occur regularly every so many minutes or response or *variable* and occur, on average, every "x" minutes or responses, but the actual gap between each reinforcement is varied (*see* Fig. 44).

In essence, the results obtained from research into the use of varying schedules of reinforcement show that variable ratio schedules produce the most persistent behaviour. It would, of course, be impossible to use variable ratio schedules as the *only* scheme for providing rewards in industry – people expect to get their salary on a regular basis! However, as Aldis (1961) suggests, it may be possible to use this method: "Take the annual Christmas bonus as an example. In many instances, this 'surprise' gift has become nothing more than a ritualized annual salary supplement. . . . Now suppose that the total bonus were distributed at irregular intervals throughout the year and in small sums dependent upon the amount of work done. Wouldn't the workers find their urge to work increased?" (quoted in Hamner, 1979, p. 167). The role of different schedules of reward in organisational settings is discussed by Hamner (1979). Much persistent human behaviour appears to be maintained on variable reinforcement schedules: seeking rewards or praise for good work, attracting members of the opposite sex and gambling, for example, can all be understood on this basis. There is also clear evidence that variable reinforcement schedules can lead to more sustained effort at work (Yukl *et al.*, 1972), although this may not always be the case (Yukl and Latham, 1975; Yukl *et al.*, 1976).

The reinforcement hierarchy

Some ideas concerning reinforcement, which seem particularly valuable within the context of organisational behaviour, have been

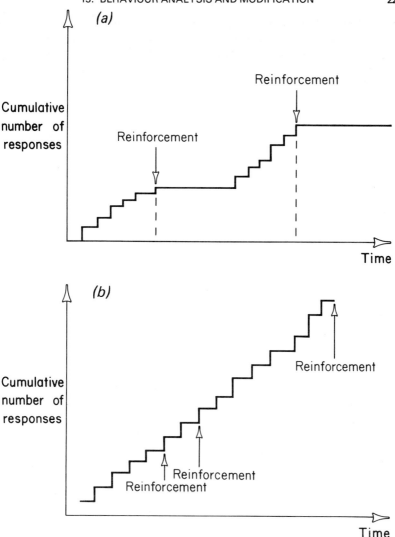

Fig. 44. *Different schedules of reinforcement: (a) A fixed interval (FI) schedule. Reinforcement occurs on a regular, timed basis. Typically, responding slows down immediately after reinforcement and begins to increase as the time for the next reinforcement approaches. (b) A variable ratio (VR) schedule. Reinforcement occurs "on average" every so many responses (e.g. VR10 = every 10 responses on average), but the occurrence of each specific reinforcement is irregular and unpredictable. Responding is frequent and regular.*

proposed and developed by Premack (1965). Premack demonstrated by experiment that an event which serves as a reinforcer for some behaviour may not have a reinforcing effect on other, different behaviour. In addition, he demonstrated that reinforcers may sometimes change places with the behaviour which produces them. For example, a thirsty laboratory animal will run to obtain water; equally an animal subjected to a long period of inactivity will drink in order to take an opportunity to run. In other words, drinking may reinforce running, but in some circumstances running may reinforce drinking. This simple example demonstrates the fact that the attraction of reinforcers may change as circumstances change. Premack has argued that there is, in effect, a hierarchy of reinforcement. The order of reinforcers in the hierarchy will change as circumstances change. Behaviours at the top of the hierarchy are things that we would like to engage in if given the opportunity – collecting £1 million from a bank, for instance. Behaviours at the bottom are those that we would rarely engage in even if the opportunity to do so were unlimited.

The reinforcement hierarchy may be used to influence or explain behaviours in many settings. Consider, for example, an employee who enjoys finishing work early and a long break from work at lunch-time. If the reinforcement provided by an early finish is further up the hierarchy than a lunch-time break, the employee may be persuaded to work through the lunch period for the reward of an early finish. In other words, one behaviour (early finish) may be used to reinforce another (work through lunch). Of course, if the employee in question had reason to attend a particularly important social event at lunch-time, the position of the two behaviours in the hierarchy might become reversed and the lunch-break might act as a reinforcer for working late. This general principle can be used to great advantage in a wide variety of settings.

Punishment

Just as a reinforcement will increase the likelihood of a response, punishment (the use of aversive or unpleasant stimuli) will decrease the likelihood of the behaviour that immediately precedes it. At first sight, punishment may seem to be a useful means for suppressing or eliminating certain behaviours. It is – but only when correctly used.

Consider the case of a supervisor who always raises disciplinary problems at the company's weekly progress meetings and, in so doing, reveals that he has consistently made bad decisions and errors of judgment when supervising his staff. At first at the meetings his manager responds with tactful and diplomatic assistance and tries to point out the errors to the supervisor, suggesting how they might be avoided in future. Eventually, however, the manager becomes exasperated, loses his temper and punishes the supervisor with strong words and a public dressing down. For the next few months there are no more reports of discipline problems and the manager begins to feel that the "short, sharp shock'' has worked. Suddenly, however, the manager is confronted with a deputation of employees from the supervisor's department who claim that discipline has grown progressively worse and that their working conditions are now intolerable. What went wrong? Had the punishment not worked? The punishment had worked, but inevitably – as anticipated above – it had decreased the likelihood of the behaviour immediately preceding it, which in this case was the reporting of problems by the supervisor at the weekly meetings. The supervisor had learned that this was not a successful thing to do. Consequently, he deliberately neglected raising the issue at meetings and thus avoided the possibility of punishment occurring, which was not the outcome the manager had intended. On the contrary, the behaviour the manager had tried to punish had continued unchecked and the supervisor continued making errors of judgment. To influence this behaviour, punishment would need to have occurred immediately after it.

In many cases it is impractical to give punishment at the appropriate time. For this and many other reasons (e.g. a classically conditioned aversion to the punisher, and the fact that avoiding punishment may provide a form of reinforcement and therefore encourage avoidance behaviour), most people feel that punishment is not a very effective means of controlling behaviour. Incidentally, punishment – *the presentation of an aversive stimulus* – should not be confused with negative reinforcement. Negative reinforcers are stimuli that have the effect of *increasing the probability of occurrence of the response that precedes them when they are removed from the situation*. If, for example, attendance at a series of lectures given jointly by lecturers A and B is very poor, but when lecturer A resigns and lecturer B carries on alone attendance increases, lecturer A was a negative reinforcer!

Fundamentals of conditioning: contiguity and contingency

The general overview of the work of the behaviourists given above has illustrated their use of certain key concepts such as response, stimulus, reinforcement and extinction. The research on punishment mentioned immediately above illustrates two important concepts, one of which is *contiguity* – that is for conditioning to occur there should be only a small delay between behaviour and reinforcement (or punishment). In broad terms, the longer the gap between these two events, the less likely it is that the target behaviour will be strengthened or diminished. The other fundamental concept, not mentioned explicitly so far, is the idea of *contingency*. This emphasises that reinforcement is contingent on response; in other words for conditioning to occur, reinforcement should be provided *only* when the desired behaviour occurs.

Reinforcing other behaviour makes it likely that this will be influenced and that the intended behaviour will not be affected. Contiguity and contingency are seen as fundamental elements involved in understanding how conditioning takes place and, taken together, with concepts of stimulus, response, reinforcement and extinction, represent the core of the behaviourist position.

APPLICATIONS

Instructional methods

Some of the basic principles developed by behaviourists have given rise to techniques that can be used to manage and control human learning in a variety of settings. Many of the techniques of programmed instruction, for example, rely heavily on behaviourist principles. Programmed instruction is essentially a method for presenting information to learners in systematic "packages" (*see* Davies, 1972, for further information). Each "package" might take the form of a page in a programmed textbook or a "frame" on the screen of a teaching-machine. A teaching-machine is merely an automated means for providing information, usually incorporating a screen to present frames of information and buttons that can be pressed to control the sequence of frames presented. The frames of information are presented in accordance with one of two basic programming techniques – linear (Skinner, 1954) or branching (Crowder, 1960). Fig. 45 provides examples.

A Linear Frame	A Branching Frame

Page 25
 	
Feedback (correct answer from p. 24.)
 	
――――― information ―――――
 	
The two main types of programmed instruction are Linear and B_____ programmes.
(Go to page 26 and check your answer.)
	Page 7
	
	Yes, Skinner did advocate linear programmes.
	
	――――― information ―――――
	
	One of the main features of programmed instruction is that it requires an active response from the trainee.
	   True — go to p.12.
	   False — go to p.14.
	   Don't know — go to p. 8.

Fig. 45. *Programmed instruction—examples of typical frames.*

The linear programming method involves presenting very small pieces of information at a level of difficulty that is low for the target population being trained. Each frame usually ends with the learner being required to make a response of some sort. Because the material is easy there is a high probability that the learner will be able to give the correct response. The next frame in the sequence provides the correct answer, and most learners will be reinforced by observing that their response was correct. Although some learners will inevitably make errors, the likelihood of errors is minimised by careful pre-testing of programmes to make sure that the difficulty level is low. In a linear programme all learners go through the same sequence of frames. In a branching programme the responses to the questions asked at the end of the frames determine which frame the learner goes to next.

Material presented in branching frames is usually more difficult and mistakes are more frequent. The questions at the end of the frame are designed to determine what, if anything, the learner has misunderstood, so that they can be directed to remedial frames which then deal with the specific misunderstanding and, in turn, direct the learner back into the mainstream of the programme.

There is evidence to suggest that programmed instruction is both efficient and cost effective when compared with conventional forms of instruction (Hartley, 1972). But despite such evidence after early enthusiastic use of the technique in Britain in the 1960s (Annett, 1971), the anticipated widespread use of programmed instruction has not occurred, although many educational and commercial organisations do make some use of the technique. This limited use of programmed instruction may be due to a range of factors, including the lack of applicability of "off-the-shelf" programmes to an organisation's specific needs, and the size of trainee population needed to make the use of programmed instruction cost effective (Beck, 1969; Annett, 1971). The first stage in the preparation of any piece of programmed instruction involves the identification of the specific target behaviours that the instruction is designed to bring about. Early and later workers in the field have continually emphasised that without clarity about the target behaviours it is impossible to prepare a systematic programme of instruction to achieve them. In keeping with the behaviourists' emphasis on observable behaviour, target behaviour should provide a clear statement of what the trainee should be able to *do* at the end of the programme (Mager, 1962). Despite the fact that programmed instruction has not in some ways fulfilled its early promise and, regardless of future developments, a lasting contribution is apparent, as Stammers and Patrick (1975) point out: "The enduring contribution of programmed instruction to training has been to focus attention on the objectives of training programmes, and to close the teaching loop by requiring responses from trainees and giving feedback to them in the light of their responses" (p. 78).

Organisational behaviour modification

The principle of operant conditioning and systematic procedures of behaviour analysis have been applied in educational and clinical settings for some time (Ulrich *et al.*, 1974; Rimm and Masters, 1979). More recently, they have also been used within organisational settings to modify behaviour. Comprehensive coverage of the application of operant techniques to Organisational Behaviour Modification (OB Mod) has been presented by Luthans and Kreitner (1975). The essence of the OB Mod approach involves focusing on critical behaviours that are important for satisfactory work performance and the application of reinforcement principles attempting to strengthen appropriate behaviour patterns. Luthans and Kreitner describe a five-step procedure for using OB Mod techniques:

(*a*) Identify the critical behaviours.
(*b*) Measure the critical behaviours.
(*c*) Carry out a functional analysis of the behaviour.
(*d*) Develop an intervention strategy.
(*e*) Evaluate.

Critical behaviours represent the activities of the personnel within the organisation that are influencing organisational performance and are to be strengthened, weakened or modified in some way. Such behaviour might be identified in a variety of ways, including discussion with relevant personnel, systematic observation or tracing the cause of performance or production deficiencies. An important point, however, is that only specific, observable behaviour is used. To say that it is critical to "have a positive attitude" would not be acceptable and the behaviour that demonstrated such qualities (low absenteeism, prompt responses to requests, instructions, etc.) would need to be identified.

Once the critical behaviours are identified, a baseline *measure* of their frequency of occurrence is obtained, either by direct observation or recording, or perhaps from existing company records. This baseline measure is important in two main ways. It provides an objective view of the current situation, indicating for example that the scale of a problem is much bigger or smaller than it was at first thought to be, and it provides a basis for examining any change that might eventually take place as a result of intervention.

Functional analysis involves identifying:

(*a*) the cues or stimuli in the work situation (antecedent conditions) that trigger the behaviour; and

(*b*) the contingent consequences, i.e. the consequences in terms of reward, punishment etc., that are maintaining the behaviour.

These can be examined using the A–B–C (Antecedent Behaviour Consequences) framework mentioned earlier. This stage is critical for the success of any programme of OB Mod, since it is essential to have an accurate picture of the antecedents and consequences that may be maintaining the behaviour in question. For example, an OB Mod programme may be considered by a sales manager as a means of encouraging sales personnel to make fewer visits' to base—visits that are spent in unproductive chats with colleagues. The sales manager may be concerned about the behaviour because of the time-wasting involved and because the sales director keeps making comments about large numbers of the sales force "sitting at base together doing nothing". The *apparent* rewarding consequences of returning to base may be the opportunity to relax and avoid the pressures of being on the road. It could be, however, that the important consequence for the sales staff is the opportunity for social interaction with colleagues and that it is the reinforcing effect of this social interaction which is maintaining their undersirable behaviour. Any attempt to modify their behaviour by providing opportunities for relaxation away from base or by staggering their visits to base so that only small numbers are there at any time would be founded on an inaccurate view of the behaviour-consequence contingencies.

Once the functional analysis has been conducted an intervention strategy designed to modify the behaviour concerned must be developed. The purpose of the intervention strategy is to strengthen desirable behaviour and weaken undesirable behaviour. A major feature of human behaviour is the range and variety of rewards that might be used to provide reinforcement. Money provides an obvious example, but many other potential rewards can be identified; Table XIV provides some examples. It is worth noting that not all of the rewards involve the organisation in direct costs, such as friendly greetings and compliments. Various intervention strategies may be used, but most involve the use of positive reinforcement in some way. Puinishment appears to have had a lesser role in most studies, although it has received some attention (*see* Arvey and Ivancevich, 1980). It is also possible to make use of Premack's reinforcement heirarchy principle mentioned earlier, whereby employees are rewarded for engaging in behaviour low down in the hierarchy (e.g. working at a job until it is finished, even if it means staying late) by being allowed to engage in behaviours

TABLE XIV. POSSIBLE REWARDS FOR USE IN ORGANISATIONAL BEHAVIOUR MODIFICATION

Contrived on-the-job rewards				Natural rewards	
Consumables	*Manipulatables*	*Visual and auditory*	*Tokens*	*Social*	*Premack*
Coffee-break treats	Desk accessories	Office with a window	Money	Friendly greetings	Job with more responsibility
Free lunches	Wall plaques	Piped-in music	Stocks	Informal recognition	Job rotation
Food baskets	Company car	Redecoration of work environment	Stock options	Formal acknowledgment of achievement	Early time off with pay
Easter hams	Watches	Company literature	Passes for films	Invitations to coffee/lunch	Extended breaks
Christmas turkeys	Trophies	Private office	Trading stamps	Solicitations of suggestions	Extended lunch period
Dinners for the family on the company	Commendations	Popular speakers or lecturers	Paid-up insurance policies	Solicitations of advice	Personal time off with pay
Company picnics	Rings/tiepins	Book club discussions	Dinner and theatre tickets	Compliment on work progress	Work on personal project on company time
After-work wine and cheese parties	Appliances and furniture for the home	Feedback about performance	Holiday trips	Recognition in house organ	Use of company machinery or facilities for personal projects
Beer parties	Home shop tools		Coupons redeemable at local stores	Pat on the back	Use of company recreation facilities
	Garden tools		Profit sharing	Smile	
	Clothing			Verbal or non-verbal recognition or praise	
	Club privileges				
	Special assignments				

Source: Luthans and Kreitner (1975).

higher up it (e.g. being given more challenging and responsible work). The choice of appropriate reinforcers is crucial for successful interventions, since the effects of specific potential rewards vary according to the people involved. To some people, for instance, the allocation of more challenging and responsible work would not be as rewarding as the opportunity to leave work on time every evening. Some people would find money more attractive than time off, etc.

Evaluation is an important element in the application of any OB Mod programme. Various designs can be used to conduct the evaluation phase of an OB Mod programme. The primary aim of the evaluation is of course to examine if, and to what extent, the intervention has modified the target behaviours. The most widely used designs are the reversal or ABAB design and the multiple baseline design. The reversal (ABAB) design involves alternating use of the OB Mod programme and removal of the programme over a period of time (*see* Fig. 46). In such a design the frequency of the

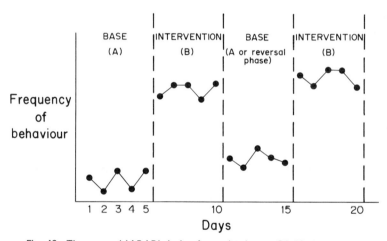

Fig. 46. *The reversal (ABAB) design for evaluating an OB Mod programme.*

target behaviour is assessed before the programme begins. This provides a baseline (the A phase). The next phase involves intervening and using reinforcement, punishment, etc., to modify behaviour (the B phase). After the intervention has produced stable new rates for the behaviour it is removed (the reversal) and conditions revert to baseline. Usually the behaviour will also revert, or at least show some return towards baseline levels. Although this design can provide impressive evidence of the effect of the intervention, there are obvious problems. The return to baseline may not always be desirable. Furthermore, the intervention may have been deliberately designed to ensure lasting behaviour change so that even when the specific reinforcers, etc., used in the intervention phase are removed, the behaviour should not revert to baseline levels (Zohar and Fussfeld, 1981).

The multiple baseline design can help to deal with these problems. In this design baseline data are collected across two or more behaviours. Then a specific intervention strategy to change each behaviour in turn is introduced (*see* Fig. 47). Each behaviour should

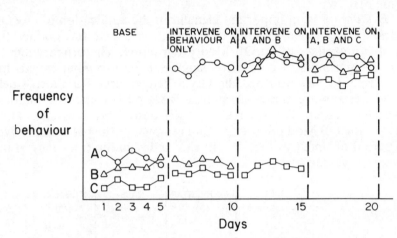

Fig. 47. *The multiple baseline design for evaluating an OB Mod programme.*

change only when the relevant intervention strategy is used. If this happens it provides convincing evidence (without the need for reversals) that the intervention is causing the change. Further details on these and other methods may be found in Kazdin (1980) and/or Luthans and Kreitner (1975).

Hamner and Hamner (1979) also provide guidance on how to apply behaviour modification procedures in organisations and they outline an approach that differs in some respects from the one described above. Programmes of behaviour modification incorporating the principles of operant conditioning in a variety of ways have been implemented in many organisations (*see* Table XV, Hamner and Hamner, 1979; Andrasik, 1981). Operant principles have been used both to change or modify undesirable behaviours and to increase the level of effort applied to desirable, productive behaviours. The application of operant principles to enhance work motivation and effort represents the major alternative to the cognitively based, expectancy theories of motivation (*see* Chapter 5) and, despite its apparent success, behaviour modification in organisations is not without its critics. One frequently raised area of concern is the ethical problems of behaviour control and modification. Is it appropriate to attempt such systematic and

TABLE XV. EXAMPLES OF BEHAVIOUR MODIFICATION PROGRAMMES
IN ORGANISATIONS

Organisation	Sample Goals	Reinforcers used	Sample Results
Weyerhaeuser Company	Teach managers how to use operant techniques to improve productivity	(a) Pay (b) Praise and recognition	Using money obtained a 33% increase in productivity in one group of workers, 18% in another and an 8% decrease in a third.
General Electric Company	To improve training and productivity. To decrease turnover and absenteeism	Social reinforcers (praise, rewards, and constructive feedback)	(a) Cost savings can be directly attributed to the programme (b) Increased productivity
B. F. Goodrich Chemical Company	To increase productivity. To meet schedules better.	Praise and recognition; freedom to choose one's own activity	Production has increased over 300%.

Source: Hamner and Hamner (1979).

controlled manipulation of people in organisations, and do such procedures undermine the freedom and dignity of the individual? Skinner (1971) provides some discussion of the behaviourist position on these issues. Another criticism of OB Mod of a more technical sort is given by Locke (1977). Whilst accepting that B Mod works, he argues that it is neither a new technique, nor is it behaviouristic. He states:

What the behaviorists call reinforcers do not condition behavior automatically, but affect action through and in conjunction with the individual's mental contents and processes . . . . While operant conditioning principles avoid the necessity of dealing with phenomena which are not directly observable, such as the minds of others, for this very reason they lack the capacity to explain human action. The typical behaviorist response to arguments like the foregoing is, in effect, "who cares why the procedures work, so long as they work?" This is the kind of pragmatic response one might expect from primitive witch doctors who are challenged to explain their "cures". One has the right to expect more from a modern day scientist (p.550).

More recently workers within the B Mod field have themselves begun to criticise and develop the theoretical basis for their own work. Early work on B Mod was based on the operant principle which emphasises that a person's behaviour is determined by external or *situational* factors (reward, punishment, etc.) and not by internal or *person* factors. More recent work (e.g. Davis and Luthans, 1980) argues that behaviour is best understood as a function of both the situation, the person and the interaction between the two. Davis and Luthans suggest that social learning theory (Bandura, 1977, *see* Chapter 5), which emphasises the interaction of situation and person factors, may be a better theoretical basis for organisational behaviour than the purely situational view based on operant conditioning only. Social learning theory differs from the traditional operant approach in many ways.

One of the important differences concerns the acceptance that internal cognitive processes are important determinants of behaviour. For example, whereas traditional reinforcement theory argues that behaviour is regulated by its immediate, external consequences only, social learning theory suggests that internal psychological factors such as *expectancies* about the eventual consequences of behaviour have a role in controlling behaviour. Bandura (1977) expresses it as follows:

> Contrary to the mechanistic view, outcomes change behavior largely through the intervening influence of thought . . . . Anticipatory capacities enable humans to be motivated by prospective consequences. Past experiences create expectations that certain actions will bring valued benefits, and that still others will avert future trouble . . . . Homeowners, for instance, do not wait until they experience the distress of a burning house to purchase fire insurance (p.18).

Social learning theorists also argue that, as well as responding to the influence of reinforcement in the environment, people often control and develop behaviour patterns through the use of self-reinforcement. "Self-appraisals of performance set the occasion for self-produced consequences. Favorable judgements given rise to rewarding self-reactions, whereas unfavorable appraisals activate punishing self-responses" (ibid., p. 133). Bandura and other social learning theorists argue that internal psychological events and processes such as self-reinforcement and expectancies help to determine behaviour. This behaviour will, to some extent, influence the situation surrounding the person, and in turn external situational factors, such as the behaviour of others, help to determine expectancies and the other internal cognitive factors. In other words, there is a constant cycle of interaction between person and situation factors, a process described by Bandura as *reciprocal determinism*. This view is quite different from the traditional operant view that "A person does not act upon the world, the world acts upon him" (Skinner, 1971, p. 211).

Another important aspect of social learning theory is the proposal that people often develop their own patterns of behaviour by observing and then copying or modelling the behaviour of others. The concept of observational learning or modelling is difficult for those holding the traditional, operant behavioural view to explain. For example, the act of copying a model provides no direct reinforcement in itself. Social learning theorists argue that this sort of action can, however, be explained if we accept that the modelling occurred because the learner had expectancies about what might eventually occur as a consequence of modelling. Thus, junior members of an organisation model their dress attitudes and behaviours on that of successful senior personnel, based on expectancies, goals and plans that they have about the eventual consequences of their behaviours. The extent to which modelling takes place is influenced by factors such as the perceived competence and success of the potential model (Weiss, 1977).

Many aspects of social learning theory seem to have considerable potential value within an organisational context. Some researchers (e.g. Goldstein and Sorcher, 1974; Latham and Saari, 1979; and Decker, 1982) have made use of the principles of modelling and observational learning to develop supervisory skills in accordance with the principles of social learning theory. Luthans and Davis (1979) have described some case studies showing how self-reinforcement can be used by people in organisations to change their own behaviour in desirable ways, and there seems little doubt that much of the future work concerned with the analysis and modification of organisational *behaviour* will incorporate concepts from social learning theory.

QUESTIONS

1. How can the processes of respondent and operant conditioning be used to explain human behaviour?

2. Describe the main phases in a programme of organisational behaviour modification (OB Mod).

3. How can OB Mod programmes be evaluated?

4. Does organisational behaviour modification work? What are the strengths and weaknesses of this approach?

5. Why does social learning theory represent an important development for work on behaviour modification?

CHAPTER FOURTEEN

Human Potential and Organisational Behaviour

OBJECTIVES

This chapter examines the influences that humanistic psychology and the human potential movement have exerted on some aspects of organisational behaviour. We examine the foundation-stones of this movement in existential philosophy and the more recent historical roots of the movement in the theory of Carl Rogers. His theory has provided a conceptual and practical base for management development and organisational behaviour. The chapter outlines a theoretical basis for the management learning process, which draws heavily on Rogers's work, and concludes with an example of experiential learning that stems from the foundation-stones laid earlier in the chapter.

THE HUMAN POTENTIAL MOVEMENT

It is sometimes argued that contemporary organisations exert a constraining influence on the growth and development of the people who work within them (e.g. Argyris, 1964). For many researchers and practitioners, one of the most important aspects of organisational life concerns the extent to which human growth and development are encouraged and threats or blocks to the full development of human potential are minimised. The work of humanistic psychologists (e.g. Maslow, 1954; Rogers, 1961) has had an enormous influence on attempts to encourage the development of human potential in organisational settings.

The human potential movement seems rooted in two historical traditions: the "phenomenological" and "scientific" (Durkin, 1964). Phenomenology emphasises the importance of each person's individual, subjective experience, and several existential philosophers (e.g. Kierkegaard, Heidegger and Buber) have played an important role in the development of phenomenological thought and philosophy. To a large extent, phenomenology provides the philosophical basis for both the human potential movement, and humanistic psychology in general (often called the "third force" to distinguish it from psychoanalysis and behaviourism) places great emphasis on the uniqueness of individuals and their personal strivings for growth and development. Medcof (1979) describes the emergence of humanistic psychology and points out that for many years psychology had been dominated by two major schools of thought.

The psychoanalysts, with their view of instinctive, irrational man doomed to conflict and the behaviourists, who saw man as a puppet, controlled by the strings of his environment. They vied with each other in their attempts to understand and explain human reactions, emotions and thoughts. These two great schools, with their sub-schools and splinter groups, were the two great forces of psychology. Then a third force appeared. It gathered strength in the fifties; it flowered in the sixties; it consolidated in the seventies: humanistic psychology. This viewpoint sees man not as a puppet, nor as driven by instincts, but as a growing, generous, healthy being in control of his own destiny (p. 227).

Psychotherapists were the first to utilise phenomenological philosophy in treating and investigating the mental life of man. The steady development of man's self-reflection and psychological introspection through psychotherapy, together with the underlying historical reaction to rationalism and the search for inner understanding, have contributed to the emergence of methods, particularly experiential learning, that provided an opportunity for self-exploration within organisational settings (Cooper, 1979).

The scientific basis of the human potential movement owes its beginnings to the nineteenth- and twentieth-century sociologists. Durkheim, for instance, emphasised the idea that the group was a "collective representation" – that is, it had an identity and existence of its own. Simmel, in the early twentieth century, stressed the importance of interaction and belongingness in the group, which later provided a basis for a theory of group conflict in terms of topological concepts. As the scientism of the twentieth century grew, these concepts and many others were formulated more rigorously and were empirically tested. Triplett (1897) and Hoede (1920, as quoted in Durkin, 1964) did the first early group studies by comparing the difference between individual and group performance and the effect of the group on the individual. Reflecting the scientific revolution and emergent interest in groups, sociologists and social psychologists performed in the late 1930s an enormous amount of empirical work on group behaviour. Sherif (1936) performed a systematic analysis of the "social norm" under controlled laboratory conditions. Newcomb performed a study of students at Bennington College to see what effect the university culture had on individual attitude change. Lippitt and White (1939) studied the effect of different types of leadership patterns on the social climate of the group and individual behaviour. In this atmosphere Kurt Lewin emerged as the main representative of group research, which he coined as "group dynamics". He developed a "field theoretical" method of examining group behaviour that provided the foundations for dealing with psychological data. He conducted numerous experiments into "group decision-making", communication patterns in groups and so on.

In the tradition of Lewin's action research a number of group psychologists came together, headed by Lewin himself, in Connecticut in 1947 to run the first experiential learning group – the precursor to the National Training Laboratory, currently the central focus of experiential learning/human relations training in the United States. They applied their own experience and research knowledge of the dynamics of the group process to the inward-orientated needs of American society. Bradford (1964) later said that "a potentially powerful medium and process of re-education had been thus inadvertently hit upon". It seemed to be capable of permitting members to achieve highly meaningful learnings about themselves and about group behaviour development. From 1946 on, the experiential learning group was established and utilised for training in industry, education, social welfare and in other fields whose work consists largely of dealing with people.

Carl Rogers

The contemporary theory that underpinned the human potential movement, which had implications for organisation behaviour, was that of Carl Rogers. His client-centred approach to understanding human behaviour has had an enormous impact on psychotherapy, teaching and management over the last two decades. His theory, or more appropriately his philosophy of human behaviour, is fairly simple. It consists of a number of constructs, which can be simply expressed as follows (and are extracted here from his most significant and early book, *Client-Centered Therapy*, 1951):

> 1. Every individual exists in a continually changing world of experience of which he is the center.
> 2. As a result of interaction with the environment, and particularly as a result of evaluational interactions with others, the structure of self formed – an organised, fluid, but consistent conceptual pattern of perceptions of characteristics and relations of the "I" or the "me", together with values attached to these concepts.

These two comments reflect Rogers's view that man's interaction with others is a main determinant of one's self-concept, and that the self-view is central to one's own behaviour with others. But even more fundamental than this is Rogers's suggestion that the organism has one basic tendency and striving – "to actualise, maintain and enhance the experiencing organism". This is a very similar concept to Maslow's (1954) concept of the self-actualisation in his hierarchy of needs (*see* Chapter 5), except that Rogers does not accept the stepwise development of man through stages. He believes that man develops by struggling to be self-actualised even in situations that do not necessarily provide the basic needs.

In addition, Rogers does acknowledge that man is limited by his heredity and social environment, but that they do not stop him from actively pursuing growth or self-fulfilment. Therefore, "behavior is basically the goal directed attempt of the organism to satisfy its needs as experienced, in the field as perceived" (ibid., p. 491). Rogers sums up his theory in the following way:

> This theory is basically phenomenological in character and relies heavily upon the concept of self as an explanatory concept. It pictures the end point of personality development as being a basic congruence between the phenomenal field of experience and the conceptual structure of the self – a situation which, if achieved, would represent freedom from internal strain and anxiety and freedom from potential strain; which would represent the maximum in realistically oriented adaptation; which would mean the establishment of an individualized value system having considerable identity with the value system of any other equally well-adjusted member of the human race (ibid., p. 532).

But by far the most widely used part of Rogerian theory is his view about how change agents should behave in trying to influence other people, whether we are talking about managers and their subordinates, or a psychotherapist and his patient. In this regard, Rogers (1957) has developed a concise schema describing the basic conditions offered by the therapist or influence agent that promotes internalised change: congruence, unconditional positive regard, and empathic understanding. The theory maintains "that these conditions are essential for the growth of personality in the therapy relationship". Rogers (1961) has, however, emphasised that therapy is only one instance of interpersonal relations and that these same conditions govern all relationships in which there is the existence of a psychological contact between influencing agent and influence, the presence of a learning situation with some anxiety and an opportunity for the influence agent to behave in accordance with these conditions.

Congruence facilitates change when the influence agent (i.e. manager) is what he is, "when in the relationship with his client he is genuine and without 'front' or facade, openly being the feelings and attitudes which at that moment are flowing in him" (ibid., 1961). When the influence agent is experiencing a warm, positive and acceptant attitude towards the influence, he is demonstrating *unconditional positive regard* in his relationship to him. And lastly, when the influence agent is sensing the feelings and personal meanings that the influencee is experiencing, "when he can perceive these from 'inside', as they seem to the client, and when he can successfully communicate something of that understanding to his client", he has fulfilled the third condition of *empathic understanding*. A relationship characterised by genuineness and transparency (Jourard, 1966), by a warm acceptance of the other person as a unique individual and by sensitivity to his inner world as he sees it, provide, for Rogers, the necessary conditions for the integration of person-relevant change.

Rogers's views have played an important role in the development of many aspects of learning and change in organisations, including the ideas and practices of management education and more "open-ended" attempts to encourage the general psychological development and growth of people in organisations. Cooper's (1976) dualistic theory of management learning provides a good example of how Rogerian ideas can be drawn on to help provide a basis for understanding and improving the management learning process.

MANAGEMENT LEARNING

Over the years there have been numerous attempts to examine the process of influence between change agents (e.g. teachers or parents) and the objects of their influence (e.g. students or children). There has not been a concomitant effort to do the same in the field of management education and training – that is, systematically to explore the learning mechanisms between a management educator and a manager. Cooper's (1976) dualistic theory of management education provides a framework for exploring the relationship between management educator and manager. The theory draws on two prominent theories concerning human personality and learning: the social learning theory of Bandura (1977) (*see* Chapter 5) and Rogers's view of human personality, growth and development.

Modelling and learning

As noted in the previous chapter, one of the central ideas in Bandura's social learning theory is the proposal that people often develop their own patterns of behaviour by observing and then copying or modelling the behaviour of others. Modelling and imitation occur when an individual observes and copies attitudes and/or behaviours from someone else (Bandura, 1977). As Bandura (1966) has suggested: ". . . informal observation of the process of social learning as it occurs in naturalistic situations reveals that the behaviour of models in one form or another is utilised to some degree in facilitating learning regardless of whether the subject is being taught the responses necessary for playing golf, swimming . . . or for conducting psychotherapeutic interviews".

In the context of management education, this process of learning takes place by an identificatory process with a management educator or indirectly by modelling the behaviour of one's boss, colleagues and subordinates. Managers learn, therefore, by modelling management educators as well as significant others in their work environment. The extent to which modelling occurs is based on factors such as the success and competence of the model (Weiss, 1977) as perceived by the "learning manager". The model is presumably seen to possess characteristics that the manager would wish to have. The individual's desire to possess these "ideal" characteristics and the relevance or salience of the trainer-trainee relationship for him provide the antecedent (prior) conditions for learning and for a willingness to accept the model's influence. The learner accepts influence in order to share "some of the positive goal states which the model commands" (Kagan, 1958). Change is adopted as part of an active attempt to establish a desired self-defining relationship with the model. According to Cooper's (1976) theory, *identification-based learning* can be defined as the acceptance of influence in order to establish or maintain a satisfying, self-defining relationship with the management's educator, and the attitudes and behaviour that the learning manager adopts in the process must be associated with and required by a role that he wishes to enact. Much of the learning gained through a modelling process remains tied to the external model and is dependent on external support. Learning is not likely to be integrated into the trainee's internal system. As Schein and Bennis (1965) suggest: ". . . when he identifies himself with a model once he has chosen the model, he limits the new information he acquires to what the particular model makes available to him. This process is more likely to lead to new attitudes which will be reinforced by the model but which may not fit as well into the rest of the personality". Thus, in an identificatory modelling process, the management educator serves as a model whom the management trainee wishes to resemble, with the resulting learning tied to the model and in the direction of the model's attitudes and behaviour.

Although an individual's managerial attitudes and behaviour can change in positive directions as a result of a process of learning based on modelling, this change tends not to be generalisable or long-lasting, since it is tied to a particular model or management educator. Transferability is likely only in subsequent working situations that closely resemble the context of the original learning environment in which the modelling took place.

In summary, a modelling or identificatory learning process is likely to take place if the management educator or significant other (e.g. boss, personnel officer, etc.) is seen as attractive or possessing the attributes the management learner or trainee desires for himself. The learning manager accepts influence in a modelling process because the management educator is salient for him; thus, by doing what he does and believing what he believes, the manager gains the satisfaction that goes with defining himself as identical with this salient figure. Change produced by this kind of learning process may not, however, be generalisable in relation to a variety of management contexts because it is essentially tied to the resources offered by the one model.

Self-directed learning

Another major process through which management learning can take place is that whereby the management educator creates the conditions for self-directed learning. Both research and experience in the field of psychotherapy, particularly client-centred, have demonstrated that personal and internalised change is facilitated when the change agent provides the conditions for self-growth by being open, discouraging dependency, and creating an atmosphere of trust. In management education (Cooper, 1981), there is a growing interest in encouraging "learning managers" to diagnose their own needs and design self-help programmes of change and development. This can be achieved if three basic antecedent conditions can be offered by the management educator:

(*a*) openness/congruence in his relationship with learning managers;

(*b*) the ability to create the conditions of *trust* in the learning community; and

(*c*) *awareness of* and *avoidance in encouraging* "dependent" learning styles.

These conditions are derived from Rogers's (1957) proposals concerning the factors that will help to promote internalised change.

The first two conditions are inextricably related. The more open and genuine the management educator or others are in their relationships with the learning manager(s), the more likely they are to help lay the foundations of trust that inevitably create the climate where self-management of learning can take place. It is important to recognise that the management educator is not asked to model openness but to *actualise* it, as "openly being the feelings and attitudes which at that moment are flowing in him", as Rogers (1961) suggests. Only when this kind of sharing of "real" information occurs can we begin to form trusting work and learning environments.

The third condition of avoiding dependent learning styles is quite different from the previous two. The onus here is on the managerial change agent to be aware of his own needs when attempting to create dependency relationships with learning managers. As we have already suggested, identifying with or modelling the management educator may help the trainee in learning new managerial styles and approaches in the short term; it may also create an unnecessarily high level of dependence on this change agent, hindering the transfer of learning to some back-home work environment. To be able to create the conditions for the self-management of learning, the managerial change agent or educator must be sensitive to "learner dependency" and be able to confront it. As Argyris (1966) suggests, some mechanism must be introduced in the learning process to act as a "springboard to get away from him [the educator/trainer] as the sole criterion for effective behaviour and look to themselves and one another as important resource people". In the self-management of learning, the trainee or learner has two major responsibilities for his own development: first, to develop the skills to diagnose his own strengths and weaknesses; and second, to plan a programme of change to utilise the full range of learning resources available in order to achieve his or her needs.

Two main consequences of encouraging self-directed management education are that:

(*a*) any change which occurs will be linked to meeting the needs of the particular individual; and

(*b*) it will tend to be transferable to a variety of contexts, since it is not tied to one resource and since the learning or change programme selected will more closely fit his subsequent work environments.

Issues arising from the theory of management learning
There are several short- and long-term management and organisational training implications in the theoretical constructs outlined above. First, in many management education contexts a modelling or identificatory relationship between educator/change agent and manager does take place and is likely to be an important element in the learning process, primarily, as Bolman (1976) argues, because the "trainer frequently appears to be powerful, if not always attractive" (p. 41). All too often trainers are not aware of this dynamic, which has several consequences:

(*a*) They encourage and foster a dependency learning style that prevents the transfer of learning back to the work environment.

(*b*) The trainer does not appreciate the potential educational value of modelling and therefore does not utilise it to the best advantage.

One can minimise the consequences of (a) by doing as Bolman suggests: ". . . what is essential, I think, is that the identification process be publicly discussable and its effectiveness publicly tested" (p. 43). If the modelling process is publicly discussed, the individual can evaluate more accurately the direct and indirect consequences of modelling, the problems involved with the transfer of learning associated with it, etc. In this way dependency can be avoided, acquired behaviour can be examined, and the whole dynamic of the teacher/student relationship can be advanced by opening it up for exploration.

There are also long-term consequences of examining the dynamics of modelling in management education. It has long been suggested by managers, for instance, that they learn most from other managers. In other words, that there is a subtle and less than conscious educative process that develops, on a day-to-day basis, whereby managers observe the consequences of the behaviour of their colleagues, internalise those that lead to successful outcomes, and discard (from some of the effective behaviours) those that are not adaptable in the particular circumstance of that particular manager. This learning sequence is essentially a modelling or identificatory one. It may be possible in the future therefore to try to harness this natural process as a tool of management development. The natural modelling dynamic could be the focal point for an approach to management-centred learning, whereby teams of managers come together to share their perceptions of the behaviour of their colleagues they see as "modellable", in the context of that particular work situation. This will not only provide managers with an enhanced awareness of effective and ineffective behaviours but will begin to create the antecedent conditions of openness, trust and interdependence that are necessary for self-managing the learning process.

Second, and finally, if we consider it desirable for managers to self-manage their own learning experience, we must take steps to ensure that top management are adequately prepared to allow this kind of development to take place. As Argyris (1966) suggests: ". . . each trainer behaves in ways that create the conditions for both psychological success and failure, which is related to his own needs and psychological make-up". The management trainer can exploit his role in the pursuance of his own needs, particularly in his desire to be liked or to exercise power. As Schein and Bennis (1965) emphasise in discussing change agents generally, "the possibilities for unconscious gratification in the change agent's role are enormous and because of their consequences, for the health of the client as well as the change agent, they must be examined". If we accept the desirability of encouraging the manager to structure to some extent his own learning environment, it will be necessary to develop management teacher/change agent development programmes that focus on the teacher's motives and how these may enable or prevent the student manager from learning in his own way.

TABLE XVI. DUALISTIC THEORY OF THE PROCESS OF
MANAGEMENT LEARNING

	Antecedent	Consequent	
		Short term	Long term
LEARNING BY MODELLING	Attractiveness (e.g. success, competence) of Management Educator	Change consistent with expectations and behaviour of model	
	Salience of Management Educator		Transferability of learning limited
SELF-MANAGING THE LEARNING PROCESS	Openness/congruence of Management Educator		
	Learning community climate of Trust	Change consistent with own needs	
	Awareness and avoidance of dependent learning styles		Learning transferable to variety of management settings

Table XVI summarises the antecedent and consequent conditions of Cooper's dualistic theory of management learning described above. It is hoped that this conceptual model may stimulate further thinking and research in the area of the processes of management learning. We have not attempted here to examine comprehensively the whole variety of learning dynamics in management education, or to establish an airtight theoretical structure, but rather to make explicit two processes of learning which have been a concern for many writers in the fields of social change and influence, and which might have applicability to management learning processes and management educators in particular.

DEVELOPING ONE'S POTENTIAL THROUGH TRAINING IN AN ORGANISATION

Let us now move from the theoretical basis for development to the practicalities of bringing about change and growth. One of the most widely utilised and significant examples of the human potential movement is the experiential learning group (or T-group), which has been used extensively in management development and training (Cooper, 1979), and to provide people with an environment in which they can learn about themselves and others. The following is an excerpt (Mangham, Hayes and Cooper, 1970) from a session of an experiential group run for a top management team of a large heavy-manufacturing plant in the north of England. The work roles of the various people described below are: Eric, *Plant Director*; John, *Joint Deputy Plant Director*; Bill, *Joint Deputy Plant Director*; Nicholas, *Works Engineer*; Harry, *Commercial Manager*; Consultant, *Group Trainer and Management Consultant.*

NICHOLAS: You [Bill] say that John and Eric are on the beam all the time. I'm not too sure, I wonder if John really does think like Eric, often John seems to agree with Eric a little too readily – so quickly that he cannot really have thought about it at all.

ERIC: No, that's quite unfair, I don't see the relationship with John in the same way you do, Nicholas. I feel that I sometimes follow John. Often when I reflect at the end of the day I realise that it's John who has got his way and not the other way round, not a case of him coming in too early, a case of him leading me along.

CONSULTANT: What is it that you are saying, Eric? Are you explaining that what Nicholas feels is not the way it is? If I were a full-time member of this group I'd be a little concerned about the relationship between you two.

JOHN: Yes, it's a good point that Nicholas brought up. He sees the role I play opposite Eric as being different from the role I play opposite other people. Sometimes, in the short run, I might appear to go along with Eric – that's while I think it through. In the long run, you know, I sometimes disagree.

NICHOLAS: This may be so, but on occasions I have felt that you have gone along with Eric even when you didn't agree. In short I feel that Eric can control this group; the two of you together are a formidable force.

JOHN: I do feel more sympathetic to Eric than to others; Harry would come at the bottom of any hierarchy of sympathy – in between, is Bill and you, Nicholas. I have sympathy with Eric because he works bloody hard. I have a sense of values and this is damned important to me – working hard – but secondly, he's an effective thinker, therefore I listen to him, I try to understand, whereas with Harry, after listening for a long time I certainly can't understand him.

NICHOLAS: However, with me, occasionally you have been jocular and sort of downputting, and this bloody irritates me.

JOHN: Well, why don't you say so at the time?

NICHOLAS: Because I feel blocked out, by you two sitting up there smiling at each other, in the know, in each other's pockets all the time. It's bloody difficult for anyone else to get a point of view across. It does surprise me sometimes that you had been putting pressure on Harry. I remember two or three weeks ago I got bloody angry towards you, John, about some issues, but basically it was because I saw you as putting a hell of a lot of pressure on Harry.

JOHN: Well, you seeing that sort of thing upsets me because I honestly didn't know we were putting that much pressure on Harry, really I didn't. Eric might have noticed it but I did not.

ERIC (*returning to the issue of the special realtionships*): I can't quite see how this special relationship that John and I are supposed to have can cause problems for the rest of the group. It might be useful to have a look at other people's relationship with me in the group, as I see them anyway. Maybe they'd like to say something about it after I've finished. Bill – you see, I'm really very neutral towards you, Bill – this could be one of the problems that's facing the group. As I see it, you don't appear to have built any relationships within the group – you have some sort of relationships outside. There's no meaningful ones within the group. Harry, well, we've said a lot about that relationship. You, Nicholas, well, there have been a few problems, not many. You're learning, you know. You've made a few mistakes, for example, with the shop stewards. You made me mad on occasions but you're doing all right, you're coming along.

CONSULTANT: Nicholas, how do you feel about that?

NICHOLAS: Like a schoolboy being patted on the head by the headmaster. It's as if Eric is saying to me "You're an up-and-coming young lad, not yet in the same league as John but you're doing all right."

ERIC: Well, that's the way it is, I'm sorry – you know, in my opinion Nicholas, you have all done well, in my opinion you aren't yet dealing with the same issues, thinking in the same way as John and I. If it's a question of you being in this group, then I'm one hundred per cent for it.

JOHN: And this is really what we're still discussing, whether or not we want this group to exist at all, and if so, who's to be in.

CONSULTANT: Well, it seems to me that the two people you are very uncertain about, and who are uncertain about their own position in all of this, are Bill and Harry. Before you try to gain their full commitment to the group or imply their rejection, it might be useful if you could spell out the pros and cons of their commitment. What's in it for them?

ERIC: I said before and I'm going to repeat it now, that really the only way forward is to make a frank assessment and I expect the same and am willing to accept the same being done on me. As I see it, Bill and Harry have little to gain in terms of promotion, so this group isn't going to be a stepping-stone to anything else. The only reward can be intrinsic, neither Bill nor Harry have a future outside this plant, as far as I know, unless they leave the company altogether. For John, I would say he is the company's next Plant Director, and there's no doubt about that. He's very intelligent, a very capable man and he's just about the right sort of age. He's got all the energy, all the drive, everything that's necessary to make a plant director. He'd make a hell of a lot better manager here than I do. Nicholas, well again, very unsure: young enough, has got enough ability, but the whole role of the engineer, and whole company structure is, as you know, currently in turmoil. Could be that this group will be very useful for him, to help him move into the area of general management, so it can make the transition to Assistant Plant Director, or even to Plant Director at some stage much easier for him. So for two of the people, Bill and Harry, the group holds no attractions in terms of extrinsic rewards, it holds the attraction of being in something that makes the decisions, implements them, that looks ahead, and that works in the very ambiguous area of general management. But the reward must essentially be inside themselves. Is this the sort of thing they really want to be doing with their time? For the other two it can clearly be of intrinsic and extrinsic use – it can give them satisfaction, it can also provide a platform for moving on. Now I can understand how many pressures there are, especially as you get older; when you're young your wife doesn't mind so much the long hours. They're expected if you're going to get on, but remember they become less sympathetic when you've reached your career ceiling. When that happens it is time to make the decision. I see the group as being one that has to meet frequently, one that has to make big decisions, one that has to take time, one which has to check out, one which has really got to learn to work together. Make no mistake about it, I basically want to work together, you see, people are one of my problems. I have accused John earlier of being unemotional, but I feel that really the unemotional one is me. I have to work with lots of people and I keep getting in the same sort of problems we've been talking about – these last two or three days. I just keep getting in these problems and I want to get out of them, and this group can help me do that. They can help me understand me and they can help me become a better plant director.

CONSULTANT: Well, you've said something about what might be in it for other people, Eric. What's in it for you?

NICHOLAS: That's the question I was just about to ask.

ERIC: Well, what's in it for me? I'm not viewing the success of this group as some sort of vehicle for promotion, no, I'm well past that sort of position. I'm not even sure that if it were offered to me I would want to take it. In some ways this group idea runs counter to what the company thinks about the way to work. In general, the boys upstairs think we should just tell people what to do. We shouldn't discuss things with them, we shouldn't try to talk things through, so I don't think they would look very favourably on it. Even if I were in the position to be promoted anyway – and I am at the point of not really wanting to go further, not wanting to do anything else, other than just be a good plant director here – team-work would not be viewed favourably. What will it do to me in other ways? I think it will make life a hell of a lot easier, because being at the top in an organisation like this is – it's a cliché, I know – a bloody lonely job, and I just want to be able to talk to people to get things sorted out, to be able to get good and honest advice. That's what I want out of it, to be part of something, not trapped in a cold image of the boss, somebody who tells you to do things. You see, I think that at the top it should be a sort of "we" thing, not an "I". We should want to do something, we should agree to it, not I want you to do something for me.

This sort of extract, taken from a session of an in-company experiential group, illustrates some of the features of the educational technique referred to as Sensitivity or T-group Training, which is the most commonly used form of experiential group method in training – although there is a range of variations being utilised today. First, as Cooper (1979) has indicated, the training is primarily "process-orientated" as distinct from "content-orientated". That is, the primary stress is on the feeling level of communications between people rather than on the informational or conceptual one. Individuals are encouraged to deal with their feelings about themselves and others and to explore the impact they have upon each other. They examine feelings, expressions, gestures, and subtle behaviours which in everyday life are often taken for granted. Second, the training is not structured in a conventional manner. The staff member does not provide the group with a topic of conversation. The individual members must decide themselves what they want to talk about, what kinds of problems they wish to deal with, and what means they want to use in reaching their goals. As they concern themselves with these problems, they begin to act in characteristic ways: some people remain silent, some are aggressive, some tend consistently to initiate discussion, and some attempt to structure the proceedings. With the aid of the staff member, these approaches or developments become the focal points for discussion and analysis. The staff member draws attention to events and behaviour in the group by occasional interventions in the form of tentative interpretations which he considers will provide information for study. He encourages members to focus attention on behaviour in the group, here and now. Who is behaving in what way and what feelings are being generated as a result? Third, the heart of a T-group approach is found in small groups, allowing a high level of participation, involvement and free communication. These groups therefore consist of between eight to twelve members.

As *Smith* (1967) has suggested, any experiential training group, as does any natural group, has a number of problems towards which its attention is focused. Below are some examples.

(*a*) *The problem of distribution of power and influence.* Shall the group be tightly structured? Who shall determine this? How shall the group deal with the staff member's power and influence?

(*b*) *The problem of intimacy.* How much of my private thoughts and feelings is it right to tell the group? How close shall the group members become to one another?

(*c*) *The problem of identity.* What sort of person am I? How do I compare with these other group members? What is the "real" me – me as I see me, or as they can see me?

As the group works on these problems, it develops a normative structure or set of rules governing the range of permissible behaviours, a more open and trusting environment and a less defensive one. When this occurs it is possible for group members to give and receive feedback with regard to one another's behaviour. The feedback process is one whereby a member of the group is told by the others what effect his behaviour has had on them. As Smith has illustrated, individuals in the group learn that the sort of feedback which is usable by the receiver does not comprise general value judgments ("I think that you are an aggressive s.o.b.") but specific statements as to what feelings and behaviour followed an act of the receiver's ("When you proposed that you should be chairman, I was very angry, but I said nothing because I feared the consequences"). In this way, each member of the group builds up a picture of how the others respond to his or her customary behaviour. Meaningful and accurate communication necessitates this kind of checking of messages which is rarely possible in ordinary everyday life.

As you might be able to predict, there are a number of possible outcomes of this form of training. Miles (1960) summarised a number of these as increases in:

Sensitivity: the ability to perceive what is actually going on in a social situation (including both behavioural events and inferred feelings of other persons).
Diagnostic ability: the skill of assessing ongoing social situations in a way that enables effective action; the employment of appropriate explanatory categories to understand reasons for presented interaction.
Action skill: the ability to intervene effectively in ongoing situations in such a way as to maximise personal and group effectiveness and satisfaction. . . .

All these experiential training goals have one thing in common: they are directed towards developing the individual, helping him to become more aware of himself and his impact on others, to behave more effectively in face-to-face situations and to reassess his fundamental interpersonal approach (specifically in relation to his needs of power, affection and aggression). In addition to these objectives, there are at least two others. First, as Redlich and Astrachan (1969) emphasise, in an issue of the *American Journal of Psychiatry* dealing specifically with this form of training, T-groups can increase one's understanding of the psychology of group and intergroup behaviour. In this context, the concepts of role differentiation, group normative structure and authority relationships can be explored in the course of the development of the ongoing self-analytic group. Thus, the skills of people in observing group and intergroup behaviour can be enhanced. And second, another primary aim of experiential group training is "to improve teamwork within the organisation" – to develop the organisation as a team rather than the individual as a person, as in the illustration given above of the British manufacturing plant. In this situation one would assemble for discussion of interpersonal problems on the job an ongoing work group. The group might include, for instance, an industrial manager and his subordinates; or a senior social worker and his/her social workers under supervision; or any other group of people who work together and whose interpersonal relationships may be or are preventing them from performing their work effectively. This area of interest is commonly referred to as "organisational development".

Broadly speaking, therefore, the T-group approach can be used to achieve a number of different outcomes, which can crudely be divided into three categories: learning about one's self, learning about group and intergroup dynamics, and improving work relations. These objectives are not achieved by relying on standard T-group training design, although a number of constituents of the method described earlier are common to all such designs. This form of training requires careful specification of the goal or problem in a particular situation and the creation of a training design that will meet these goals or resolve problems. In addition, the training programme required to achieve a particular goal can vary greatly from situation to situation. For example, a training programme to improve work group relations among a group of waiters and waitresses might differ substantially in design from one for the board of directors of a large multinational industrial organisation. The objectives of the training may be relatively similar – to reduce interpersonal obstacles and improve the work group or organisational climate – but the approach employed may, within limits, differ in quite a number of ways: in the balance of conceptual and experiential learning; in the inclusion or exclusion of boss, subordinates, colleagues or related staff; and in the orientation of the training staff (person-centred versus group-centred), etc.

QUESTIONS

1. From which two historical traditions does the human potential movement come?

2. What are the basic tenets of Carl Rogers's theory of personality?

3. Describe briefly the dualistic theory of management education.

4. What are the issues that arise from the theory of management learning?

References

INTRODUCTION

Argyris, C. "Problems and new directions for industrial psychology" in M. D. Dunnette (Ed.), *Handbook of Industrial and Organisational Psychology*. Chicago, Ill.: Rand McNally, 1976.

Wedderburn, Z. "Who are we? An analysis of the division of occupational psychology 1981 register of members." *Occupational Psychology Newsletter, 10,* 1982, 5–12.

CHAPTER 1

Ackoff, R. L., and Emery, F. E. *On Purposeful Systems.* London: Tavistock, 1972.

Argyris, C. "Personality *vs* organization." *Organizational Dynamics, 3,* 1974, 2–5.

Bedeian, A. G. *Organizations: Theory and Analysis.* Hinsdale, Ill.: Dryden Press, 1980.

Buckley, W. *Sociology and Modern Systems Theory.* Englewood Cliffs, N.J.: Prentice-Hall, 1967.

Burns, T., and Stalker, G. M. *The Management of Innovation.* London: Tavistock, 1961.

Davis, L. E., and Taylor, J. C. "Technology organization and job structure" in R. Dubin (Ed.), *Handbook of Work, Organization and Society.* Chicago, Ill.: Rand McNally, 1976.

Duncan, W. J. *Organizational Behavior* (2nd Ed.). Boston, Mass.: Houghton Mifflin, 1981.

Fayol, H. *Industrial and General Administration* (Translated by J. A. Coubrough). Geneva: International Management Institute, 1930 (originally published 1916).

Filley, A. C., House, R. J., and Kerr, S. *Managerial Process and Organizational Behaviour* (2nd Ed.). Glenview, Ill.: Scott, Foresman, 1976.

James, L. R., and Jones, A. P. "Organizational structure: A review of structural dimensions and their conceptual relationships with individual attitudes and behaviour." *Organizational Behavior and Human Performance, 16,* 1976, 74–113.

Katz, D., and Kahn, R. L. *The Social Psychology of Organizations* (2nd Ed.). New York: John Wiley, 1978.

Kotter, J. P. *Organizational Dynamics: Diagnosis and Intervention.* Reading, Mass.: Addison-Wesley, 1978.

Lawrence, P. R., and Lorsch, J. W. "Differentiation and integration in complex organizations." *Administrative Science Quarterly, 12,* 1967, 1–47.

Payne, R. L., and Pugh, D. S. "Organizations as psychological environments" in P. B. Warr (Ed.), *Psychology at Work*. Harmondsworth, Middx: Penguin, 1971.

——. "Organizational structure and climate" in M. D. Dunnette (Ed.), *Handbook of Industrial and Organizational Psychology*. Chicago, Ill.: Rand McNally, 1976.

Perrow, C. *Organizational Analysis*. Belmont, Calif.: Wadsworth, 1970.

Pugh, D. S., and Hickson, D. J. *Organization Structure in Its Context*. Farnborough: Saxon House, D. C. Heath, 1976.

Schein, E. H. *Organizational Psychology* (3rd Ed.). Englewood Cliffs, N.J.: Prentice-Hall, 1980.

Silverman, D. *The Theory of Organizations*. London: Heinemann, 1970.

Taylor, F. W. *The Principles of Scientific Management*. New York: Harper, 1911.

Trist, E. L, and Bamforth, K. W. "Some social and psychological consequences of the longwall method of coal getting." *Human Relations*, 4, 1951, 3–38.

Trist, E. L., Susman, G. I., and Brown, G. R. "An experiment in autonomous working in an American underground coal mine." *Human Relations*, 30, 1977, 201–36.

Weber, M. *The Theory of Social and Economic Organization* (Edited and translated by A. M. Henderson and T. Parsons). Oxford: Oxford University Press, 1947 (originally published 1922).

Weick, K. E. "Enactment processes in organizations" in B. M. Staw and G. R. Salancik (Eds.), *New Directions in Organizational Behavior*. Chicago, Ill.: St Clair Press, 1977.

Woodward, J. *Management and Technology*. London: HMSO, 1958.

——. *Industrial Organization: Theory and Practice*. Oxford: Oxford University Press, 1965.

CHAPTER 2

Argyle, M. *The Psychology of Interpersonal Behaviour*. Harmondsworth, Middx: Penguin, 1967.

——. *The Social Psychology of Work*. Harmondsworth, Middx: Penguin, 1973.

Argyle, M., and Dean, J. "Eye contact, distance and affiliation." *Sociometry*, 28, 1965, 289–304.

Berne, E. *Games People Play*. Harmondsworth, Middx: Penguin, 1964.

Bossard, J., and Boll, E. *The Large Family System*. Philadelphia, Pa: University of Pennsylvania Press, 1956.

Cooper, C. L. *Psychology and Management*. London: Macmillan, 1982.

Cooper, C. L., and Alderfer, C. *Advances in Experiential Social Processes*. New York, John Wiley, 1978.

French, J. R., and Caplan, R. D. "Psychosocial factors in coronary heart disease." *Industrial Medicine*, 39, 1970, 383–97.

Hall, E. T. "A system for the notation of proxemic behavior." *American Anthropologist*, 65, 1963, 1003–26.

Handy, C. *Understanding Organisations*. Harmondsworth, Middx: Penguin, 1976.

Harlow, H. "Social deprivation in monkeys." *Scientific American, 207,* 1962, 136–46.

Krech, D., Crutchfield, R., and Ballachey, E. *Individual in Society*. New York: McGraw-Hill, 1962.

Krout, M. "An experimental attempt to produce unconscious manual symbolic movements." *Journal of General Psychology, 51,* 1954, 93–120.

Margolis, B. L., and Kroes, W. H. L. "Work and the health of man" in J. O'Toole (Ed.) *Work and the Quality of Work Life*. Cambridge, Mass: MIT Press, 1974.

Mehrabian, A. "Significance of posture and position in the communication of attitude and status relationships." *Psychological Bulletin, 71,* 1968, 359–72.

Richards, C., and Dobyns, H. "Topography and culture." *Human Organization Vol. 16, No. 1,* 1957.

Roethlisberger, F. J., and Dickson, W. J. *Management and the Worker*. Cambridge, Mass.: Harvard University Press, 1939.

Sarbin, T., and Hardyk, C. "Contributions to role taking theory" in G. Lindzey (Ed.), *Handbook of Social Psychology*. Reading, Mass.: Addison-Wesley, 1953.

Schein, E. *Organizational Psychology*. Englewood Cliffs, N.J.: Reading, Mass.: Prentice-Hall, 1965.

Schlosberg, A. "The description of facial expressions in terms of two dimensions." *Journal of Experimental Psychology, 44,* 1952, 229–37.

Sherif, M. "A study of the social factors in perception." *Archives of Psychology, No. 187,* 1935.

Slater, P. "Role differentiation in small groups" in P. Hare (Ed.), *Small Groups*. New York: Knopf, 1955.

Sommer, R. "Leadership and group geography." *Sociometry, 24,* 1961, 99–109.

Wallen, N. "Analysis and investigation of teaching methods" in N. Gage (Ed.), *Handbook of Research in Teaching*. Chicago, Ill.: Rand McNally, 1963.

CHAPTER 3

Anastasi, A. "More on heritability: Addendum to the Hebb and Jensen interchange." *American Psychologist, 26,* 1971, 1036–37.

Boring, E. G. "Intelligence as the tests test it." *New Republic, 35,* 1923, 35–7.

Burt, C. *The Factors of Mind*. London: University of London Press, 1940.

Entwistle, N. J. *Styles of Learning and Teaching*. Chichester: Wiley, 1981.

Erlenmeyer-Kimling, L., and Jarvik, L. F. "Genetics and intelligence: A review." *Science, 142,* 1963, 1477–9.

Eysenck, H. J., and Kamin, L. *Intelligence: The Battle for the Mind*. London, Pan, 1981.

Getzels, J. W., and Jackson, P. W. *Creativity and Intelligence*. New York: John Wiley, 1962.

Guilford, J. P. *The Nature of Human Intelligence*. New York: McGraw-Hill, 1967.

Hudson, L. *Contrary Imaginations*. London: Methuen, 1966.

Kagan, J., Rosman, B. L., Day, D., Albert, J., and Phillips, W. "Information processing in the child: Significance of analytic and reflective attitudes." *Psychological Monographs, 78, Whole No. 1,* 1964.

Kamin, L. J. *The Science and Politics of IQ*. New York: John Wiley, 1974.

Loehlin, J. C., Lindzey, G., and Spuhler, J. N. *Race Differences in Intelligence*. San Francisco, Calif.: Freeman, 1975.

Mintzberg, H. "Planning on the left side and managing on the right." *Harvard Business Review, 54,* 1976, 49–58.

Pask, G. "Styles and strategies of learning." *British Journal of Educational Psychology, 46,* 1976, 128–48.

Robey, D., and Taggart, W. "Measuring managers' minds: The assessment of style in human information processing." *Academy of Management Review, 6,* 1981, 375–83.

Satterly, D. J. "Covariation of cognitive styles, intelligence and achievement." *British Journal of Educational Pschology, 49,* 1979, 179–81.

Scarr, S., and Carter-Saltzman, L. "Twin-method: Defense of a critical assumption." *Behavior Genetics, 9,* 1979, 527–42.

Skodak, M., and Skeels, H. "A final follow-up study of children in adoptive homes." *Journal of Genetic Psychology, 75,* 1949, 85–125.

Spearman, C. *The Abilities of Man*. London: Macmillan, 1927.

Thurstone, L. L. "Primary mental abilities." *Psychometric Monographs, No. 1,* 1938.

Vernon, P. E. *The Measurement of Abilities*. London: University of London Press, 1956.

——. *The Structure of Human Abilities* (2nd Ed.). London: Methuen, 1961.

——. *Intelligence and Cultural Environment*. London: Methuen, 1969.

Wallach, M. A., and Kogan, N. *Modes of Thinking in Young Children*. New York: Holt, Rinehart & Winston, 1965.

Wheeler, L. R. "A comparative study of the intelligence of East Tennessee mountain children." *Journal of Educational Psychology, 33,* 1942, 321–34.

Witkin, H. A. "Cognitive style in academic performance and in teacher-student relations" in S. Messick (Ed.) *Individuality in Learning*. San Francisco, Calif.: Jossey-Bass, 1976.

Witkin, H. A., Moore, C. A., Goodenough, D. R., and Cox, P. W. "Field-dependent and field-independent cognitive styles and their educational implications." *Review of Educational Research,* 1977, 1–64.

CHAPTER 4

Carlson, E. R., and Abelson, H. "Attitude change through modification of attitude structure." *Journal of Abnormal and Social Psychology*, *52*, 1956, 256–61.

Cohen, A. R. *Attitude Change and Social Influence*. New York: Basic Books, 1964.

Converse, P., and Campbell, A. "Political standards in secondary groups" in T. M. Newcomb and R. E. Hartley (Eds), *Readings in Social Psychology*. Evanston, Ill.: Row & Peterson, 1960.

Cooper, C. L. *Learning from Others in Groups*. London: ABP, 1979.

Dabbs, J., and Leventhal, H. "Effects of varying the recommendations in fear-arousing communication." *Journal of Personality and Social Psychology*, *4*, 1966, 525–31.

Fishbein, M., and Ajzen, I. *Belief, Attitude and Behavior*. Reading, Mass.: Addison-Wesley, 1975.

Homans, G. *The Human Group*. New York: Harcourt, Brace & World, 1950.

Hovland, C. *The Order of Presentation in Persuasion*. New Haven, Conn.: Yale University Press, 1957.

Hovland, C., Lumsdaine, A., and Sheffield, F. *Experiments on Mass Communication*. Princeton, N.J.: Princeton University Press, 1949.

Hovland, C., and Pritzker, H. "Extent of opinion change as a function of amount of change advocated." *Journal of Abnormal and Social Psychology*, *54*, 1957, 257–61.

Hovland, C., and Weiss, W. "The influence of source credibility on communication effectiveness." *Public Opinion Quarterly*, *15*, 1952, 635–50.

Janis, I., and Feshback, S. "Effects of fear arousing communications." *Journal of Abnormal and Social Psychology*, *48*, 1953, 78–92.

Karlins, M., and Abelson, H. *Persuasion*. London: Crosby Lockwood, 1970.

Katz, E., and Lazarsfield, P. F. *Personal Influence*. New York: Free Press, 1955.

Kelley, H. H., and Woodruff, C. "Members' reactions to apparent group approval of a counternorm communication." *Journal of Abnormal and Social Psychology*, *52*, 1956, 67–74.

Koeske, G., and Crano, W. "The effect of congruous and incongruous source statement combinations upon the judged credibility of a communication." *Journal of Experimental Social Psychology*, *4*, 1968, 384–399.

Krech, D., Crutchfield, R. S., and Ballachey, E. L. *Individual in Society*. New York: McGraw-Hill, 1962.

Lewin, K. "Studies in group decision" in D. Cartwright and A. Zander, *Group Dynamics*. Evanston, Ill.: Row & Peterson, 1953.

McGinnies, E. "Studies in persuasion: Reactions of Japanese students to one sided and two sided communications." *Journal of Social Psychology*, *70*, 1966.

Menzel, H., and Katz, E. "Social reactions and innovation in the medical profession." *Public Opinion Quarterly, 19,* 1956, 337–52.

Ottoway, R. N. *Change Agents at Work.* London: Associated Business Press, 1979.

Rogers, C. R. *Personal Power.* London: Constable, 1978.

Rosnow, R., and Robinson, E. *Experiments in Persuasion.* New York: Academic Press, 1967.

Schuessler, K. F. *Measuring Social Life Feelings.* San Francisco, Calif.: Jossey-Bass, 1982.

Secord, P. F., and Backman, C. W. *Social Psychology,* New York: McGraw-Hill, 1969.

Tannenbaum, P. "Initial attitude toward source and concept as factors in attitude change through communication." *Public Opinion Quarterly, 20,* 1956, 413–26.

Weiss, W. "Opinion congruence with a negative source of one issue as a factor influencing agreement on another issue." *Journal of Abnormal and Social Psychology, 54,* 1957, 180–6.

Wright, P. "Attitude change under direct and interpersonal influence." *Human Relations, 19,* 1966, 199–211.

CHAPTER 5

Alderfer, C. P. *Existence, Relatedness and Growth.* New York: Free Press, 1972.

Bandura, A. *Social Learning Theory.* Englewood-Cliffs, N.J.: Prentice-Hall, 1977.

Beck, J. E. "Changing a manager's construction of reality" in J. E. Beck and C. J. Cox, *Advances in Management Education.* Chichester: Wiley, 1980.

Belbin, R. M. *Management Teams: Why They Succeed or Fail.* London: Heinemann, 1981.

Campbell, J. P., and Pritchard, R. D. "Evidence pertaining to expectancy -instrumentality-valence theory" in R. M. Steers and L. W. Porter, *Motivation and Work Behavior.* New York: McGraw-Hill, 1979.

Cattell, R. B. *The Scientific Analysis of Personality.* Harmondsworth, Middx: Penguin, 1965.

Cooper, C. L. "A dualistic theory of the processes of management learning." *Management Decision, 14,* 1976, 54–62.

Dachler, H. P., and Hulin, C. L. "A reconsideration of the relationship between satisfaction and judged importance of environmental and job characteristics." *Organisational Behavior and Human Performance, 4,* 1969, 252–66.

De Board, R. *The Psychoanalysis of Organisations.* London: Tavistock, 1978.

Dickson, N. S. *The Psychology of Military Incompetence.* London: Cape, 1976.

Dollard, J., and Miller, N. E. *Personality and Psychotherapy.* New York: McGraw-Hill, 1950.

Dunham, R. B. "The measurement and dimensionality of job characteristics." *Journal of Applied Psychology, 61,* 1976, 404–9.

Dunnette, M. D., Campbell, J. P., and Hakel, M. D. "Factors contributing to job satisfaction and job dissatisfaction in six occupational groups." *Organizational Behavior and Human Performance, 2,* 1967, 143–74.

Endler, N. S., and Magnusson, D. (Eds). *Interactional Psychology and Personality.* Washington DC: Hemisphere (Halstead-Wiley), 1976.

Eysenck, H. J. *The Structure of Human Personality.* London: Methuen, 1970.

Eysenck, H. J., and Eysenck, S. B. G. *The Eysenck Personality Inventory.* London: University of London Press, 1964.

Eysenck, H. J., and Wilson, G. D. *The Experimental Study of Freudian Theories.* London: Methuen, 1973.

Fein, M. "Job enrichment: A reevaluation" in R. M. Steers and L. W. Porter, *Motivation and Work Behavior.* New York: McGraw-Hill, 1979.

Hackman, J. R., and Oldham, G. R. "Development of the job diagnostic survey." *Journal of Applied Psychology, 60,* 1975, 159–70.

Hall, D. T., and Nougaim, K. E. "An examination of Maslow's need hierarchy in the organizational setting." *Organizational Behavior and Human Performance, 3,* 1968, 12–35.

Herzberg, F. "One more time: How do you motivate employees?" *Harvard Business Review, 46,* 1968, 53–162.

Herzberg, F., Mausner, B., and Snyderman, B. B. *The Motivation to Work.* New York: John Wiley, 1959.

Hull, C. L. *Principles of Behavior.* New York: Appleton-Century-Crofts, 1943.

Kelly, G. A. *The Psychology of Personal Constructs.* New York: Norton, 1955.

Lawler, E. E. *Motivation in Work Organizations.* Belmont, Calif.: Brooks/Cole, 1973.

Lawler, E. E. III, and Suttle, J. L. "A causal correlational test of the need hierarchy concept." *Organizational Behavior and Human Performance, 7,* 1972, 265–87.

Le Francois, G. R. *Psychology.* Belmont, Calif.: Wadsworth, 1980.

Magnusson, D., and Endler, N. S. (Eds). *Personality at the Crossroads: Current Issues in Interactional Psychology.* Hillsdale, N.J.: Erlbaum, 1977.

Maslow, A. H. *Motivation and Personality,* New York: Harper, 1954.

Mischel, W. *Personality Assessment.* New York: John Wiley, 1968.

——. "Self-control and the Self" in T. Mischel (Ed.), *The Self: Psychological and Philosophical Issues.* Totowa, N. J.: Rowman & Littlefield, 1977.

Nadler, D. A., and Lawler, E. E. III. "Motivation: A diagnostic approach" in R. M. Steers and L. W. Porter, *Motivation and Work Behavior.* New York: McGraw-Hill, 1979.

Payne, R. "Factor analysis of a Maslow-type need satisfaction questionnaire." *Personnel Psychology, 23,* 1970, 251–68.

Pervin, L. A. *Personality: Theory Assessment and Research* (3rd Ed.). New York: John Wiley, 1980.

Rauschenberger, J., Schmitt, N., and Hunter, J. "A test of the need hierarchy concept by a Markov model of change in need strength." *Administrative Science Quarterly*, *25*, 1980, 654–70.

Schneider, J., and Lock, E. A. "A critique of Herzberg's incident classification system and a suggested revision. *Organizational Behavior and Human Performance*, *6*, 1971, 441–57.

Skinner, B. F. *About Behaviorism*, New York: Knopf, 1974.

Slater, P. (Ed.) *Dimensions of Intrapersonal Space*. London: John Wiley, 1977.

Smith, M. "Applications and uses of repertory grids in management education" in J. E. Beck and C. J. Cox, *Advances in Management Education*. Chichester: Wiley, 1980.

Smith, M., Hartley, J., and Stewart, B. "A case study of repertory grids used in vocational guidance." *Journal of Occupational Psychology*, *51*, 1978, 97–104.

Smith, M., and Stewart, B. J. M. "Repertory grids a flexible tool for establishing the structure of a manager's thoughts." *Management Bibliographies and Reviews*, *3*, 1977, 209–28.

Steers, R. M., and Porter, L. W. *Motivation and Work Behavior*. New York: McGraw-Hill, 1979.

Stewart, V., and Stewart, A. *Business Applications of Repertory Grids*. London: McGraw-Hill, 1981.

Wahba, M. A., and Bridwell, L. G. "Maslow reconsidered: A review of research on the need hierarchy theory" in R. M. Steers and L. W. Porter, *Motivation and Work Behavior*. New York: McGraw-Hill, 1979.

Wall, T. D., Clegg, C. W., and Jackson, P. R. "An evaluation of the job characteristics model." *Journal of Occupational Psychology*, *51*, 1978, 183–96.

CHAPTER 6

Annett, J., Duncan, K. D., Stammers, R. B., and Gray, M. J. *Task Analysis. Training Information Paper No. 6*. London: HMSO, 1971.

Arvey, R. D., and Hoyle, J. "A Guttman approach to the development of behaviorally based rating scales for systems analysts and programmers/ analysts." *Journal of Applied Psychology*, *59*, 1974, 61–8.

Ash, R. A., and Edgell, S. L. "A note on the readability of the PAQ." *Journal of Applied Psychology*, *60*, 1975, 765–6.

Blanz, F., and Ghiselli, E. "The mixed standard scale: A new rating system." *Personnel Psychology*, *25*, 1972, 155–99.

Blum, M. L., and Naylor, J. C. *Industrial Psychology: Its Theoretical and Social Foundations*. New York: Harper & Row, 1968.

Bottomley, M. *Personnel Management*. Plymouth: Macdonald & Evans, 1983.

Dickinson, T. L., and Zellinger, P. M. "A comparison of the behaviorally anchored rating and mixed standard scale formats." *Journal of Applied Psychology*, *65*, 1980, 147–54.

Dunnette, M. D. "A note on the criterion." *Journal of Applied Psychology*, *47*, 1963, 251–4.

Fay, C. H., and Latham, G. P. "Effects of training and rating scales on rating errors." *Personnel Psychology*, *35*, 1982, 105–16.

Fine, S. A., and Wiley, W. W. "An introduction to functional job analysis" in E. A. Fleishman and A. R. Bass (Eds), *Studies in Personnel and Industrial Psychology*. Homewood, Ill.: Dorsey Press, 1974.

Flanagan, J. C. "The critical incident technique." *Psychological Bulletin*, *51*, 1954, 327–58.

Fordham, K. G. "Job advertising" in B. Ungerson (Ed.), *Recruitment Handbook* (2nd Ed.). Guildford: Gower Press, 1975.

Ghiselli, E. E. *The Validity of Occupational Aptitude Tests*. New York: Wiley, 1966.

——. "The validity of aptitude tests in personnel selection." *Personnel Psychology*, *26*, 1973, 461–77.

Guion, R. M. *Personnel Testing*. New York: McGraw-Hill, 1965.

Hemphill, J. K. "Job descriptions for executives." *Harvard Business Review*, *37*, 1959, 55–67.

Kelly, G. A. *The Psychology of Personal Constructs*. New York: Norton, 1955.

Landy, F. J., and Trumbo, D. A. *Psychology of Work Behavior*. Homewood, Ill.: Dorsey Press, 1980.

Latham, G. P., and Wexley, K. N. *Increasing Productivity through Performance Appraisal*. Reading, Mass.: Addison-Wesley, 1981.

Lawshe, C. H., Bolda, R. A., Brune, R. L., and Auclair, G. "Expectancy Charts II: Their theoretical development." *Personnel Psychology*, *11*, 1958, 545–60.

McCormick, E. J. "Job and task analysis" in M. D. Dunnette (Ed.), *Handbook of Industrial and Organizational Psychology*, Chicago, Ill.: Rand McNally, 1976.

McCormick, E. J., Jeanneret, P., and Mecham, R. C. "A study of job characteristics and job dimensions as based on the position analysis questionnaires." *Journal of Applied Psychology*, *36* (monograph), 1972, 347–68.

Makin, P. J., and Robertson, I. T. "Self-assessment, realistic job previews and occupational decisions." Paper presented at the 20th International Congress on Applied Psychology. Edinburgh, July 1982.

Munro-Fraser, J. *Employment Interviewing* (4th Ed.). Plymouth: Macdonald & Evans, 1966.

Naylor, J. C., and Shine, C. C. "A table for determining the increase in mean criterion score obtained by using a selection device." *Journal of Industrial Psychology*, *3*, 1965, 33–42.

Nemeroff, W. F., and Wexley, K. N. "An exploration of the relationships between performance feedback interview characteristics and interview outcomes as perceived by managers and subordinates." *Journal of Occupational Psychology*, *52*, 1979, 25–34.

Patrick, J., Spurgeon, P., Barwell, F., and Sparrow, J. *Re-deployment by Upgrading to Technician. Grouping of Skills (Sub-project 1)*. Report submitted to Manpower Services Commission. Applied Psychology

Department, University of Aston, Birmingham, June 1980.

Platt, T. E. "The job specification" in B. Ungerson (Ed.), *Recruitment Handbook*, Guildford: Gower Press, 1975.

Prien, E. P. "Development of a clerical position description questionnaire." *Personnel Psychology*, *18*, 1965, 91–8.

Prien, E. P., and Ronan, W. W. "Job analysis: A review of research findings." *Personnel Psychology*, *24*, 1971, 371–96.

Rodger, A. *The Seven Point Plan* (with 1968 postscript). Slough: National Foundation for Educational Research, on behalf of the National Institute of Industrial Psychology, 1974.

Rosinger, G., Myers, L. B., Levy, G. W., Loar, M., Mohrman, S. A., and Stock, J. R. "Development of a behaviorally based performance appraisal system." *Personnel Psychology*, *35*, 1982, 75–88.

Saal, F. E., Downey, R. G., and Lahey, M. A. "Rating the ratings: Assessing the psychometric quality of rating data." *Psychological Bulletin*, *88*, 1980, 413–28.

Schwab, D. P., Heneman, H. G. III, and De Cotis, T. A. "Behaviourally anchored rating scales: A review of the literature." *Personnel Psychology*, *28*, 1975, 549–62.

Shepherd, A. "An improved tabular format for task analysis." *Journal of Occupational Psychology*, *47*, 1976, 93–104.

Smith, M. "An analysis of three managerial jobs using repertory grids." *Journal of Management Studies*, *17*, 1980, 205–13.

Smith, P. C., and Kendall, L. M. "Retranslation of expectations: An approach to the construction of unambiguous anchors for rating scales." *Journal of Applied Psychology*, *47*, 1963, 149–55.

Stewart, R. *Managers and Their Jobs*. London: Macmillan, 1967.

Taylor, H. C., and Russell, J. T. "The relationship of validity coefficients to the practical effectiveness of tests in selection: Discussion and tables." *Journal of Applied Psychology*, *22*, 1939, 565–78.

Zammuto, R. F., London, M., and Rowland, K. M. "Organization and rater differences in performance appraisals." *Personnel Psychology*, *35*, 1982, 643–58.

CHAPTER 7

Anastasi, A. *Psychological Testing* (5th Ed.). London: Collier Macmillan, 1982.

Arvey, R. D., and Campion, J. E. "The employment interview: A summary and review of recent literature." *Personnel Psychology*, *35*, 1982, 281–322.

Asher, J. J. "The biographical item: Can it be improved?" *Personnel Psychology*, *25*, 1972, 251–69.

Asher, J. J., and Sciarrino, J. A. "Realistic work sample tests: A review." *Personnel Psychology*, *27*, 1974, 519–33.

Bartram, D., and Dale, H. C. A. "The Eysenck personality inventory as a selection test for military pilots." *Journal of Occupational Psychology*, *55*, 1982, 287–96.

British Psychological Society/Runnymede Trust. *Discriminating Fairly.* Leicester: British Psychological Society, 1980.

Carlson, R. E. "Selection interview decisions: The relative influence of appearance and factual written information on an interviewer's final rating." *Journal of Applied Psychology, 51,* 1967, 461–8.

Carlson, R. E., Thayer, P. W., Mayfield, E. C., and Peterson, D. A. "Improvements in the selection interview." *Personnel Journal, 50,* 1971, 268–75.

Cederblom, D., and Lounsbury, J. W. "An investigation of user acceptance of peer evaluation." *Personnel Psychology, 33,* 1980, 567–79.

Dulewicz, V., and Fletcher, C. "The relationship between previous experience and intelligence and background characteristics of participants and their performance in an assessment centre." *Journal of Occupational Psychology, 55,* 1982, 197–207.

Elliott, A. G. P. "Some implications of lie scale scores in real-life selection." *Journal of Occupational Psychology, 54,* 1981, 9–16.

Farr, J. L., and York, C. M. "Amount of information and primacy-recency effects in recruitment decisions." *Personnel Psychology, 28,* 1975, 233–8.

Forbes, R. J., and Jackson, P. R. "Non-verbal behaviour and the outcome of selection interviews." *Journal of Occupational Psychology, 53,* 1980, 65–72.

Ghiselli, E. E. *The Validity of Occupational Aptitude Tests.* New York: John Wiley, 1966.

——. "The validity of aptitude tests in personnel selection." *Personnel Psychology, 26,* 1973, 461–77.

Gill, R. W. T. "The in tray (in basket) exercise as a measure of management potential." *Journal of Occupational Psychology, 52,* 1979, 185–97.

Heneman, H. G. III. "The impact of interviewer training and interview structure on the reliability and validity of the selection interview." *Proceedings of the Academy of Management,* 1975, 231–3.

Howard, G. S., and Dailey, P. R. "Response-shift bias: A source of contamination of self-report measures." *Journal of Applied Psychology, 64,* 1979, 144–50.

Howard, G. S., Dailey, P. R., and Gulanick, N. A. "The feasibility of informed pretests in attenuating response shift bias." *Applied Psychological Measurement, 3,* 1979, 481–94.

Huck, J. R. "Assessment centres: A review of the external and internal validities." *Personnel Psychology, 26,* 1973, 191–212.

Jessup, G., and Jessup, H. *Selection and Assessment at Work.* London: Methuen, 1975.

Jones, A. "Inter-rater reliability in the assessment of group exercises at a UK assessment centre." *Journal of Occupational Psychology, 54,* 1981, 79–86.

Keenan, A., and Wedderburn, A. A. I. "Putting the boot on the other foot: Candidate's descriptions of interviewers." *Journal of Occupational Psychology, 53,* 1980, 81–9.

Kilmoski, R., and Strickland, W. J. "Assessment centers—valid or merely prescient?" *Personnel Psychology*, *30*, 1977, 353–61.

Kingston, N. *Selecting Managers: A Survey of Current Practice in 200 Companies. Management Survey Report 4*. London: British Institute of Management, 1971.

Latham, G. P., Saari, L. M., Purcell, E. D., and Campion, M. A. "The situational interview." *Journal of Applied Psychology*, *65*, 1980, 422–7.

Latham, G. P., Wexley, K. N., and Purcell, E. D. "Training managers to minimize rating errors in the observation of behavior." *Journal of Applied Psychology*, *60*, 1975, 550–5.

Leonard, R. L. "Cognitive complexity and the similarity—attraction paradigm." *Journal of Research in Personality*, *10*, 1976, 83–8.

Mayfield, E. C. "The selection interview: A re-evaluation of published research." *Personnel Psychology*, *17*, 1964, 239–60.

Mayfield, E. C., Brown, S. H., and Hamstra, B. W. "Selection interviewing in the life insurance industry: An update of research and practice." *Personnel Psychology*, *33*, 1980, 725–39.

Miner, J. B. *Personnel Psychology*. New York: Macmillan, 1969.

Muchinsky, P. M. "The use of reference reports in personnel selection: A review and evaluation." *Journal of Occupational Psychology*, *52*, 1979, 287–97.

Owens, W. A. "Background data" in M. D. Dunnette (Ed.), *Handbook of Industrial and Organizational Psychology*. Chicago, Ill.: Rand McNally, 1976.

Parisher, D., Rios, B., and Reilly, R. R. "Psychologists and psychological services in urban police departments: A national survey." *Professional Psychology*, *10*, 1979, 6–7.

Parker, M. J. "Improved methods for the recruitment and selection of operatives." Unpublished MPhil Thesis: University of Aston in Birmingham, 1980.

Pearn, M. A. "Changes in the law on race relations: Practical implications for employers." *BACIE Journal*, Oct. 1976, 163–6.

——. *Selecting and Training Coloured Workers. Training Information Paper No. 9*. London: HMSO, 1977.

Peters, L. H., and Terborg, J. R. "The effects of temporal placement of unfavourable information and attitude similarity on personnel selection decisions. *Organizational Behaviour and Human Performance*, *13*, 1975, 279–93.

Reilly, R. R., and Chao, G. T. "Validity and fairness of some alternative employee selection procedures." *Personnel Psychology*, *35*, 1982, 1–62.

Robertson, I. T., and Kandola, R. S. "Work sample tests: Validity, adverse impact and applicant reaction." *Journal of Occupational Psychology*, *55*, 1982, 171–83.

Schmitt, N. "Social and situational determinants of interview decisions: Implications for the employment interview." *Personnel Psychology*, *29*, 1976, 79–101.

Schwab, D. P., and Heneman, H. G. III. "Relationship between interview structure and interview reliability in an employment situation." *Journal of Applied Psychology*, 53, 1969, 214–17.

Sneath, F., Thakur, M., and Medjuck, B. *Testing People at Work*. London: Institute of Personnel Management, 1976.

Ulrich, L., and Trumbo, D. "The selection interview since 1949." *Psychological Bulletin*, 53, 1965, 100–16.

Valenzi, E., and Andrews, I. R. "Individual differences in the decision process of employment interviewers." *Journal of Applied Psychology*, 58, 1973, 49–53.

Vance, R. J., Kuhnert, K. W., and Farr, J. L. "Interview judgements: Using external criteria to compare behavioral and graphic scale ratings." *Organizational Behavior and Human Performance*, 22, 1978, 279–94.

Wagner, R. "The employment interview: A critical review." *Personnel Psychology*, 2, 1949, 17–46.

Webster, E. C. *Decision Making in the Employment Interview*. Montreal, Quebec: Eagle, 1964.

Wexley, K. N., Sanders, R. E., and Yukl, G. A. "Training interviewers to eliminate contrast effects in employment interviews." *Journal of Applied Psychology*, 57, 1973, 233–6.

Wright, C. R. Jr. "Summary of research on the selection interview since 1964." *Personnel Psychology*, 22, 1969, 391–413.

Wysocki, B. "More companies try to spot leaders early, guide them to the top." *Wall Street Journal*, Feb. 25, 1981.

CHAPTER 8

Batstone, E., Boraston, I., and Frenkel, S. *Shop Stewards in Action*. Oxford: Blackwell, 1977.

Brown, W., and Jacques, E. *Glacier Project Papers*. London: Heinemann, 1965.

Clegg, H. A., Killick, A. J., and Adams, R. *Trade Union Officers*. Oxford: Blackwell, 1966.

Cooper, C. L. *The Stress Check*. London and Englewood Cliffs, N.J.: Prentice-Hall, 1980.

——. *Executive Families Under Stress*. London and Englewood Cliffs, N.J.: Prentice-Hall, 1981.

Cooper, C. L., and Davidson, M. J. *High Pressure*. London: Fontana, 1982.

Davidson, M. J., and Cooper, C. L. "The extra pressure of women executives." *Personnel Management*, June, 1980a, 48–51.

——. "Type A coronary prone behaviour and stress in senior female managers and administrators." *Journal of Occupational Medicine*, 22, 1980b, 801–6.

Fogarty, M. P., Rapoport, R., and Rapoport, R. N. *Sex, Career and Family*. Beverly Hills, Calif.: Sage, 1971.

Foster, L. W., Latack, J. C., and Riendl, L. J. "The effects and promises of the shortened work week." *Proceedings of the Academy of Management Annual Conference*, Aug. 1979.

Friedman, M., and Rosenman, R. H. *Type A Behaviour and Your Heart*. London: Wildwood House, 1974.

Goodman, J., and Whittingham, T. G. *Shop Stewards in British Industry*. London: McGraw-Hill, 1969.

Hall, D. T., and Hall, F. "Stress and the two career couple" in C. L. Cooper and R. L. Payne (Eds), *Current Concerns in Occupational Stress*. London: Wiley, 1980.

Handy, C. *Understanding Organisations*. Harmondsworth, Middx: Penguin, 1976.

Haynes, S. G., and Feinleib, M. "Women, work and coronary heart disease: Prospective findings from the Framingham Heart Study." *American Journal of Public Health, 70*, 1980, 133–41.

Heller, Joseph. *Catch-22*. New York, Simon & Schuster, 1961; London: Cape, 1962.

Hennig, M., and Jardim, A. *The Managerial Woman*. London: Pan, 1978.

Lancet, The. "Women, Work and Coronary Heart Disease" (editorial), 12 July 1979, 76–7.

Mant, A. *The Rise and Fall of the British Manager*. London: Pan, 1977.

Mills, C. Wright. *The Power Elite*. New York: Oxford University Press, 1959.

Newberry, P., Weissman, M., and Myers, J. "Working wives and housewives: Do they differ in mental status and social adjustment?" *American Journal of Orthopsychiatry, 49*, 1979, 282–91.

Rosenman, R. H., Friedman, M., and Strauss, R. "CHD in the Western Collaborative Group Study." *Journal of the American Medical Association, 195*, 1966, 86–92.

Staines, G. L., Pleck, J. H., Shepard, L., and O'Connor, P. "Wives' employment status and marital adjustment." University of Michigan: Institute of Social Research Working Paper, 1978.

Terkel, S. *Working*. New York: Avon, 1972.

Torrington, D., and Chapman, J. *Personnel Management*. London: Prentice-Hall, 1979.

Welner, A., Marten, S., Wochnick, E., Davis, M., Fishman, R., and Clayton, J. "Psychiatric disorders among professional women." *Archives of General Psychiatry, 36*, 1979, 169–73.

CHAPTER 9

Barber, R. "Who would marry a Director?" *Director*, March 1976, 60–2.

Beattie, R. T., Darlington, T. G., and Cripps, D. M. *The Management Threshold* (BIM Paper OPN 11, 1974).

Breslow, L., and Buell, P. "Mortality from coronary heart disease and physical activity of work in California." *Journal of Chronic Diseases, 11*, 1960, 615–26.

Brook, A. "Mental stress at work." *The Practitioner, 210*, 1973, 500–6.

Brummet, R. L., Pyle, W. C., and Flamholtz, E. G. "Accounting for human resources." *Michigan Business Review, 20*, 1968, 20–5.

Buck, V. *Working Under Pressure*. London: Staples Press, 1972.

Caplan, R. D., Cobb, S., and French, J. R. P. "Relationships of cessation of smoking with job stress, personality and social support." *Journal of Applied Psychology*, *60*, 1975, 211–19.

Constandse, W. J. "A neglected personnel problem." *Personnel Journal*, *51*, 1972, 129–33.

Cooper, C. L. *Executive Families under Stress*. Englewood Cliffs, N.J.: Prentice-Hall, 1981.

Cooper, C. L., and Davidson, M. *High Presure: Working Lives of Women Managers*. London: Fontana, 1982.

Cooper, C. L., and Marshall, J. *Understanding Executive Stress*. London: Macmillan, 1978.

Cooper, C. L., and Payne, R. L. (Eds). *Stress at Work*. New York: John Wiley, 1978.

Donaldson, J., and Gowler, D. "Prerogatives, participation and managerial stress" in D. Gowler, and K. Legge (Eds), *Managerial Stress*, Epping: Gower Press, 1975.

French, J. R. P., and Caplan, R. D. "Psychosocial factors in coronary heart disease." *Industrial Medicine*, *39*, 1970, 383–97.

——. "Organisational stress and individual strain" in A. J. Marrow (Ed.), *The Failure of Success*, 30–66. New York: AMACOM, 1973.

French, J. R. P., Tupper, C. J., and Mueller, E. I. "Workload of university professors." Unpublished Research Report, University of Michigan, 1965.

Friedman, M. *Pathogenesis of Coronary Artery Disease*. New York: McGraw-Hill, 1969.

Goffman, E. "On cooling the mark out." *Psychiatry*, *15*, 1952, 451–63.

Gowler, D., and Legge, K. "Stress and external relationships—the 'Hidden contract'" in *Managerial Stress*. Epping: Gower Press, 1975.

Guest, D., and Williams, R. "How home affects work." *New Society*, Jan. 1973.

Handy, C. "The family: Help or hindrance" in C. L. Cooper and R. Payne (Eds), *Stress at Work*. London: Wiley, 1978.

Howard, J. H., Cunningham, D. A., and Rechnitzer, P. A. "Health patterns associated with Type A behaviour: A managerial population." *Journal of Human Stress*, March 1976, 24–31.

Immundo, L. V. "Problems associated with managerial mobility." *Personnel Journal*, *53*, 1974, 910.

Jenkins, C. D. "Psychological and social precursors of coronary disease." *New England Journal of Medicine*, *284*, 1971, 307–17.

Kahn, R. L., Wolfe, D. M., Quinne, R. P., Snoek, J. D., and Rosenthal, R. A. *Organizational Stress*. New York: John Wiley, 1964.

Kasl, S. V. "Mental health and the work environment." *Journal of Occupational Medicine*, *15*, 1973, 509–18.

Kay, E. "Middle management" in J. O'Toole (Ed.), *Work and the Quality of Life*. Cambridge, Mass.: MIT Press, 1974.

Kearns, J. L. *Stress in Industry*. London: Priory Press, 1973.

Lazarus, R. S. *Psychological Stress and the Coping Process*. New York: McGraw-Hill, 1966.

Levinson, H. "Problems that worry our executives" in A. J. Marrow (Ed.), *The Failure of Success*. New York: AMACOM, 1973.

McMurray, R. N. "The executive neurosis" in R. L. Noland (Ed.), *Industrial Mental Health and Employee Counselling*. New York: Behavioural Publications, 1973.

Margolis, B. L., and Kroes, W. H. "Work and the health of man" in J. O'Toole (Ed.), *Work and the Quality of Life*. Cambridge, Mass.: MIT Press, 1974.

Margolis, B. L., and Kroes, W. H., and Quinn, R. P. "Job stress: An unlisted occupational hazard." *Journal of Occupational Medicine, 16*, 1974, 654–61.

Marshall, J., and Cooper, C. L. *Executives under Pressure*. London: Macmillan, 1979.

——. "Work experiences of middle and senior managers: The pressures and satisfactions." *Management International Review, 19*, 1979, 81–96.

Mettlin, C., and Woelfel, J. "Interpersonal influence and symptoms of stress." *Journal of Health and Social Behavior, 15*, 1974, 311–19.

Middle Class Housing Estate Study, Civil Service College, United Kingdom, unpublished paper, 1975.

Miller, J. G. "Information input overload and psychopathology." *American Journal of Psychiatry, 8*, 1960, 116.

Mintzberg, H. *The Nature of Managerial Work*. New York: Harper & Row, 1973.

Morris, J. "Managerial stress and the cross of relationships" in D. Gowler and K. Legge (Eds), *Managerial Stress*. Epping: Gower Press, 1975.

Neff, W. S. *Work and Human Behaviour*. New York: Atherton Press, 1968.

Pahl, J. M., and Pahl, R. E. *Managers and Their Wives*. London: Allen Lane, 1971.

Quinn, R. P., Seashore, S., and Mangione, I. *Survey of Working Conditions*. UK Government Printing Office, 1971.

Rosenman, R. H., Friedman, M., and Jenkins, C. D. "Clinically unrecognized myocardial infarction in the Western Collaborative Group Study." *American Journal of Cardiology, 19*, 1967, 776–82.

Rosenman, R. H., Friedman, M., and Strauss, R. "A predictive study of CHD." *Journal of the American Medical Association, 189*, 1964, 15–22.

——. "CHD in the Western Collaborative Group Study." *Journal of the American Medical Association, 195*, 1966, 86–92.

Russek, H. I., and Zohman, B. L. "Relative significance of hereditary, diet and occupational stress in CHD of young adults." *American Journal of Medical Science, 235*, 1958, 266–75.

Seidenberg, R. *Corporate Wives—Corporate Casualities*. New York: American Management Association, 1973.

Shirom, A., Eden, D., Silberwasser, S., and Kellerman, J. J. "Job stress and the risk factors in coronary heart disease among occupational categories in kibbutzim." *Social Science and Medicine, 7*, 1973, 875–92.

Sleeper, R. D. "Labour mobility over the life cycle." *British Journal of Industrial Relations, 13*, 1975.

Sofer, C. *Men in Mid-Career*. Cambridge: Cambridge University Press, 1970.

Stewart, R. *Constrasts in Management*. New York: McGraw-Hill, 1976.

Uris, A. "How managers ease job pressures." *International Management*, June 1972, 45–6.

Wardwell, W. I., Hyman, M., and Bahnson, C. B. "Stress and coronary disease in three field studies." *Journal of Chronic Diseases*, *17*, 1964, 73–84.

CHAPTER 10

Agervold, M. "Swedish Experiments in Industrial Democracy" in I. E. Davis and A. B. Cherns (Eds), *The Quality of Working Life*, Vol. 2, 46–65. New York: Free Press, 1975.

Butera, F. "Environmental factors in job and organization design: The case of Olivetti" in I. E. Davis and A. B. Cherns (Eds), *The Quality of Working Life*, Vol. 1, 166–200. New York: Free Press, 1975.

Butteriss, M. *The Quality of Working Life: The Expanding International Scene. Work Research Unit Paper No. 5*. London, 1975.

Clutterbuck, D. "Creating a factory with a factory." *International Management*, Oct. 1973.

Coch, L., and French, J. R. P. "Overcoming resistance to change." *Human Relations*, *1*, 1948, 512–32.

Cooper, C. L., and Mumford, E. *Quality of Worklife in Eastern and Western Europe*. London: Associated Business Press, 1979.

Davis, L. E., and Cherns, A. B. *The Quality of Working Life*, Vols 1–2. New York: Free Press, 1975.

Elden, M., and Taylor, J. "Participatory research at work." *Journal of Occupational Behaviour*, *4 (1)*, 1983, 1–8.

French, J. R. P., and Caplan, R. D. "Organizational stress and individual strain" in A. J. Marrow (Ed.), *The Failure of Success*, 52. New York: AMACOM, 1973.

Herrick, N. Q., and Maccoby, M. "Humanizing Work: A priority goal of the 1970s" in I. E. Davis and A. B. Cherns (Eds), *The Quality of Working Life*, Vol. 1, 63–77. New York: Free Press, 1975.

Hertog, F. J. den. "Work structuring Philips Gloeilampenfabrieken." *Industrial Psychology*, 1974.

Hill, P. *Towards a New Philosophy of Management*. New York: Barnes & Noble, 1972.

Jenkins, D. *Industrial Democracy in Europe*. Geneva: Business International SA, 1974.

Kato, H. "Job enlargement as viewed from industrial engineering." Paper delivered to the Japan Psychological Association, 38th National Conference, 1974.

Mire, J. "Trade unions and worker participation in management" in I. E. Davis and A. B. Cherns (Eds), *The Quality of Working Life*, Vol. 1, 416–38. New York: Free Press, 1975.

Morse, N. C., and Reimer, E "The experimental change of a major organisational variable." *Journal of Abnormal and Social Psychology*, *52*, 1956, 120–9.

Norstedt, J., and Aguren, S. *The Saab-Scania Report*. Stockholm: Swedish Employers Confederation, 1974.

O'Toole, J. *Work in America*. Boston, Mass.: MIT Press, 1973.

Paul, W. J., and Robertson, K. B. *Job Enrichment and Employee Motivation*. London: Gower Press, 1970.

Powell, R. M., and Schacter, J. L. Self-determination at work. *Academy of Management Journal, 15*, 1975, 165–73.

Preston, L. E., and Post, J. E. "The third managerial revolution." *Academy of Management Journal, 17*, 1974, 476–86.

Ruehl, G. "Work structuring II." *Industrial Engineering*, Feb. 1974, 52–6.

Strauss, G., and Rosenstein, E. "Worker participation: A critical view." *Industrial Relations, 9*, 1970, 197–214.

Takezawa, S. "The quality of working life: Trends in Japan." Unpublished paper, Rikkyo University, 1974.

Takezawa, S. *et al. Improvements in QWL in Three Industries*. Geneva: ILO, 1982.

Taylor, J. C. "Experiments in work system design: Economic and human results." Unpublished paper, University of California. Los Angeles, 1975.

Trist, E. L., and Bamforth, K. "Some social and psychological consequences of the long wall method of coal getting." *Human Relations, 4*, 1951, 3–38.

Wright, B. *Executive Ease and Disease*. Epping: Gower Press, 1975.

N.B. Some of the material in this chapter was drawn from an article by C. L. Cooper in D. Torrington's *Comparative Industrial Relations*. London: Associated Business Press, 1977.

CHAPTER 11

Allport, D. A., Antonis, B., and Reynolds, P. "On the division of attention: A disproof of the single channel hypothesis." *Quarterly Journal of Experimental Psychology, 24*, 1972, 225–35.

Anderson, J. R. *Cognitive Psychology and Its Implications*. San Francisco, Calif.: Freeman, 1980.

Bartlett, F. C. *Remembering*. Cambridge: Cambridge University Press, 1932.

Bousfield, W. A. "The occurrence of clustering in the recall of randomly arranged associates." *Journal of General Psychology, 49*, 1953, 229–40.

Bower, G. H., Clark, M. C., Lesgold, A. M., and Winzenz, D. "Hierarchical retrieval schemes in recall of categorical word lists." *Journal of Verbal Learning and Verbal Behavior, 8*, 1969, 323–43.

Broadbent, D. E. *Perception and Communication*. London: Pergamon, 1958.

Brown, J. "Some tests of the decay theory of immediate memory." *Quarterly Journal of Experimental Psychology, 10*, 1958, 12–21.

Bryan, W. L., and Harter, N. "Studies on the telegraphic language: The acquisition of a hierarchy of habits." *Psychological Review*, 6, 1899, 345–75.

Cherry, E. C. "Some experiments on the recognition of speech with one and with two ears." *Journal of the Acoustical Society of America*, 25, 1953, 975–9.

Ekstrand, B. R. "To sleep perchance to dream" (about why we forget) in C. P. Duncan, L. Sechrest and A. W. Melton (Eds), *Human Memory Festschrift in Honour of Benton J. Underwood*. New York: Appleton-Century-Crofts, 1972.

Entwistle, N. J. *Styles of Learning and Teaching*. Chichester: Wiley, 1981.

Fitts, P. M., and Posner, M. I. *Human Performance*, Belmont, Calif.: Brooks/Cole, 1967.

Gagné, R. M. *The Conditions of Learning* (3rd Ed.). New York: Holt, Rinehart & Winston, 1977.

Gagné, R. M., and Briggs, L. J. *Principles of Instructional Design*. New York: Holt, Rinehart & Winston, 1974.

Groot, A. D. de. *Thought and Choice in Chess*. The Hague: Mouton, 1965.

James, W. *Principles of Psychology*. London: Macmillan, 1890.

Jenkins, J. G., and Dallenbach, K. M. "Oblivescence during sleep and waking." *American Journal of Psychology*, 35, 1924, 605–12.

Legge, D., and Barber, P. J. *Information and Skill*. London: Methuen, 1976.

Mandler, G. "Organization and memory" in K. W. Spence and J. A. Spence (Eds), *The Psychology of Learning and Motivation*, Vol. 1. New York: Academic Press, 1967.

Mandler, G., and Pearlstone, Z. "Free and constrained concept learning and subsequent recall." *Journal of Verbal Learning and Verbal Behavior*, 5, 1966, 126–31.

Miller, G. A. "The magical number seven, plus or minus two: Some limits in our capacity for processing information." *Psychological Review*, 63, 1956, 81–97.

Miller, G. A., Galanter, E., and Pribram, K. *Plans and the Structure of Behavior*, New York: Holt, Rinehart & Winston, 1960.

Neisser, U. *Cognition and Reality*. San Francisco, Calif.: Freeman, 1976.

Ostry, D., Moray, N., and Marks, G. "Attention, practice and semantic targets." *Journal of Experimental Psychology: Human Perception and Performance*, 2, 1976, 326–36.

Owens, J., Bower, G. H., and Black, J. B. "The 'soap opera' effect in story recall." *Memory and Cognition*, 7, 1979, 185–91.

Rogers, C. R. *Client Centred Therapy*. London: Constable, 1951.

Schrank, R. C., and Abelson, R. *Scripts, Plans, Goals and Under standing*. Hillsdale, N.J.: Lawrence Erlbaum, 1977.

Shaffer, L. H. "Multiple attention in continuous verbal tasks" in P. M. A. Rabbitt and S. Dornic (Eds), *Attention and Performance V*. London: Academic Press, 1975.

Sperling, G. "The information available in brief visual presentations." *Psychological Monographs*, 74, *Whole No. 11*, 1960.

Stroop, J. R. "Studies of interference in serial verbal reactions." *Journal of Experimental Psychology, 18*, 1935, 643–62.

Sulin, R. A., and Dooling, D. J. "Intrusion of a thematic idea in retention of prose." *Journal of Experimental Psychology, 103*, 1974, 255–62.

Tolman, E. C. "Cognitive maps in rats and men." *Psychological Review, 55*, 1948, 189–208.

Underwood, B. J. "Interference and forgetting." *Psychological Review, 64*, 1957, 49–60.

CHAPTER 12

Annett, J., Duncan, K. D., Stammers, R. B., and Gray, M. J. *Task Analysis. Training Information Paper No. 6.* London: HMSO, 1971.

Bandura, A. *Social Learning Theory.* Englewood Cliffs, N.J.: Prentice-Hall, 1977.

Bass, B. M., and Vaughan, J. A. *Training in Industry: The Management of Learning.* Belmont, Calif.: Wadsworth, 1966.

Boydell, T. *The Identification of Training Needs.* London: British Association of Commercial and Industrial Education, 1973.

Campbell, J. P., Dunnette, M. D., Lawler, E. E., and Weick, K. E. *Managerial Behavior, Performance and Effectiveness.* New York: McGraw-Hill, 1970.

Cantalanello, R. F., and Kirkpatrick, D. L. "Evaluating training programmes—the state of the art." *Training and Development Journal,* May 1968, 9.

Cooper, C. L. "Dualistic theory of the processes of management learning." *Management Decision, 14*, 1976, 54–62.

Davies, I. K. *The Management of Learning.* London: McGraw-Hill, 1972.

Downs, S. "Work-sampling techniques" in C. J. Brotherton (Ed.), *Towards Fairness in Selection and Placement.* London: Wiley, 1982.

Duncan, K. D. "Strategies for analysis of the task" in J. Hartley (Ed.), *Strategies for Programmed Instruction: An Educational Technology.* London: Butterworth, 1972.

Gagné, R. M. "Military training and the principles of learning." *American Psychologist, 18*, 1962, 83–91.

——. *The Conditions of Learning* (3rd Ed.). New York: Holt, Rinehart & Winston, 1977.

Gill, R. W. T. "The in-tray (in-basket) exercise as a measurement of management potential." *Journal of Occupational Psychology, 52*, 1979, 185–97.

Goldstein, I. L. "The pursuit of validity in the evaluation of training programs." *Human Factors, 20*, 1978, 131–44.

Hamblin, A. C. *The Evaluation and Control of Training.* London: McGraw-Hill, 1974.

Holding, D. H. *Principles of Training.* Oxford: Pergamon, 1965.

Industrial Training Research Unit (Rev. Ed.) *CRAMP: A Guide to Training Decisions. A User's Manual.* Cambridge: ITRU, 1981.

Johnson, S. E. A. "Development and application of a technique for analysing jobs." Unpublished MPhil Thesis, University of Aston in Birmingham, 1979.

Latham, G. P., and Saari, L. M. "Application of social learning theory to training supervisors through behavioral modeling." *Journal of Applied Psychology*, *64*, 1979, 239–46.

Leifer, M. S., and Newstrom, J. W. "Solving the transfer of training problems." *Training and Development Journal*, *34*, 1980, 42–6.

McCormick, E. J., Jeanneret, P., and Mecham, R. C. "A study of job characteristics and job dimensions as based on the position analysis questionnaires." *Journal of Applied Psychology*, *36* (monograph), 1972, 347–68.

Mager, R. F. *Preparing Objectives for Instruction*. Palo Alto, Calif.: Fearon, 1962.

Michalak, D. E. "The neglected half of training." *Training and Development Journal*, *35*, 1981, 22–8.

Robertson, I. T., and Downs, S. "Learning and the prediction of performance: Development of trainability testing in the United Kingdom." *Journal of Applied Psychology*, *64*, 1979, 42–50.

Rogers, C. A. "Feedback precision and post-feedback interval duration." *Journal of Experimental Psychology*, *102*, 1974, 604–8.

Sarason, I. G. "Test anxiety, attention and the general problem of anxiety" in C. D. Spielberger and I. G. Sarason (Eds), *Stress and Anxiety*, Vol. 1. New York: Hemisphere, 1975.

Seymour, W. D. *Industrial Skills*. London: Pitman, 1966.

Shepherd, A. "An improved tabular format for task analysis." *Journal of Occupational Psychology*, *47*, 1976, 93–104.

Stammers, R. B., and Patrick, J. *The Psychology of Training*. London: Methuen, 1975.

Warr, P. B., Bird, M. W., and Rackham, N. *The Evaluation of Management Training*. London: Gower Press, 1970.

CHAPTER 13

Aldis, O. "Of pigeons and men." *Harvard Business Review*, *39*, 1961, 59–63.

Andrasik, F. "Organizational behavior modification in business settings: A methodological and content review" in F. Luthans and K. R. Thompson, *Contemporary Readings in Organizational Behavior*. New York: McGraw-Hill, 1981.

Annett, J. "Learning in practice" in P. B. Warr (Ed.), *Psychology at Work*. Harmondsworth, Middx: Penguin, 1971.

Arvey, R. D., and Ivancevich, J. M. "Punishment in organizations: A review, propositions and research suggestions." *Academy of Management Review*, *5*, 1980, 123–32.

Bandura, A. *Social Learning Theory*. Englewood Cliffs, N.J.: Prentice-Hall, 1977.

Beck, J. E. "A survey of problems encountered by a number of industrial and commercial users of programmed instruction" in A. P. Mann and C. K. Brunstrom (Eds), *Aspects of Educational Technology III*. London: Pitman, 1969.

Breland, K., and Breland, M. "A field of applied animal psychology." *American Psychologist*, *6*, 1951, 202–4.

Crowder, N. A. "Automatic tutoring by intrinsic programming" in A. A. Lunsdaine and R. Glaser (Eds), *Teaching Machines and Programmed Learning*. Washington DC: N.E.A., 1960.

Davies, I. K. *The Management of Learning*. London: McGraw-Hill, 1972.

Davis, T. R. V., and Luthans, F. "A social learning approach to organizational behavior." *Academy of Management Review*, 5, 1980, 281–90.

Decker, P. J. "The enhancement of behaviour modeling training of supervisory skills by the inclusion of retention processes." *Personnel Psychology*, 35, 1982, 323–32.

Goldstein, A. P., and Sorcher, M. *Changing Supervisory Behavior*. New York: Pergamon, 1974.

Hamner, W. C. "Reinforcement theory and contingency management in organizational settings" in R. M. Steers and L. W. Porter, *Motivation and Work Behavior*. New York: McGraw-Hill, 1979.

Hamner, W. C., and Hamner, E. P. "Behavior modification on the bottom line." *Organizational Dynamics*. 3, 1976, 3–21.

Hartley, J. "Evaluation" in J. Hartley (Ed.), *Strategies for Programmed Instruction: An Educational Technology*. London: Butterworth, 1972.

Kazdin, A. E. *Behavior Modification in Applied Settings* (Rev. Ed.) Homewood, Ill.: Dorsey Press, 1980.

Latham, G. P., and Saari, L. M. "Application of social learning theory to training supervisors through behavioral modeling." *Journal of Applied Psychology*, 64, 1979, 239–46.

Lewis, D. J., and Duncan, C. P. "Effect of different percentages of money reward on extinction of a lever pulling response." *Journal of Experimental Psychology*, 52, 1956, 23–7.

Locke, E. A. "The myths of behavior modeling in organizations. *Academy of Management Review*, 4, 1977, 543–53.

Luthans, F., and Davis, T. R. V. "Behavioral self-management: The missing link in managerial effectiveness." *Organizational Dynamics*, 8, 1979, 42–60.

Luthans, F., and Kreitner, R. *Organizational Behavior Modification*. Glenview, Ill.: Scott, Foresman, 1975.

Mager, R. F. *Preparing Objectives for Instruction*. Palo Alto, Calif.: Fearon, 1962.

Premack, D. "Reinforcement theory" in D. Levine (Ed.), *Nebraska Symposium on Motivation*. Lincoln, Neb.: University of Nebraska Press, 1965.

Rimm, D. C., and Masters, J. C. *Behavior Therapy: Techniques and Empirical Findings* (2nd Ed.). New York: Academic Press, 1979.

Skinner, B. F. "The science of learning and the art of teaching." *Harvard Educational Review*, 24, 1954, 86–97.

——. *Beyond Freedom and Dignity*. New York: Knopf, 1971.

——. *About Behaviorism*. New York: Knopf, 1974.

Stammers, R., and Patrick, J. *The Psychology of Training*. London: Methuen, 1975.

Ulrich, R., Stachnik, T., and Malory, J. (Eds). *Control of Human Behavior*. Glenview, Ill.: Scott, Foresman, 1974.

Watson, J. B., and Rayner, R. "Conditioned emotional reactions." *Journal of Experimental Psychology*, *3*, 1920, 1–14.

Weiss, H. M. "Subordinate imitation of supervisory behavior: The role of modeling in organizational socialization." *Organizational Behavior and Human Performance*, *19*, 1977, 89–105.

Yukl, G. A. and Latham, G. P. "Consequences of reinforcement schedules and incentive magnitudes for employee performance: Problems encountered in an industrial setting." *Journal of Applied Psychology*, *60*, 1975, 294–8.

Yukl, G. A., Latham, G. P., and Pursell, E. D. "The effectiveness of performance incentives under continuous and variable ratio schedules of reinforcement." *Personnel Psychology*, *29*, 1976, 221–31.

Yukl, G. A., Wexley, K. N., and Seymour, J. D. "Effectiveness of pay incentives under variable ratio and continuous reinforcement schedules." *Journal of Applied Psychology*, *56*, 1972, 19–23.

Zohar, D., and Fussfeld, N. A. "A systems approach to organisational behavior modification: Theoretical considerations and empirical evidence." *International Review of Applied psychology*, *30*, 1981, 491–505.

CHAPTER 14

Argyris, C. *Integrating the Individual and the Organization*. New York: John Wiley, 1964.

——. *Explorations and Issues in Laboratory Education*. Washington DC: National Training Laboratories, 1966.

Bandura, A. "Social learning through imitation" in M. R. Jones (Ed.), *Nebraska Symposium on Motivation*. Lincoln, Neb.: University of Nebraska Press, 1966.

——. *Social Learning Theory*. Englewood Cliffs, N.J.: Prentice-Hall, 1977.

Bolman, L. "Group leader effectiveness" in C. L. Cooper (Ed.), *Developing Social Skills in Managers*. London: Macmillan, 1976.

Bradford, L. P., Gibb, J. R., and Benne, K. D. *T-Group Theory and Laboratory Method: Innovation in Re-education*. New York: John Wiley, 1964.

Cooper, C. L. *Developing Social Skills in Managers*. London: Macmillan, 1976.

——. *Learning from Others in Groups*. London: Associated Business Press, 1979.

——. *Developing Managers for the 1980s*. London: Macmillan, 1981.

Durkin, H. E. *Groups in Depth*. New York: International University Press, 1964.

Jourard, S. M. "To be or not to be: Transparent." Paper presented at the American Psychological Association, New York City, Sept. 1966.

Kagan, J. "The concept of identification." *Psychological Review*, *65*, 1958, 296–305.

Lippitt, R., and White, R. K. "Patterns of aggression in behaviour in experimentally created climates." *Journal of Social Psychology*, *10*, 1939, 271–99.

Mangham, I., Hayes, J., and Cooper, C. L. "Developing executive relationships." *Interpersonal Development 1* (3), 1970.

Maslow, A. *Motivation and Personality*. New York: Harper, 1954.

Medcof, J. "The humanist approach" in J. Medcof and J. Roth, *Approaches to Psychology*. Milton Keynes: Open University Press, 1979.

Miles, M. "Human relations training: Processes and outcomes." *Journal of Counselling Psychology*, *7*, 1960, 301–6.

Redlich, F. C., and Astrachan, B. "Group dynamics training." *American Journal of Psychiatry*, *125*, 1969, 1501–7.

Rogers, C. R. *Client-centered Therapy*. Boston, Mass.: Houghton Mifflin, 1951.

——. "The necessary and sufficient conditions of therapeutic personality change." *Journal of Consulting Psychology*, *21*, 1957, 95–103.

——. *On Becoming a Person*. Boston, Mass.: Houghton Mifflin, 1961.

Schein, E. H., and Bennis, W. G. *Personal Learning and Organisational Change through Group Methods*. New York: John Wiley, 1965.

Sherif, M. *The Psychology of Social Norms*. New York: Harper, 1936.

Smith, P. B. "The use of T-groups in effecting individual and organizational change." *Psychology Scene*, *1*, 1967, 23–6.

Triplett, H. "The dynamogenic factors in pacemaking and competition." *American Journal of Psychology, 9*, 1897, 507–33.

Weiss, H. M. "Subordinate imitation of supervisor behavior: The role of modeling in organizational socialization." *Organizational Behavior and Human Performance*, *19*, 89–105, 1977.

Index of Authors

Index